THE
SHERLOCK
HOLMES
QUIZ BOOK

Kathleen Kaska

FUN FACTS

PUZZLES

TRIVIA

& MORE

THE SHERLOCK HOLMES

QUIZ BOOK

KATHLEEN KASKA

LP
LYONS
PRESS

Guilford, Connecticut

This book is dedicated to The Dogs in the Nighttime:
The Sherlock Holmes Society of Anacortes, Washington.

A special dedication to Sherlockian Sheila Holtgrieve 1944–2020

An imprint of The Rowman & Littlefield Publishing Group, Inc.
4501 Forbes Blvd., Ste. 200
Lanham, MD 20706
www.rowman.com

Distributed by NATIONAL BOOK NETWORK

Parts of this book were originally published in *The Sherlock Holmes Triviography and Quiz Book* by Kathleen Kaska. Copyright © 2000 by Kathleen Kaska

British Library Cataloguing in Publication Information available

Library of Congress Cataloging-in-Publication Data available

ISBN 978-1-4930-5315-5 (paper)
ISBN 978-1-4930-5316-2 (electronic)

CONTENTS

ACKNOWLEDGEMENTS

In writing this book, I discovered enough Sherlock Holmes trivia to fill the Tower of London. The more I researched, the more I uncovered. This book includes both questions that are "elementary" and those that are challenging, for readers of Sherlock Holmes range from young school-age children to veteran Sherlockians who spend much of their time dissecting the Canon. *The Sherlock Holmes Quiz Book* was written to entertain and enhance Sherlock Holmes fans of any age.

A special acknowledgement to Margie Deck (Sherlockian Extraordinaire) of the Seattle Sound of the Baskervilles Sherlock Holmes Society and The John H. Watson Society for her thorough reading of the manuscript and setting the record straight.

William Gillette as Sherlock Holmes in the Broadway production of
Sherlock Holmes 1899-1900

ONE
THE WORLD OF SHERLOCK HOLMES

"My name is Sherlock Holmes.
It is my business to know what other people don't."
—SHERLOCK HOLMES

K NOWING WHAT OTHERS DON'T and disclosing his deductions in such a simple and logical manner has made Sherlock Holmes the most popular detective of all time. Since the publication of Sir Arthur Conan Doyle's first novel, *A Study in Scarlet*, in 1887, the public's enjoyment and fascination have not waned over the past century. In fact, Sherlock Holmes fans have an insatiable appetite for the clever sleuth and his sidekick, the prolific Dr. Watson.

Conan Doyle's short stories and novels continue to be published today and have been adapted for radio, stage, television, and film, as well as for books and TV programs for children. According to author Martin Fido in his recently published book, *The World of Sherlock Holmes*, 200 to 300 Sherlock Holmes films and 1,000 to 2,000 radio and TV programs have been produced. Conan Doyle's works have been translated into sixty-five languages, as well as into braille, shorthand, and pig Latin. More than 100 books, along with dozens of articles, essays, and parodies about Sherlock Holmes, Dr. Watson, the villain Moriarty, and Conan Doyle have been written. Today over 300 Sherlock Holmes societies exist worldwide, and dozens of Holmes websites have brought the Great Detective into cyberspace. Numerous authors have continued writing Sherlock Holmes stories in Conan Doyle's style. It seems that the more Sherlockians have, the more they want. No other character in recent literature continues so to grow in popularity and demand.

What makes Sherlock Holmes the greatest detective of all time? Why has his name become a household word, synonymous with cleverness and deductive reasoning? His creator, Conan Doyle, did little more than mass produce his stories and send them off to his publisher for the next monthly edition. To Conan Doyle, Holmes was a stepping-stone to his writing career, and once established, his passion for writing historical fiction took precedence over producing adventures for his detective. Nevertheless, once the *Strand Magazine* provided its readership with monthly tales of Holmes and Watson, these two fictional characters seemed to take on lives of their own.

QUIZ 1
A STUDY IN STATISTICS

Rarely is there a person, young or old, who could not instantly identify the man with the chiseled facial features wearing a deerstalker cap, puffing on a curved pipe, and staring intently through a magnifying lens, as Sherlock Holmes. When the words, "Elementary, my dear Watson," are spoken, no explanation as to the phrase's origin or meaning is necessary. And even if one has never seen the film or read the story, everyone knows that *The Hound of the Baskervilles* is a spine-chilling mystery involving the world's greatest detective.

Test your knowledge of twenty Sherlock Holmes facts. The short-answer questions in this quiz are divided into three levels: easy, moderate, and difficult.

EASY

1. What is the name of Sherlock Holmes's older brother?
2. What musical instrument does Holmes play?
3. Who is Holmes's archenemy?
4. Who is the woman who proved to be a challenging opponent and possible romantic interest for Holmes's in "A Scandal in Bohemia"?
5. What is the name of Holmes's tobacco shop?
6. What is the name of Holmes's second landlady?
7. For which branch of science does Holmes have a passion?

MODERATE

8. What are Holmes's first words to Dr. Watson?

9. Of which beverage does Holmes drink large quantities?

10. Who gives Holmes his gold snuff box with an amethyst in the center?

11. What type of liquor does Holmes occasionally drink?

12. Who is the landlady of 221B Baker Street mentioned only in "A Scandal in Bohemia"?

13. Which section of the newspaper does Holmes peruse daily, looking for clues?

14. According to Holmes, how many different perfume scents exist?

DIFFICULT

15. How many steps lead from the outer hall of Holmes's house on Baker Street to his room?

16. At which bank does Holmes have his account?

17. What after dinner drink does Holmes enjoy on occasion?

18. How many windows are in Holmes's sitting room?

19. In which story does Holmes actually say to Watson, "Come, Watson, come! The game is afoot."?

20. In which publication does Holmes publish two monographs on the differences of the human ear?

QUIZ 2
CHARACTERS ACCORDING TO HOLMES

Character descriptions are Dr. Watson's forte, but occasionally Holmes uses his art of observation to bring a character to life. His concise, sharp descriptions leave no mystery as to the type of character he is dealing with, be it a notorious villain or an innocent victim. In this quiz, who are the fifteen characters described by Holmes and in which story or novel does each appear?

1. "He is one of the most dangerous men in England—a ruined gambler, an absolutely desperate villain, a man without heart or conscience."

2. "I managed to see him on a plausible pretext, but I seemed to read in his dark, deep-set, brooding eyes that he was perfectly aware of my true business. He is a man of fifty, strong, active, with iron-gray hair, great bunched black eyebrows, the step of a deer, and the air of an emperor—a fierce, masterful man, with a red-hot spirit behind his parchment face. He is either a foreigner or has lived long in the tropics, for he is yellow and sapless, but tough as whipcord."

3. "This man is the greatest financial power in the world, and a man, as I understand, of most violent and formidable character."

4. "a little wizened fellow with a cringing manner and a shambling style of walking. He wore an open jacket, with a splotch of tar on the sleeve, a red-and-black check shirt, dungaree trousers, and heavy boots worn. His face was thin and brown and crafty, with a perpetual smile upon it, which showed an irregular line of yellow teeth, and his crinkled hands were half closed in a way that is distinctive of sailors."

5. "He was a man of excellent birth and education, who had squandered a fortune upon the turf, and who lived now by doing a little quiet and genteel book-making in the sporting clubs of London."

6. "a big, ginger moustached man of the slow, solid Sussex breed—which covers much good sense under a heavy, silent exterior."

7. "I only caught a glimpse of her at the moment, but she was a lovely woman, with a face that a man might die for."

8. "His appearance, you see, is so remarkable that no one can pass him without observing him. A shock of orange hair, a pale face disfigured by a horrible scar, which, by its contraction, has turned up the outer edge of his upper lip, a bulldog chin, and a pair of very penetrating eyes, which present a singular contrast to the colour of his hair, all mark him out from amid the common crowd of mendicants, and so, too, does his wit, for he is ever ready with a reply to any piece of chaff which may be thrown at him by the passers-by."

9. "He has an extraordinary faculty for figures, and audits the books in some of the government departments. [He] lodges in Pall Mall, and he walks round the corner into Whitehall every morning and back every evening. From year's end to year's end he takes no exercise, and is seen nowhere else, except only in the Diogenes Club, which is just opposite his rooms."

10. "He was not generally popular among the undergraduates, though it always seemed to me that what was set down as pride was really an attempt to cover extreme natural diffidence. In appearance he was a man of an exceedingly aristocratic type, thin, high-nosed, and large-eyed, with languid and yet courtly manners."

11. "He is extremely tall and thin, his forehead domes out in a white curve, and his two eyes are deeply sunken in his head. He is clean-shaven, pale, and ascetic-looking, retaining something of the professor in his features. His shoulders are rounded from much study, and his face protrudes forward and is forever slowly oscillating from side to side in a curiously reptilian fashion."

12. "He was a hearty, full-blooded fellow, full of spirits and energy, the very opposite to me in most respects, but we had some subjects in common, and it was a bond of union when I found that he was as friendless as I."

13. "Women have seldom been an attraction to me, for my brain has always governed my heart, but I could not look upon her perfect clear-cut face, with all the soft freshness of the downlands in her delicate colouring, without realizing that no young man would cross her path unscathed."

14. "He is a poorly educated man, small, active, with his right leg off, and wearing a wooden stump which is worn away upon the inner side. His left boot has a coarse, square-toed sole, with an iron band round the heel. He is a middle-aged man, much sunburned, and has been a convict."

15. "a steady, solid, bovine man with thoughtful eyes, which looked at me now with a very troubled expression."

QUIZ 3
SHERLOCK HOLMES GAZETTEER

Sherlock Holmes and Dr. Watson ventured through the streets of London from the wealthy Hyde Park district to the opium dens in the seedy side of town. Below are twenty locations and addresses mentioned in the canon. They are divided into two parts: the early Sherlock Holmes stories and the stories published after Conan Doyle resurrected his detective. Match the following places with the correct character or incident.

PART 1
Place
1. No. 3 Lauriston Gardens
2. Hotel Dulong
3. King's Pyland Stable in Devonshire
4. Grimpen Mire
5. Lancaster Gate

6. Hurlstone Manor

7. Pondicherry Lodge

8. Great Alkali Plain

9. Stoke Moran

10. Englischer Hof in the village of Meiringen, Switzerland

Person/Incident

A. Hotel in Lyons, France, where Holmes was convalescing—"The Reigate Squires"

B. Location where the body of Enoch J. Drebber was found—*A Study in Scarlet*

C. Area where Holmes hid out while conducting his investigation—*The Hound of the Baskervilles*

D. Residence of Reginald Musgrave—"The Musgrave Ritual"

E. Residence of Grimesby Roylott and Helen Stoner—"The Adventure of the Speckled Band"

F. Dartmoor stables owned by Colonel Ross—"Silver Blaze"

G. Residence of Hatty Doran—"The Adventure of the Noble Bachelor"

H. Hotel near Reichenbach Falls where Holmes and Watson stayed—"The Final Problem"

I. Home of Major Sholto—*The Sign of Four*

J. Desert where John Ferrier and Lucy were rescued—*A Study in Scarlet*

PART 2

Place

1. Fighting Cock Inn
2. The Haven in Lewisham
3. Fulworth Cove
4. 45 Lord Street in Brixton
5. 427 Park Lane
6. Simpson's Tavern
7. Camden House
8. Tuxbury Old Park
9. Skibbareen
10. Lower Gill

Person/Incident

A. Inn owned by Reuben Hays—"The Adventure of the Priory School"

B. Restaurant in the Strand frequented by Holmes and Watson—"The Adventure of the Dying Detective" and "The Adventure of the Illustrious Client"

C. Residence of Colonel Emsworth—"The Adventure of the Blanched Soldier"

D. Holmes's retirement village—"The Adventure of the Lion's Mane"

E. Address of Inspector Stanley Hopkins—"The Adventure of Black Peter"

F. Moor near the Priory School—"The Adventure of the Priory School"

G. House across the street from 221B Baker Street from which Sebastian Moran tried to shoot Holmes—"The Adventure of the Empty House"

H. Home of Josiah Amberley—"The Adventure of the Retired Colourman"

I. Coastal town in Ireland where Holmes spied for the British government—"His Last Bow"

J. Murder site of Ronald Adair—"The Adventure of the Empty House"

QUIZ 4
WORDS OF WISDOM

"When you have eliminated the impossible, whatever remains, however improbable, must be the truth." Wit and wisdom came as naturally to Sherlock Holmes as studying a man's hat and deducing that he was once well off, had recently fallen on hard times, had turned to drink, and that his wife no longer loved him. This short-answer quiz contains twenty Sherlock Holmes quotes. From which story or novel was each quote taken?

HOLMES ON THOUGHT AND TRUTH

1. "It is, of course, a trifle, but there is nothing so important as trifles."

2. "Circumstantial evidence is occasionally very convincing, as when you find a trout in the milk, to quote Thoreau's example."

3. "It is an old maxim of mine that when you have excluded the impossible, whatever remains, however improbable, must be the truth."

4. "Snarling people have snarling dogs, dangerous people have dangerous ones. And their passing moods may reflect the passing moods of others."

5. "I play the game for the game's own sake."

HOLMES ON CRIMES AND CRIMINALS

6. "If criminals would always schedule their movements like railway trains, it would certainly be more convenient for all of us."

7. "Crime is common. Logic is rare."

8. "When the crime is coolly premeditated, then the means of covering it are coolly premeditated also."

9. "We should get the big fish, but the smaller would dart right and left out of the net."

10. "This empty house is my tree, and you are my tiger."

HOLMES ON PHI LOSOPHY AND RELIGION

11. "Well, moonshine is a brighter thing than fog."

12. "There is nothing in which deduction is so necessary as in religion. It can be built up as an exact science by the reasoner. Our highest assurance of the goodness of Providence seems to me to rest in the flowers. All other things, our powers, our desires, our food, are all really necessary for our existence in the first instance. But this rose is an extra. Its smell and its colour are an embellishment of life, not a condition of it. It is only goodness which gives extras, and so I say again that we have much to hope from the flowers."

13. "A loaf of bread and a clean collar. What does man want more?"

14. "The wages of sin, Watson—the wages of sin!" said he. "Sooner or later it will always come. God knows, there was sin enough."

15. "I confess that I have been as blind as a mole, but it is better to learn wisdom late than never to learn it at all."

HOLMES ON WOMEN

16. "There is a danger for him who taketh the tiger cub, and danger also for whoso snatches a delusion from a woman."

17. "Women are never to be entirely trusted—not the best of them."

18. "One of the most dangerous classes in the world," said he, "is the drifting and friendless woman. She is the

most harmless and often the most useful of mortals, but she is the inevitable inciter of crime in others. She is migratory. She has sufficient means to take her from country to country and from hotel to hotel. She is lost, as often as not, in a maze of obscure pensions and boarding houses. She is a stray chicken in a world of foxes. When she is gobbled up she is hardly missed."

19. "You can't play with edged tools forever without cutting those dainty hands."

20. "Women have seldom been an attraction to me, for my brain has always governed my heart."

QUIZ 5
DR. JOHN WATSON

Dr. John Watson, like Sherlock Holmes, has many characteristics in common with his creator. Both Dr. Watson and Conan Doyle started their careers as medical doctors and ended as writers; Conan Doyle wrote historical fiction, books on spiritualism, and pamphlets and articles expressing his political beliefs, while Watson was content in chronicling Sherlock Holmes's cases. Both served as surgeons in the military, both were married more than once, and both men were tall, well-built, and athletic. As they aged, both men put on weight, although they continued to maintain a strong, healthy constitution. Holmes often commented on Watson's way with the ladies as being attributable to his "natural advantages." This quiz contains fifteen short-answer questions about Dr. Watson, his family, background, and experiences as Holmes's sidekick.

1. What is the approximate year in which Dr. Watson was born?

2. Where did Watson receive his medical degree and in what year?

3. At which hospital did Watson serve as a staff surgeon?

4. What sport did Watson play when he lived in Blackheath Common?

5. What type of gun does Watson own?

6. Where was Watson stationed when he was injured in battle?

7. What type of pipe tobacco does Watson prefer?

8. In the entire canon Watson mentions three different medical practices. What are their locations, and in what year was he at each?

9. In what month and year does Watson marry Mary Morstan?

10. In which story does Watson consult his wife about bringing a case to Holmes's attention?

11. In which story does Watson's wife refer to him as James rather than John?

12. What is the name of Dr. Watson's inefficient housekeeper, who is given notice by Mrs. Watson?

13. In what year did Watson reenlist in the army?

14. Where does Watson keep his written records of Holmes's cases?

15. How many total years have Watson and Holmes worked together?

QUIZ 6
PROFESSOR MORIARTY

Considered by many Holmes fans as the only Conan Doyle character who could give Holmes a mental run for his money, Professor Moriarty is the master criminal in the Sherlock Holmes canon. Details about the professor are revealed in the book *The Valley of Fear*, when Inspector MacDonald comes to Holmes for assistance in a case. But not until the story "The Final Problem" do Holmes and Moriarty face off in a battle to the death. In this story Holmes professes his desire to rid society of this notorious character: "But I could not rest, Watson, I could not sit quiet in my chair, if I thought that such a man as Professor Moriarty were walking the streets of London unchallenged." This quiz contains ten short-answer questions about Sherlock Holmes's archenemy.

1. What is Professor Moriarty's first name?
2. How many brothers does Moriarty have?
3. What subject did Moriarty teach when he was a college professor?
4. What is the name of the book Moriarty wrote, which Holmes describes as "a book which ascends to such rarefied heights of pure mathematics that it is said that there was no man in the scientific press capable of criticizing it"?
5. What is the professor's teaching salary?
6. Who is the French painter who painted the portrait which hangs over Moriarty's writing desk?
7. What happens to any member of Moriarty's gang who breaks the rules of the organization?
8. Who is Moriarty's chief of staff, and how much does he get paid?
9. How many times has Holmes been inside Moriarty's house?
10. When is the only time that Dr. Watson actually sees Moriarty?

QUIZ 7
MYCROFT HOLMES

Mycroft Holmes, Sherlock's older brother, makes an appearance in two stories: "The Greek Interpreter" and "The Adventure of the Bruce-Partington Plans." Holmes clearly looks up to his older brother with admiration and trust. During Holmes's Great

Hiatus, Mycroft was the only person whom Holmes trusted with his secret. And the feeling of admiration and respect are definitely mutual, for Mycroft relies on Holmes on two occasions in the abovementioned stories. While both men are gifted in the area of deductive reasoning, the similarity ends there. Where Holmes tackles problem solving with an intense nervous energy, Mycroft takes an indifferent view of any case which causes him to stray from his daily routine. According to Holmes, "If the art of the detective began and ended in reasoning from an armchair, my brother would be the greatest criminal agent that ever lived. But he had no ambition and no energy."

Mycroft Holmes has been the subject of many parodies and pastiches through the years, and one of the most enjoyed speculations is that Mycroft Holmes might very well have been the father of Rex Stout's Nero Wolfe. This quiz contains ten short-answer questions about Sherlock Holmes's only sibling.

1. How much older is Mycroft than Sherlock Holmes?
2. To which private club does Mycroft Holmes belong?
3. At what time could you find Mycroft at his club?
4. What does Mycroft claim as his livelihood?
5. In which part of London does Mycroft live?
6. What color are Mycroft's eyes?
7. Of what finish is Mycroft's snuff box?
8. What type of handkerchief does Mycroft carry?
9. What odd rule do members of Mycroft's club have to obey?
10. How much money does Mycroft earn each year?

QUIZ 8
HOLMES RETURNS

After an absence of almost ten years, Conan Doyle brought Holmes back to entertain his public with thirty-four additional adventures. As Holmes explains to Dr. Watson after the good doctor recovers from his shock, he conceived of the idea to allow the world to think that he had died in the accident while tumbling down the cliff. Holmes wanted to put some distance between himself and the Moriarty gang. Within hours of his return, Holmes and Watson are back on the streets of London pursuing a murderous villain. This quiz contains ten short-answer questions about Holmes's Great Hiatus and his return to London.

1. What does Watson do after seeing Holmes for the first time after he was presumed dead?

2. How was Holmes able to release himself from Professor Moriarty's grasp when they were wrestling on the cliffs of Reichenbach Falls?

3. How long was Holmes's hiatus?

4. Where did Holmes spend his time?

5. What topic did Holmes research?

6. At what time does Holmes return to Baker Street?

7. Why does Holmes return to London?

8. Who knew that Holmes was still alive?

9. What alias did Holmes use while exploring in the north?

10. How is Holmes's first case after his return linked with his past?

QUIZ 9
MESSAGES AND SECRET CODES

Perhaps the best secret message was written in the forgotten riddle of "The Musgrave Ritual," an edict which was memorized by every Musgrave family member since its origination in the seventeenth century.

"Whose Was It? His who is gone.
Who shall have it? He who will come.
Where was the sun? Over the oak.
Where was the shadow? Under the elm.
How was it stepped? North by ten and by ten,
east by five and by five, south by two and by two,
west by one and by one, and so under.
What shall we give for it? All that is ours.
Why should we give it? For the sake of trust."

The meaning was lost over time and came to be considered trivial and insignificant, even with regard to the mystery continuing to haunt the Musgrave family. Holmes and the Musgrave butler, however, believed otherwise. Connect the following fifteen codes and messages with the story and the individuals involved.

1. "THE OLD MAN IS DEAD."
2. "There is danger-may-come-very-soon-one. Douglas'-rich—country-now-at-Birlstone-House-Birlstone-confidence-is-pressing."
3. "Jagged or torn."
4. "I will be at Thor Bridge at nine o'clock."
5. "Will come without fail to-night and bring new sparking plugs."
6. "Come at once if convenient—if inconvenient come all the same."
7. "Be at the third pillar from the left outside the Lyceum Theatre tonight at seven o'clock."
8. "I will be there, you may be sure. Maudie"
9. "Our own colours, green and white. Green open, white shut. Main stair, first corridor, seventh right, green baize. Godspeed. D."
10. "Come at once without fail. Can give you information as to your recent loss. Elman."

11. "You will see me when all is ready. Come at once.
    F.H.M."

12. "S. H. for J. O."

13. "The cottage is still tenanted [it said]. Have seen the
    face again at the window. Will meet the seven-o'clock
    train and will take no steps until you arrive."

14. "Put the papers on the sundial."

15. "The game is up. Hudson has told all. Fly for your
    life."

QUIZ 10
FIRST WORDS

It is easy to picture Conan Doyle developing that very first line
and then spinning the rest of the tale as effortlessly as a passenger
climbing aboard a train and sitting back to enjoy the ride. In the
early days of writing Sherlock Holmes tales, Conan Doyle quickly
cranked out the stories almost in first draft. As he grew tired of
writing about his detective, he continued with the same rapidity,
except with the intention of submitting them to his publishers as
quickly as possible so that he could write other things which held
his interest more. His attitude toward Sherlock Holmes, however, did not deter his fans from absorbing every word and then
demanding more. The following quiz contains thirty of the most
interesting first lines of the Sherlock Holmes tales. Your task is to
identify the tale.

1. "It was a bitterly cold night and frosty morning,
   towards the end of the winter of '97, that I was
   awakened by a tugging at my shoulder."

2. "I have never known my friend to be in better form,
   both mental and physical, than in the year '95."

3. "In the third week of November, in the year 1895, a
   dense yellow fog settled down upon London."

4. "When I glance over my notes and records of the Sherlock Holmes cases between the years of '82 and '90, I am faced by so many which present strange and interesting features that it is no easy matter to know which to choose and which to leave."

5. "My dear fellow," said Sherlock Holmes as we sat on either side of the fire in his lodging at Baker Street, "life is infinitely stranger than anything which the mind of man could invent."

6. "It was the year 1878 I took my degree of Doctor of Medicine of the University of London, and proceeded to Netley to go through the course prescribed for surgeons in the Army."

7. "It is years since the incident of which I speak took place, and yet it is with diffidence that I allude to them."

8. "I don't think that any of my adventures of Mr. Sherlock Holmes opened quite so abruptly, or so dramatically, as that which I associate with . . . "

9. "Of all the problems which have been submitted to my friend, Mr. Sherlock Holmes, for solution during the years of our intimacy, there were only two which I was the means of introducing to his notice—that of Mr. Hatherley's thumb, and that of Colonel Warburton's madness."

10. "To Sherlock Holmes she is always *the* woman."

11. "The July which immediately succeeded my marriage was made memorable by three cases of interest, in which I had the privilege of being associated with Sherlock Holmes and of studying his methods."

12. "It was some time before the health of my friend Mr. Sherlock Holmes recovered from the strain caused by his immense exertions in the spring of '87."

13. "I find it recorded in my notebook that it was a bleak and windy day towards the end of March in the year 1892."

14. "It was in the spring of the year 1894 that all London was interested, and the fashionable world dismayed, by the murder of the Honorable Ronald Adair under most unusual and inexplicable circumstances."

15. "We were fairly accustomed to receive weird telegrams at Baker Street, but I have a particular recollection of one which reached us on a gloomy February morning some seven or eight years ago, and gave Mr. Sherlock Holmes a puzzled quarter of an hour."

16. "It was with a heavy heart that I take up my pen to write these the last words in which I shall ever record the singular gifts by which my friend Mr. Sherlock Holmes was distinguished."

17. "To the man who loves art for its own sake," remarked Sherlock Holmes, tossing aside the advertisement sheet of the *Daily Telegraph*, "it is frequently in its least important and lowliest manifestations that the keenest pleasure is to be derived."

18. "We were seated at breakfast one morning, my wife and I, when the maid brought in a telegram."

19. "Sherlock Holmes took his bottle from the corner of the mantelpiece, and his hypodermic syringe from its neat morocco case."

20. "Holmes," said I as I stood one morning in our box-window looking down the street, "here is a madman coming along. It seems rather sad that his relatives should allow to him to come out alone."

21. "During my long and intimate acquaintance with Mr. Sherlock Holmes I had never heard him refer to his relations, and hardly ever to his own early life."

22. "Mr. Sherlock Holmes, who was usually very late in the mornings, save upon those not infrequent occasions when he was up all night, was seated at the breakfast table. I stood upon the hearth-rug and picked up the stick which our visitor had left behind him the night before."

23. "Somewhere in the vaults of the bank of Cox and Co., at Charing Cross, there is a travel-worn and battered tin dispatch-box with my name, John H. Watson, M. D., Late Indian Army, printed upon the lid."

24. "From the point of view of the criminal expert," said Mr. Sherlock Holmes, "London has become a singularly uninteresting city since the death of the late lamented Professor Moriarty."

25. "In recording from time to time some of the curious experiences and interesting recollections which I associate with my long and intimate friendship with Mr. Sherlock Holmes, I have continually been faced by difficulties caused by his own aversion to publicity."

26. "Holmes had been seated for some hours in silence with a long, thin back curved over a chemical vessel in which he was brewing a particularly malodorous product."

27. "It may have been a comedy, or it may have been a tragedy."

28. "From the years 1894 to 1901 inclusive, Mr. Sherlock Holmes was a very busy man."

29. "It was pleasant to Dr. Watson to find himself once more in the untidy room of the first floor in Baker Street which had been the starting-point of so many remarkable adventures."

30. "It is a most singular thing that a problem which was certainly as abstruse and unusual as any which I have faced in my long professional career should have come to me after my retirement, and be brought, as it were, to my very door."

Quiz 11
CHARACTERS ACCORDING TO WATSON—PART 1

Deductive reasoning is to Sherlock Holmes what character descriptions are to Dr. Watson. This brilliant attribute is rarely, if ever, discussed in the numerous essays written about Watson. Holmes's chronicler had a gift for matching adjective with character: "A lean, ferret-like man"; "fresh-complexioned young fellow"; "a bright, quick face, freckled like a plover's egg." His simple but vivid words flowed within the story, bringing the characters to life as if they had stepped from the page into reality. Here are fifteen character descriptions from *A Study in Scarlet*, *The Sign of Four*, *Adventures of Sherlock Holmes*, and *Memoirs of Sherlock Holmes*, the stories written before the Great Hiatus. Identify the character and the story or novel.

1. "He was a man of about fifty, tall, portly, and imposing, with a massive, strongly marked face and a commanding figure. He was dressed in a sombre yet rich style, in black frock-coat, shining hat, neat brown gaiters, and well-cut pearl-gray trousers. Yet his actions were in absurd contrast to the dignity of his dress and features, for he was running hard, with occasional little springs, such as a weary man gives who is little accustomed to set and tax upon his legs."

2. "entered the room with a firm step and an outward composure of manner. She was a blonde young lady, small, dainty, well gloved, and dressed in the most perfect taste. There was, however, a plainness and simplicity about her costume which bore with it a suggestion of limited means. The dress was a sombre grayish beige, untrimmed and unbraided, and she wore a small turban of the same dull hue, relieved only by a suspicion of white feather in the side. Her face had neither regularity of feature nor beauty of complexion,

but her expression was sweet and amiable, and her large blue eyes were singularly spiritual and sympathetic. In an experience of women which extends over many nations and three separate continents, I have never looked upon a face which gave a clearer promise of a refined and sensitive nature."

3. "In height he was rather over six feet, and so excessively lean that he seemed to be considerably taller. His eyes were sharp and piercing, save during those intervals of torpor to which I have alluded; and his thin, hawk-like nose gave his whole expression an air of alertness and decision. His chin, too, had the prominence and squareness which mark the man of determination."

4. "She was rather above the middle height, slim, with dark hair and eyes, which seemed the darker against the absolute pallor of her skin. I do not think that I have ever seen such deadly paleness in a woman's face. Her lips, too, were bloodless, but her eyes were flushed with crying. As she swept silently into the room she impressed me with a greater sense of grief than the banker had done in the morning, and it was the more striking in her as she was evidently a woman of strong character, with immense capacity for self-restraint."

5. "Looking over his shoulder, I saw that on the pavement opposite there stood a large woman with a heavy fur boa round her neck, and a large curling red feather in a broad-brimmed hat which was tilted in a coquettish Duchess of Devonshire fashion over her ear. From under this great panoply she peeped up in a nervous, hesitating fashion at our windows, while her body oscillated backward and forward, and her fingers fidgeted with her glove buttons."

6. "She was a striking-looking woman, a little short and thick for symmetry, but with a beautiful olive complexion, large, dark, Italian eyes, and a wealth of

deep black hair. Her rich tints made the white face of her companion the more worn and haggard by the contrast."

7. "a small man with a very high head, a bristle of red hair all round the fringe of it, and a bald, shining scalp which shot out from among it like a mountain-peak from fir-trees."

8. "A lean, ferret-like man, furtive and sly-looking, was waiting for us upon the platform. In spite of the light brown dustcoat and leather leggings which he wore in deference to his rustic surroundings, I had no difficulty in recognizing . . . "

9. "His costume was a peculiar mixture of the professional and of the agricultural, having a black top-hat, a long frock-coat, and a pair of high gaiters, with a hunting-crop swinging in his hand. So tall was he that his hat actually brushed the cross bar of the doorway, and his breadth seemed to span it across from side to side. A large face, seared with a thousand wrinkles, burned yellow with the sun, and marked with every evil passion, was turned from one to the other of us, while his deep-set, bile-shot eyes, and his high, thin, fleshless nose, gave him somewhat the resemblance to a fierce old bird of prey."

10. "A pale, taper-faced man with sandy whiskers rose up from a chair by the fire as we entered. His age may not have been more than three or four and thirty, but his haggard expression and unhealthy hue told of a life which had sapped his strength and robbed him of his youth. His manner was nervous and shy, like that of a sensitive gentleman, and the thin white hand which he laid on the mantelpiece as he rose was that of an artist rather than of a surgeon. His dress was quiet and sombre—a black frock-coat, dark trousers, and a touch of colour about his necktie."

11. "She was plainly but neatly dressed, with a bright, quick face, freckled like a plover's egg and with the brisk manner of a woman who has had her own way to make in the world."

12. "I entered my consulting-room and found a gentleman seated by the table. He was quietly dressed in a suit of heather tweed, with a soft cloth cap which he had laid down upon my books. Round one of his hands he had a handkerchief wrapped, which was mottled all over with bloodstains. He was young, not more than five-and-twenty, I should say, with a strong, masculine face; but he was exceedingly pale and gave me the impression of a man who was suffering from some strong agitation, which it took all his strength of mind to control."

13. "A man entered who could hardly have been less than six feet six inches in height, with the chest and limbs of a Hercules. His dress was rich with a richness which would, in England, be looked upon as akin to bad taste. Heavy bands of astrakhan were slashed across the sleeves and fronts of his double-breasted coat, while the deep blue cloak which was thrown over his shoulders was lined with flame-coloured silk and secured at the neck with a brooch which consisted of a single flaming beryl. Boots which extended halfway up his calves, and which were trimmed at the tops with rich brown fur, completed the impression of barbaric opulence which was suggested by his whole appearance."

14. "Our visitor bore every mark of being an average commonplace British tradesman, obese, pompous, and slow. He wore rather baggy gray shepherd's check trousers, a not over-clean black frock-coat, unbuttoned in the front, and a drab waistcoat with a heavy brassy Albert chain, and a square pierced bit of metal dangling down as an ornament. A frayed tophat and a faded brown overcoat with a wrinkled velvet collar lay upon

a chair beside him. Altogether, look as I would, there was nothing remarkable about the man save his blazing red head, and the expression of extreme chagrin and discontent upon his features."

15. "He was a large man with rounded shoulders, a massive head, and a broad, intelligent face, sloping down to a pointed beard of grizzled brown. A touch of red in nose and cheeks, with a slight tremor of his extended hand, recalled Holmes's surmise as to his habits. His rusty black frock-coat was buttoned right up in front, with a collar turned up, and his lank wrist protruded from his sleeves without a sign of cuff or shirt."

Basil Rathbone as Sherlock Holmes and Nigel Bruce as Dr. Watson in
Universal Studios' *Dressed to Kill* 1946

TWO

SHERLOCK HOLMES NOVELS

"It is a capital mistake to theorize
before you have all the evidence."
—SHERLOCK HOLMES

THE PUBLIC IS INTRODUCED TO Sherlock Holmes and Dr. Watson in Conan Doyle's first Sherlock Holmes tale, *A Study in Scarlet.* Published in *Beeton's Christmas Annual* in 1887 and in novel form a year later, this two-part tale begins with Dr. Watson, recently discharged from the army, recovering from a battle wound. He is looking for direction in his life; Sherlock Holmes is looking for a roommate. A mutual friend named Stamford introduces them (preparing Watson beforehand about Holmes's eccentric habits), and the two characters begin a partnership that continues for thirty-nine years on the written page and forever in the minds and hearts of Sherlockians.

Conan Doyle's second Sherlock Holmes novel, *The Sign of Four,* published in 1890, sends Holmes and Watson on a chivalrous treasure hunt which turns into a murderous chase. Considered one of the best mysteries in the entire canon, *The Sign of Four* consists of romance and riches, bloodhounds and boat chases, and, of course, murder and mayhem. In chronicling this case, Watson gives insight into Holmes's drug habit and his antagonistic attitude toward women. The good doctor himself, in the wake of danger, falls in love, and Scotland Yard, in what appears to be a recurring measure, takes credit for capturing the bad guy and solving the crime.

Considered the best written and the most popular of all Sherlock Holmes cases, *The Hound of the Baskervilles* first appeared in the *Strand* in monthly episodes in 1901 and was published as a novel in 1902. Conan Doyle had not written a Holmes story in almost seven years, having left his detective in a fatal struggle in Switzerland. The inspiration for this mystery originated from an actual Dartmoor legend and, after considerable research with friend Bertram Fletcher Robinson, Conan Doyle wrote the most famous book of his career. When published in the *Strand,* the story increased the magazine's circulation to over 30,000. Conan Doyle's intention was not, however, to bring Holmes back; rather his intention was to tell a great Gothic tale, using his detective as a catalyst. In fact, the story was set in 1889, two years before Holmes would meet his demise. But little did Conan Doyle realize that his fantastic book would cause such an enthusiastic reaction from Sherlockians worldwide. With publishers on the author's doorstep offering "big bucks," Sherlock Holmes was, at last, reintroduced into the world of literature.

The last Sherlock Holmes novel, *The Valley of Fear*—probably the least popular of all four novels—was published thirteen years after *The Hound of the Baskervilles.* Two completely different tales linked together by a fine thread tell of a conspiracy and an apparent murder. In part one, "The Tragedy of Birlstone," Holmes solves the mystery with Watson's assistance. Part two, "The Scowrers," recounts a chain of events that began in America some thirteen years earlier, leading to the present crime in London.

All four novels show Conan Doyle at his best, his story-telling ability capturing the essence of London around the turn of the twentieth century.

QUIZ 12
A STUDY IN SCARLET

Published in Beeton's Christmas Annual, *1887;*
novel published in 1888

Conan Doyle approached his writing career as a professional approaches a business venture. He felt that the literary market lacked a good detective serial and proceeded to develop Sherlock Holmes and Dr. Watson in their first investigation. *A Study in Scarlet* was rejected by five publishers before Ward, Lock & Co. picked up the story and published it in the *Beeton's Christmas Annual* the following year, 1887. Conan Doyle was paid a mere twenty-five pounds, and although the reviews were few in number, the print run sold out. Ward, Lock & Co. reprinted the story in book form in July 1888 with an added bonus—this volume included illustrations by Charles Doyle, the author's father. The following two-part quiz contains forty short-answer questions concerning characters, clues, and circumstances.

Story Date: London 1881
Part I: "The Brixton Mystery"
CHARACTERS

1. Which Scotland Yard detective writes to Holmes asking for his assistance in solving the mystery surrounding the body found in an abandoned house off Brixton Road?
2. Who found the body?
3. Whom did the constable see on the streets when he called for help after discovering the body?
4. Who answers the ad Holmes placed in the paper?
5. Who comes rushing up to the apartment at breakfast time, with a report on the crime?
6. Whom does Inspector Gregson arrest for the murder of Drebber?
7. Who reluctantly gives Inspector Gregson information as to when Drebber left the house and where he was going?
8. How was Joseph Stangerson murdered?
9. Who saw the murderer leave from Stangerson's window?
10. Who found the cab driver who was at the scene of the crime?

CLUES

1. What are the two main observations Holmes makes about the body?
2. What item falls from the body as it is being moved?
3. Of the many items found in the pockets of the dead man, which two gave the inspectors helpful leads?

4. From information found on the body, where was the victim planning to travel?

5. What clue does Inspector Lestrade find in the back room of the house?

6. What does Holmes pick up from the floor and place in an envelope?

7. What type of tobacco does the murderer smoke?

8. How does Holmes know that the message written on the wall was meant to be a red herring?

9. How did Inspector Gregson discover where Drebber was staying?

10. What piece of evidence, discovered by Lestrade and considered insignificant, gives Holmes the link he needs to tie up the case?

CIRCUMSTANCES

1. What is the first thing Holmes does when he arrives on the scene?

2. What nickname does Holmes give the two men, possibly the murderers, who placed the body in the house?

3. Why does Holmes want to speed up his investigation?

4. What does Holmes do to encourage the constable to give accurate information?

5. Why did the constable decide to investigate the abandoned house in Lauriston Gardens?

6. How does Holmes lure the man who dropped the ring to come to Baker Street?

7. According to the *Daily Telegraph*, what political faction is responsible for the "Brixton Mystery"?

8. According to the *Standard*, what political faction is responsible for the crime?

9. According to the *Daily News*, what political faction is responsible for the crime?

10. What did Arthur Charpentier say happened after he followed Drebber?

Story Date: 1847 to 1860 in Utah
Part 2: "The Country of the Saints"
1. Where does part two of the story take place?
2. Why were John Ferrier and Lucy alone in the desert?
3. Who rescued John Ferrier and Lucy?
4. What happened to John Ferrier when the Mormons settled and began their community?
5. Why was Jefferson Hope in Utah?
6. Who visited John Ferrier after Jefferson Hope left, and what was the reason for this visit?
7. What type of threats did John Ferrier begin receiving?
8. What was the Mormons' secret code and response, allowing travelers to pass the sentinels?
9. What happened to Lucy?
10. Why did Jefferson Hope not stand trial for the two murders?

QUIZ 13
THE SIGN OF FOUR

Published in Lippincott Magazine,
February 1890; book published 1890

After the success of *A Study in Scarlet,* Lippincott Publishers of Pennsylvania asked Conan Doyle for another Sherlock Holmes story. Pleased with the request, but still struggling with his reputation as a novice writer, Conan Doyle did not immediately accept the offer. However, a short time later, he had the opportunity to meet Oscar Wilde at a party sponsored by Lippincott Publishers. Wilde had just read Conan Doyle's novel *Micah Clarke* and sang the praises of the young author to the others attending. By the end of the evening, both Wilde and Conan Doyle received an offer from Lippincott to write a book. The results were *The Picture of Dorian Gray* by Oscar Wilde and *The Sign of Four* by Conan Doyle. The Sherlock Holmes author signed the contract that very day, and less than six months later, in February 1890, the story appeared in the magazine and then in book form later that year. Here are thirty short-answer questions.

Story Date: 1888
CHARACTERS

1. Whom did Mary contact after her father disappeared?

2. Why is Thaddeus's twin brother, Bartholomew, angry with him?

3. Because of the treasure, Major Sholto was afraid to go out alone. Whom did he hire to protect him?

4. According to Major Sholto, what killed Captain Morstan?

5. How are Holmes, Watson, Mary, and Thaddeus able to gain entrance into Bartholomew's house after McMurdo, the bodyguard, refuses to let them in?

6. Who alerts Holmes and Thaddeus that Bartholomew has bolted himself in his room and refuses to answer?

7. What does Holmes ask that Watson fetch to assist them in tracking the criminals?

8. Whom does the overzealous Inspector Jones arrest for the murder of Bartholomew Sholto?

9. Whom does Holmes hire to help him find the missing boat?

10. Who shoots the aborigine as he is about to blow a poison dart?

CLUES

1. How does Holmes know that the person who wrote the letter also addressed the six boxes that were sent to Mary?

2. When did Thaddeus and Bartholomew realize that their father was involved with a secret agency?

3. How did Bartholomew Sholto find the hidden treasure?

4. What message is left by Bartholomew's body?

5. What evidence does Holmes find that indicates that someone entered through the window?

6. How does Holmes know that the man escaping from the scene of the crime slid down the rope too quickly?

7. How does Holmes know that another person is involved in the crime?

8. How does Holmes know that the poison used to kill Sholto is a type of strychnine?

9. What is peculiar about the footprint found in the attic?

10. Why is the tiny-footed person so easy to track?

CIRCUMSTANCES

1. How much time had passed between the time Mary's father disappeared and the day that she called upon Holmes for assistance?

2. What happened as Major Sholto was about to tell his sons where the treasure was hidden?

3. Why is Watson not excited about Mary's good fortune?

4. Why does the dog fail in his first attempt to track the criminal?

5. What is the name of the boat which the criminals hired?

6. How are Holmes, Watson, and Jones able to capture their fugitive?

7. What happens to the Agra treasure?

8. How many years does Jonathan Small wait to take possession of the treasure?

9. How did Small lose his leg?

10. What is the most valued jewel of the treasure?

QUIZ 14
THE HOUND OF THE
BASKERVILLES

Published in the Strand, *August 1901–April 1902;*
book published in 1902

The dark, eerie setting, the frightful legend of the devil hound, and the classic Victorian characters make *The Hound of the Baskervilles* the best of Conan Doyle's Sherlock Holmes mysteries. It is one of the few Holmes tales based on an actual legend. In 1901, Conan Doyle was on holiday in Norfolk where he became reacquainted with a colleague he knew during the South African War.

Bertram Fletcher Robinson told Conan Doyle of the old legend of Dartmoor. The two men became so excited over the prospect of turning the legend into a Holmes story, that they walked the moor for hours developing the plot. The novel was first published in the *Strand* in 1901 as a magazine serial, then in book form in 1902. There was some speculation as to why Robinson's name was not mentioned as a coauthor to the story, but because Conan Doyle was considered an honest and highly moral man, the issue was not pursued. This legendary tale merits thirty short-answer questions.

TRIVIA FACTS : DID YOU KNOW THAT . . .

1. Arthur Conan Doyle never had Sherlock Holmes smoking a calabash pipe or wearing a deerstalker cap. These signature items were added as others adapted the Holmes stories and published sketches of the detective.

2. In all the writings by Arthur Conan Doyle, Sherlock Holmes never said, "Elementary, my dear Watson."

3. When Conan Doyle submitted A Study in Scarlet to the London publication *Cornhill Magazine*, editor James Payne turned it down claiming it was "shilling dreadful."

4. Conan Doyle's initial name for his Great Detective was Sherringford Holmes.

Story Date: 1889

CHARACTERS

1. Who wrote the Baskerville manuscript?
2. Who discovered Sir Charles's body?
3. Who is the messenger that Holmes hires?
4. Who does the passenger picked up in Trafalgar Square claim to be?
5. Who are the suspects that Holmes names in the case?
6. Who found out about the stranger on the moor?
7. Whom does Holmes bring with him to help in the investigation?
8. Who sends Sir Henry the warning?
9. How does Holmes know who is behind the mystery of Baskerville Hall?
10. Who is sucked into the mire?

CLUES

1. How does Dr. Mortimer know that Sir Charles stood at the gate in the alley for about five or ten minutes?
2. How does Holmes know that Sir Charles was running in the alley before his death?
3. How does Holmes know that the newsprint is from the *Times*?
4. What two items of Sir Henry's are stolen from his hotel?
5. What is the disturbing noise that Watson hears on the first night that he stays in the hall?
6. Why was Sir Charles at the alley gate on the night he was killed?
7. How does Holmes know that Watson is waiting in the hut?
8. Why does the hound chase Selden?
9. What scent does Holmes smell on the warning letter?
10. What complicates the case for Holmes?

CIRCUMSTANCES

1. During which year does the story take place?

2. Whom does Holmes assign to find the newspaper from which the warning message to Sir Henry was clipped?

3. What warning does Holmes give Sir Henry as he boards the train for Devonshire?

4. What is the first eerie sight that Dr. Mortimer, Dr. Watson, and Sir Henry notice when they arrive at Baskerville Hall?

5. What is the name of the mire on the moor?

6. The remains of which prehistoric man are found on the moor?

7. Why does Stapleton invite Watson for a visit?

8. What does Watson find when he enters the hut on the moor?

9. Where is the hound kept?

10. How is Beryl prevented from warning Sir Henry?

QUIZ 15
THE VALLEY OF FEAR

Published in the Strand, *September 1914–May 1915; novel published in 1915*

In part one of *The Valley of Fear,* Holmes's investigative genius comes through without a hitch. Considered by many critics as one of the best detective stories written by Conan Doyle, "The Tragedy of Birlstone" takes place in a country manor in Sussex, where Holmes outsmarts Inspector MacDonald of Scotland Yard; White Mason, Sussex's chief of police; and friends and lovers who reside in the manor. Bringing everyone together in the library, as all good detectives do, Holmes coaxes John Douglas to tell his story. Anxious to free himself and his wife from the "rat trap," Douglas takes his audience back almost twenty years to Vermissa Valley, California, where greed and power ruled with an iron fist.

Part two, "The Scowrers," is a lengthy tale explaining the sordid circumstances surrounding *The Valley of Fear.* This quiz contains forty short-answer questions.

Story Date: Late 1890s
Part 1: "The Tragedy of Birlstone"
CHARACTERS
1. Who sends Holmes a message in code regarding a tragedy about to occur at Birlstone Manor?

2. Which Scotland Yard detective assists Holmes in this case?

3. How was the victim murdered?

4. Where did John Douglas make the acquaintance of his longtime friend Cecil James Barker?

5. What is the name of the Sussex police chief who summoned Scotland Yard to assist in this case?

6. What name did Mr. Douglas utter when he was delirious while recovering from a hunting accident?

7. What odd question does Mrs. Douglas ask Watson about Holmes?

8. What does Holmes believe about the story that Mrs. Douglas and Mr. Barker tell concerning the death of Mr. Douglas?

9. Who resembles the description the hotel employees gave of Mr. Hargrave, the owner of the bicycle?

10. Which servant allows Holmes to spend time in Mr. Douglas's study, contemplating the case?

CLUES
1. What clue did Barker find on the windowsill of Douglas's study?

2. What is left near the dead man's body?

3. What did the murderer steal after he killed his victim?

4. What fact about the crime puzzles Inspector MacDonald?

5. What appears on the dead man's body that causes Holmes to reason that Douglas may have been nervous that day?

6. What object does Holmes notice missing from the study?

7. What peculiar reaction does Mrs. Douglas show when told that her husband's wedding ring is missing?

8. What does Holmes notice about Mrs. Douglas on the evening he ponders the case in Mr. Douglas's study?

9. What is found in the bundle that was thrown in the moat?

10. After finding the clothing in the moat, with the coat's label indicating that it came from the United States, what does Holmes deduce that the initials V. V. stand for?

CIRCUMSTANCES

1. At what time is the moat bridge surrounding the manor usually lowered?

2. What is the odd marking on Mr. Douglas's arm?

3. What ironic circumstance may have prevented Douglas from defending himself?

4. What is Holmes's mood during the investigation?

5. What time do the servants usually retire for the evening?

6. According to Holmes, what happens to the sound of a gun if it is fired at a very close range?

7. What odd question does Holmes ask Watson when Holmes returns from a late night investigation?

8. What message, concerning the moat, does Holmes send to Mr. Barker?

9. When does Mr. Douglas's story begin?

10. What happened to Mr. Douglas when the truth was revealed?

Story Date: 1875
Part 2: "The Scowrers"

1. Who was the boss at the Union House?
2. Where did McMurdo stay when he reached the valley?
3. What job did McMurdo find after he settled in the valley?
4. How did McGinty make his money?
5. Why did McMurdo leave Chicago?
6. What talent did McMurdo have that McGinty felt may be useful?
7. What initiation ritual proclaimed McMurdo as a member of the lodge?
8. Why did Captain Marvin arrest McMurdo?
9. What special assignment did the bodymaster give McMurdo?
10. What became of McGinty and Baldwin?

TRIVIA FACTS : DID YOU KNOW THAT . . .

1. Conan Doyle considered calling *The Sign of the Four* either *The Sign of Six* or *The Problem of the Sholtos*.

2. Conan Doyle was an avid dog lover and often used his dogs for models in his Holmes stories. For instance, the sleuth-dog Toby in the book *The Sign of Four* was modeled after the author's half spaniel, half lurcher.

3. In creating his detective stories, Conan Doyle always developed the solution to his mysteries first and then wrote the stories leading up to their conclusions.

4. In 1911 a man named Oscar Slater was convicted of murdering an elderly woman in Edinburgh and was sentenced to death. Conan Doyle was convinced of his innocence and, after conducting his own investigation, was able to gain Slater's release from prison. The endeavor took sixteen years.

Jeremy Brett as Sherlock Holmes in the British Granada television series
Sherlock Holmes 1984-94

THREE

THE FIRST COLLECTION:
THE ADVENTURES OF SHERLOCK HOLMES

"You see, but you do not observe."
—SHERLOCK HOLMES

IN THIS FIRST COLLECTION of stories, Sherlock Holmes and Dr. Watson are reunited after a brief separation due to Dr. Watson's recent marriage and his return to the practice of medicine. On his way home after visiting a patient, Watson passes through his old neighborhood and drops in at Baker Street, unannounced, to find Holmes in the middle of a deductive pursuit. While they catch up on current news and domestic developments, Watson receives a benign lecture on the art of observation, fueling the fire for adventure. The following afternoon finds them hot on the trail of a dainty, but notorious, woman whose memory will forever strike a sensitive nerve for Holmes. The collection begins with "A Scandal in Bohemia," and the subsequent adventures of "The Red-Headed League," "A Case of Identity," "The Boscombe Valley Mystery," "The Five Orange Pips," "The Man with the Twisted Lip," "The Adventure of the Blue Carbuncle," "The Adventure of the Speckled Band," "The Adventure of the Engineer's Thumb," "The Adventure of the Noble Bachelor," "The Adventure of the Beryl Coronet," and "The Adventure of the Copper Beeches" find Holmes and Watson solving cases involving fraud, deception, murder, and robbery.

The Adventures of Sherlock Holmes was released in book form in 1892. It contains twelve Sherlock Holmes stories accompanied by 104 illustrations by Sidney Paget, the artist responsible for immortalizing the visual image of the Great Detective. Conan Doyle dedicated this book to his medical school teacher, Dr. Joseph Bell, whom he credited for providing the inspiration for the character of Sherlock Holmes.

Dr. Bell reciprocated Conan Doyle's gesture by writing perhaps one of the book's most accurate reviews, explaining in simple terms why Sherlock Holmes became the most popular detective in literary history, which is also why, after over one hundred years, his popularity continues to soar. Bell's review, which appeared in *Bookman Magazine,* compliments Conan Doyle's ability to weave an intriguing plot in the briefest manner, using the fewest possible words. He writes that Conan Doyle "has given us stories that we can read at a sitting between dinner and coffee, and we have not a chance to forget the beginning before we reach the end."

Conan Doyle was writing during an era when literature, and the discussion of such, made a delightful evening of entertainment. But as entertainment has evolved over the past century into electronic media, so has the adaptation of Sherlock Holmes stories. The current generation of Holmes's readership can enjoy his original adventures, along with new creations, on television, in theatres, and over the Internet. In 1995, young children flicked on the tube after school and watched a spunky little Jack Russell terrier entertain and teach them about the power of observation and the joys of literature as he dressed up like the Great Detective and solved the mystery of *The Hound of the Baskervilles,* "Wishbone" style.

QUIZ 16
"A SCANDAL IN BOHEMIA"

Published in the Strand *in July 1891*

The year was 1891, Conan Doyle's first two Sherlock Holmes books, *A Study in Scarlet* and *The Sign of Four,* along with his historical novel *The White Company,* were selling very well. His medical practice located at 23 Montague Place, however, was faltering. Conan Doyle's heart was not in his practice, and he was becoming bored with his role as doctor. Upon the advice of his wife and his mother, he began another Sherlock Holmes story, the first in the collection *The Adventures of Sherlock Holmes.* "A Scandal in Bohemia" was written in a few days, and he was so pleased with the results that he completed four more stories in less than three weeks. The following quiz contains ten multiple choice questions.

Story Date: March 1888

1. Since Watson's marriage, Holmes and Watson had not seen each other for some time; what change does Holmes notice about his friend that causes the detective to reply, "Wedlock suits you."
   A. Watson declines Holmes's offer of a cigar.
   B. Watson has gained seven and a half pounds.
   C. Watson's clothes are expertly cared for and mended.
   D. Watson has developed a light gait to his step.

2. When the nobleman, using the name Count Von Kramm, visits Holmes, what disguise does he wear to hide his true identity?
   A. He is dressed in a harlequin costume.
   B. He wears a white hood over his head.
   C. The visitor wears a black mask over his face.
   D. He wears a cape which he holds over his face.

3. What is the King of Bohemia, Wilhelm Gottsreich Sigismond von Ormstein, trying to recover from Irene Adler in order to prevent a scandal?
   A. A photograph of the King and Miss Adler, which proves that they had an affair
   B. Love letters that he wrote Miss Adler
   C. A piece of royal jewelry that the King gave to his ex-lover
   D. His dressing gown with his monogram

4. How many attempts are made to steal the item(s) from Miss Adler?
   A. Three
   B. Four
   C. Two
   D. Five

5. What does Miss Adler plan to do that would cause a scandal for the King?

    A. Irene Adler plans to send the item(s) to the King's fiancée on the day of the wedding.

    B. She plans to send the item(s) to the newspaper two days prior to the wedding.

    C. She plans to crash the wedding and personally deliver the item(s) to the bride.

    D. Irene Adler plans to send the item(s) to the fiancée's father, the King of Scandinavia.

6. What two disguises does Holmes use in this story?

    A. A cabby and a street beggar

    B. A constable and a drunk

    C. An ill-kept groom and a benevolent clergyman

    D. An old woman and a chimney sweep

7. What does Holmes do that causes Miss Adler to reveal her hiding place?

    A. Holmes has Watson throw a smoke rocket into her room and shout "Fire!"

    B. Holmes tells her that he has stolen the item(s) during the night, and she rushes to the hiding place to check.

    C. Holmes bribes Miss Adler's housekeeper to spy on her.

    D. Holmes tells her that he believes that the item(s) are not in her possession any longer and pretends to leave her apartment. He hides in the hall and watches her reflection in the glass of the door as she goes to retrieve them.

8. Why does Irene Adler decide not to continue with her plan to ruin the King?

    A. She falls in love with another man and marries him.

    B. The King is able to discover information about Miss Adler that she does not want revealed to her new lover.

C. The King agrees to pay her for the item(s).

D. Holmes retrieves the item(s) that Miss Adler planned to use to ruin the King.

9. What memento does Irene Adler give to Holmes? He proclaims to Watson that he plans to wear it on his watch chain.

A. A button from her frock

B. An earring of which the matching one was lost

C. An emerald ring which the King had given her when they were lovers

D. The sovereign that she gave Holmes for assisting her in the Church of St. Monica

10. What payment does Holmes request for assisting the King?

A. The King's emerald snake ring

B. The photograph that Irene Adler left behind

C. The King's gold watch

D. An invitation to the King's wedding

QUIZ 17
"THE RED-HEADED LEAGUE"

Published in the Strand *in August 1891*

The plot for "The Red-Headed League" was based on a well-known bank robbery staged by Adam Worth, who ran an intricate crime network in the United States in the 1860s and 70s. He rented a house next to the Boylestone Bank in Boston and tunneled through the basement, robbing the bank of $450,000 and an enormous amount of gold coins. Many of the details of this case make their way into Conan Doyle's story. The following quiz contains ten short-answer questions.

Story Date: 1890

1. How does Sherlock Holmes know that Jabez Wilson had been to China?

2. Who is Ezekiah Hopkins?

3. What does Jabez Wilson do for a living?

4. What work was Mr. Wilson asked to perform as a member of the league? And what hours was he required to work?

5. When Jabez Wilson tracked Duncan Ross to the address he gave as his home, what did Wilson find?

6. Which Scotland Yard detective assists Holmes on this case?

7. What are the thieves after?

8. What does Holmes notice about the knees of Vincent Spaulding's trousers?

9. Who is the other man Holmes recruits to help with the capture?

10. When reflecting upon this case, Holmes mentions to Watson that the solution "was perfectly obvious from the start." What clue put Holmes on the right track?

Quiz 18
"A CASE OF IDENTITY"

Published in the Strand *in September 1891*

Conan Doyle often refused to assist people requesting help in Sherlock Holmes–type cases. He was even able to resist the temptation of a Polish nobleman who offered him a blank check if Conan Doyle would come to Poland and help clear his name in connection with a murder. However, Conan Doyle did agree to help a young girl named Joan Paynter, who wrote to him about her fiancé, who had disappeared. She could not afford to hire a detective, and Conan Doyle was her only hope. He was able to locate the man and in doing so convinced Miss Paynter that he was not worth the trouble. The story of Miss Paynter is similar to "A Case of Identity." This quiz contains ten true/false statements about young lovers who are so easily deceived.

Story Date: 1890

1. Mary Sutherland met Hosmer Angel at the gasfitters' ball.
2. Mary's father was a minister before he died.
3. Mary and Hosmer plan to marry in a small chapel in Torquay.
4. Holmes realizes that Mary's stepfather and her boyfriend are the same man when he notices that both of their letters were typed from the same typewriter.
5. Mary's stepfather, James Windibank, is a travelling representative for the wine exporter Westhouse and Marbank.

TRIVIA FACTS : DID YOU KNOW THAT . . .

1. Sir Arthur Conan Doyle based Sherlock Holmes on a real person. While in medical school at Edinburgh Royal Infirmary, Conan Doyle studied under Dr. Joseph Bell, a surgeon who used his phenomenal powers of deduction to diagnose his patients' maladies with profound accuracy.

2. Conan Doyle, along with his family and several close friends, celebrated his knighthood at the Hotel Métropole in London. Conan Doyle was apprehensive about receiving the honor and even more so about the party given in his honor. His pent-up frustration was released through a barrage of shouts when he opened a package that contained beautiful handmade shirts and an anonymous message that read, "With greeting to Sir Sherlock Holmes."

3. Conan Doyle's inspiration in writing *The Valley of Fear* came from the true story of the Pinkerton Detective Agency and its conflict with the secret society called the Molly Maguires.

---

6. Before she contacts Holmes for help Mary attempts to find Hosmer by running an ad in the *London Times*.

7. Mary supplements her inheritance as a part-time governess for the children of a minister and his wife.

8. Mary does not use her inheritance because she allows her mother and stepfather to use the interest from her money for household expenses, since she lives with them.

9. Holmes threatens to choke Windibank with his bare hands when he finds out what Windibank has done.

10. The solution is obvious to Holmes when he becomes aware of Mary Sutherland's stock investments.

QUIZ 19
"THE BOSCOMBE VALLEY MYSTERY"

Published in the Strand *in October 1891*

"The Boscombe Valley Mystery" is the last of a series of four stories written by Conan Doyle while in a writing frenzy. He was producing one Holmes story a week in the spring of 1891. By this time he had physically drained himself and was forced to spend several weeks in bed with a life-threatening case of the flu. After a six-week convalescence, he finished just two more stories, but it wasn't due to lack of enthusiasm—quite the contrary, he took a few weeks away from his writing to close down his medical practice at Montague Place. Conan Doyle had made the decision to write full-time. He moved his family to a quiet suburb in south London and never looked back. "There we settled down, and there I made my first effort to live entirely by pen. It soon became evident that I had been playing the game well within my powers and that I should have no difficulty in providing a sufficient income. It seemed as if I had settled into a life which might be continuous." The following quiz contains ten multiple choice questions.

Story Date: June 1889

1. What did John Turner and Charles McCarthy have in common?

   A. They were wounded while fighting in the Crimean War.
   B. Both men had served in Parliament and were raised in Scotland.
   C. Both John Turner and Charles McCarthy were widowers with one teenaged child each, a daughter and a son, respectively.
   D. Their deceased wives were sisters.

2. Who saw James McCarthy carrying a gun and following his father on his way to Boscombe Pool?

   A. John Turner, James McCarthy's landlord
   B. Patience Moran, the daughter of the lodgekeeper of the Boscombe Valley estate
   C. Alice Turner, John Turner's daughter
   D. William Crowder, the gamekeeper

3. Who saw Charles McCarthy and his son, James, quarreling?

   A. John Turner
   B. Patience Moran
   C. Alice Turner
   D. William Crowder

4. What did Charles McCarthy mumble before he died?

   A. Something about paying for what someone did
   B. Something about a rat
   C. Something about learning a lesson
   D. Something about stealing land

5. While making his statement to the police, what did James McCarthy say that he saw on the ground near his father's body, an item which had disappeared before he left to get help?

A. A plaid hunting cap
B. A brown leather smoking pouch
C. A gold watch chain
D. A gray coat of some sort

6. Why were Charles McCarthy and his son, James, quarreling?

   A. James had lost another job.
   B. James refused to enlist in the service and follow in his father's footsteps.
   C. James refused to marry Alice Turner.
   D. Mr. McCarthy had threatened to disinherit his son.

7. How does Holmes know that the murderer was left-handed?

   A. Charles McCarthy was struck from behind on the left side of his head.
   B. Holmes finds a bloody left-handed glove near the scene of the crime.
   C. There is a bloody left thumbprint on the murder weapon.
   D. By analyzing the scene of the crime, position of footprints, location where the body fell, and the broken stems of the bushes, Holmes is able to determine that fact.

8. How is Holmes able to identify the rock as the murder weapon?

   A. Using his lens, Holmes finds strands of hair on the rock.
   B. The large rock is unlike the other small, pebble-sized rocks in the area. Holmes deduces that the murderer brought it with him in planning the murder.
   C. The rock had been moved because there is grass growing under it.
   D. There is a dark brown blood stain on the rock.

9. What crime did John Turner commit when he was young?

    A. John Turner had forged bank documents, swindling several miners.

    B. One evening John Turner was drunk and killed a man who was beating his wife.

    C. John Turner had jumped several claims at a gold-mining camp.

    D. John Turner was a member of a gang of wagon robbers.

10. Which two terms or phrases helped Holmes solve the case?

    A. Victoria and goldmines

    B. Cooee and rat

    C. Bristol and Bermuda Dockyard

    D. Boats and Boscombe Pool

QUIZ 20
"THE FIVE ORANGE PIPS"

Published in the Strand *in November 1891*

Shortly before Conan Doyle wrote "The Five Orange Pips," a horrid incident occurred in New Orleans where eleven Italians were hanged by an angry mob who believed them to have Mafia connections. A political upheaval between the United States and Italy ensued as a result of the American government's refusing to thoroughly investigate the incident. The Italian government withdrew its minister from Washington in protest. Racism in America was a very newsworthy issue, possibly influencing Conan Doyle to write this intriguing story involving the long arm of the Ku Klux Klan, which reached all the way to England. The following quiz contains ten short-answer questions.

Story Date: September in the late 1890s

1. How is Holmes recommended to John Openshaw?

2. What did John Openshaw's Uncle Elias do when he lived in America?

3. What happened on March 10, 1883, and a few weeks later on May 2, 1883?

4. How many men received the strange message with the five orange pips included in the envelope?

5. What evidence does John Openshaw present Holmes that puts him on the right track in solving this case?

6. What does Holmes write in the letter he sends Captain Calhoun?

7. How is Holmes able to track down the leader of the gang responsible for the murders?

8. What was the name of Captain Calhoun's ship?

9. What is odd about the deaths of the men who received the message?

10. According to the Holmes encyclopedia, what is the origin of the name Ku Klux Klan?

QUIZ 21
"THE MAN WITH THE TWISTED LIP"

Published in the Strand *in December 1891*

Conan Doyle would often peruse the court case announcements in *Cornhill Magazine* for information that he could use in creating his Sherlock Holmes stories. On one occasion, there appeared a description of two men: a gentleman who was involved in a political scandal, and a street beggar who was grotesquely scarred. Conan Doyle combined these two characters, creating the man with the twisted lip. The following quiz contains ten true/false statements.

Story Date: June 1889

1. Isa Whitney became addicted to opium when he broke his back in a riding accident, taking the drug as a pain remedy.

2. Dr. Watson finds Whitney at the Bar of Gold opium den, in Swandam Lane.

3. Coincidentally, Watson finds Holmes in the opium den looking for the same man.

4. St. Clair's wife knew that her husband had been to the Bar of Gold opium den because a colleague of her husband's had spotted him going into the establishment.

5. Inspector Barton discovers the gift that St. Clair had promised to bring home to his son in the pockets of St. Clair's discarded coat.

6. When Mrs. St. Clair saw her husband in Swandam Lane, she noticed that he was not wearing his shirt or jacket.

7. When Holmes calls on Mrs. St. Clair to tell her that her husband is probably dead, she surprises Holmes by telling him that she hopes that her husband is dead.

8. To confirm his theory, Holmes brings a Gladstone bag (sponge) to the prison when he visits Boone.

9. Neville St. Clair conceived of his plan to make money in an unconventional manner when he was assigned to write an article for a London evening paper.

10. St. Clair did not tell his family where he was going when he went to work because he did not want his children to be ashamed of him.

QUIZ 22
"THE ADVENTURE OF THE BLUE CARBUNCLE"

Published in the Strand *in January 1892*

By the end of 1891, Conan Doyle had published six Sherlock Holmes stories, and it was evident that the partnership between the writer and the *Strand Magazine* would last a long time. Editor

Herbert Greenhough Smith, one of the founders of the magazine recalled, "there came to me an envelope containing the first two stories of a series which were destined to become famous all over the world as *The Adventures of Sherlock Holmes*. What a God-send to an editor jaded with wading through reams of impossible stuff! The ingenuity of plot, the limpid clearness of style, the perfect art of telling a story!"

"The Adventure of the Blue Carbuncle" is the seventh story in the collection, and upon completion, Conan Doyle asked the magazine for fifty pounds for this story and subsequent submissions in the collection. The magazine gladly accepted his terms. The following quiz contains ten multiple choice questions.

Story Date: Late 1880s, Early 1890s

1. What does Commissionaire Peterson bring Holmes on Christmas morning along with the goose?

    A. A tobacco pouch
    B. An old felt hat
    C. A cracked pipe
    D. A ring of keys

2. Among the many facts Holmes deduces from the lost item, what astonishes Watson the most about Holmes's summary of the man to whom the item belongs?

    A. He has probably taken to drink.
    B. He was well-to-do up until three years ago.
    C. His wife no longer loves him.
    D. His grizzled hair has been cut within the last few days.

3. How much is the reward for the return of the blue carbuncle?

    A. 500 pounds
    B. A choice of one of the Countess of Morcar's paintings
    C. 1,000 pounds
    D. A small diamond of lesser value

4. Where was the blue carbuncle originally discovered?
   A. Near Victoria Falls in southern Rhodesia
   B. On the banks of the Amoy River in southern China
   C. On the banks of the Ganges in India
   D. On the banks of the Blue Nile in Ethiopia

5. From where was the diamond stolen?
   A. The Hotel Cosmopolitan
   B. The Countess of Morcar's safe
   C. It was stolen en route to the Countess's safety deposit box.
   D. It was stolen from under the Countess's pillow while she slept.

6. What other crimes, associated with the jewel, were committed?
   A. Three blackmails, two burglaries
   B. An arson, two robberies, and two assaults
   C. Three cases of bigamy
   D. Two murders, a vitriol-throwing (acid), suicide, several robberies

7. What does James Ryder's goose look like?
   A. It is white with a barred tail.
   B. It is white with a scarred left foot.
   C. It is the only white goose with a black marking over its right eye.
   D. It is a white goose that is missing several tail feathers.

8. Who is arrested for stealing the diamond?
   A. Catherine Cusack, the Countess's maid
   B. James Ryder, the head attendant at the Hotel Cosmopolitan
   C. Henry Baker, the man who lost his goose
   D. John Horner, the plumber who came to the Countess's dressing room to solder a grate

9. Where does Henry Baker get his prized goose?

   A. Henry Baker is a member of the Alpha Inn goose club, whose members contributed a few pence each week to the inn's owner in return for a goose on Christmas.

   B. He steals the goose from his neighbor because his neighbor refused to pay for the repairs of a fence that he had broken.

   C. Henry Baker's boss has given Henry the goose as a Christmas bonus.

   D. He has purchased the goose at a local church bazaar that was trying to raise money for a new organ.

TRIVIA FACTS : DID YOU KNOW THAT . . .

1. Conan Doyle may have conceived of the idea for his story "A Scandal in Bohemia" after his trip to Vienna in 1891. At that time all of Europe was in shock over the apparent double suicide of Austrian Archduke Rudolph and his mistress.

2. In 1893 Conan Doyle and Robert Louis Stevenson began corresponding by mail. Stevenson had read "The Adventure of the Engineer's Thumb" to his native overseer, telling him that it was a true story. When Conan Doyle planned a visit to Samoa, his identity as the creator of Sherlock Holmes had to be kept secret, for Stevenson did not wish to confess his lie and disappoint the Samoan.

3. Conan Doyle used to enjoy telling the story about Sherlock Holmes meeting St. Peter at the gates of heaven. St. Peter was overjoyed that the Great Detective was finally in heaven, because now he would be able to help solve the mystery of who, among the millions of men in heaven, was Adam. Holmes's response, "Elementary, my dear St. Peter. He is the only one of the millions who lacks a certain *je ne sais quoi* in the middle of his stomach."

10. What does Holmes say and do to the man who stole the diamond after he confesses and begins sobbing?

   A. Holmes throws open the door and shouts at him to leave.
   B. Holmes lights his pipe and sends Watson for the police.
   C. Holmes starts laughing and tells the man that he is not fit to be a respectable thief.
   D. Holmes slaps him on the back and tells him to sit down and join him for Christmas dinner.

QUIZ 23
"THE ADVENTURE OF THE SPECKLED BAND"

Published in the Strand *in February 1892*

Conan Doyle enjoyed reading the magazine *Nineteenth Century,* and he often clipped and saved articles for his reference file. In this file was an article written by Sir Joseph Fayrer, in which he describes a deadly snake called the Indian adder. Intrigued by this venomous snake, Conan Doyle used the reptile as one of the more important and pivotal house guests of Dr. Grimesby Roylott in "The Adventure of the Speckled Band." The following quiz contains ten multiple choice questions.

Story Date: April 1893

1. At the beginning of the story Dr. Watson is reviewing Holmes's case notes and reflects on their time together. How many years had Holmes and Watson been working together?

   A. Five
   B. Eleven
   C. Eight
   D. Nine

2. Who recommended Sherlock Holmes to Helen Stoner?

   A. Helen Stoner's sister, Julia, mentioned Holmes before she died.
   B. Mrs. Farintosh from the case of the opal tiara
   C. Helen Stoner's aunt, Miss Honoria Westphail
   D. Percy Armitage, Helen's fiancé

3. What does Helen Stoner believe caused her sister's death?

   A. Helen believes that her sister died of fright and nervous shock.
   B. Helen believes that her sister must have been poisoned.
   C. Helen believes that her sister had accidentally taken an overdose of sleeping draught.
   D. Helen fears that her sister's death may have been caused by one of her stepfather's exotic pets.

4. What incident caused Miss Stoner to call upon Holmes for assistance?

   A. She had spent the night in the room of her deceased sister and heard the strange whistle that her sister had heard a few days before she died.
   B. She found a letter written by Julia, expressing fear of their stepfather.
   C. The man to whom Julia was engaged told Helen that Julia feared for her life.
   D. When Helen announced her engagement to her stepfather, he flew into a rage and threatened to kill her fiancé.

5. What unusual pets does Dr. Roylott own?

   A. A black bear and a grizzly bear
   B. Several different species of birds, all imported from the Amazon
   C. A cheetah and a baboon
   D. Two female lions and a jackal

6. How did Dr. Roylott convince his stepdaughter to sleep in her sister's room?

   A. He started repairing the west wing of the manor, which required the wall of Miss Stoner's room to be replaced.
   B. He told her that he was having terrifying nightmares and pleaded with her to sleep in the room next to his in case he started screaming during the night.
   C. He told her that there was evidence of someone trying to pry open the window, and until he could secure the lock, she would be safer in another room.
   D. He told Helen that he kept hearing Julia's voice and pleaded for Helen to sleep in Julia's room to see if she could also hear the voice.

7. What is unusual about the condition of the bed in the sister's room?

   A. The legs of the frame are sawed off, placing the mattress close to the floor.
   B. Dr. Roylott insisted that the bed remain in the center of the room.
   C. It is nailed to the floor.
   D. Every evening when Helen retires, the bed cover is covered with black fur.

8. To what is the fake bellrope fastened?

   A. A light on Dr. Roylott's desk
   B. A small shaft used for ventilation
   C. A door of an animal cage
   D. A bell which hung over Dr. Roylott's bed

9. What clue, concerning the chair in Dr. Roylott's room, leads Holmes to the solution of the mystery?

   A. The placement of the chair in the room.
   B. The chair is covered with a coat of fine dust.

C. Holmes finds small leaves from the tree located right outside Dr. Roylott's room.

D. Because of the scuff marks on the seat of the chair, Holmes knows that Dr. Roylott stood on the chair many times.

10. What does Dr. Roylott do in an attempt to intimidate Holmes?

A. Dr. Roylott bends Holmes's fireplace poker with his bare hands.

B. Dr. Roylott arm wrestles Holmes and wins.

C. Dr. Roylott shows Holmes a trophy he won while fighting in the navy.

D. Dr. Roylott tears through an encyclopedia volume with his bare hands.

QUIZ 24
"THE ADVENTURE OF THE ENGINEER'S THUMB"

Published in the Strand *in March 1892*

In this story about conspirators and counterfeiters, a ceiling is slowly lowered by levers in an attempt to crush the victim, Victor Hatherley. Conan Doyle developed the idea from a similar scene in Wilkie Collins's story "A Terribly Strange Bed." The following quiz contains ten short-answer questions.

Story Date: Summer 1892

1. What does Victor Hatherley do for a living?

2. For whom did Hatherley work before he became self-employed?

3. How much is Hatherley paid for his work and secrecy?

4. What does Colonel Stark tell Hatherley that he is excavating near Berkshire?

5. Who tries to warn Hatherley so that he can make his escape before it is too late?

6. What clue does Hatherley find, leading him to believe that Colonel Stark is excavating something other than what he claimed?

7. How does Hatherley lose his thumb?

8. What evidence does Holmes find to corroborate Hatherley's story?

9. Who helps Hatherley escape?

10. What is Colonel Stark making in the house?

QUIZ 25
"THE ADVENTURE OF THE NOBLE BACHELOR"

Published in the Strand *in April 1892*

Conan Doyle had a great interest and fascination for the American West, and in several stories, Native American tribes are mentioned. For instance, the Blackfeet and the Pawnee are referred to in part 2, "The Country of the Saints" in *A Study in Scarlet*. In "The Noble Bachelor" an Apache tribe is responsible for setting in motion a chain of events that leads from the western United States to London. The following quiz contains ten true/false statements about a story in which a tenacious young American girl, although tough and free-spirited, is no match for the Great Detective.

Story Date: October 1886

1. Hatty Doran's father became wealthy overnight by gambling in California.

2. Hatty's maid, Alice, assists Hatty in escaping after the wedding breakfast.

3. Flora Miller, the woman who was jilted by Lord St. Simon, is suspected of luring Hatty away and then murdering her.

4. Inspector Lestrade believes that Hatty Doran's body will be found in the Serpentine River because a witness saw a woman matching her description climbing aboard a boat.

5. Hatty Doran uses the phrase "jumping a claim" to describe her predicament.

6. A partial address on the back of the message gives Holmes the clue as to where to find Hatty.

7. Frank shook Hatty's hand at the wedding, and as he did so, he slipped her a note.

8. Hatty was shocked when she saw Frank at her wedding because she believed that he was killed by another miner who stole his claim.

9. Holmes solves the murder before Inspector Lestrade arrives with a plethora of clues.

10. Holmes finds Hatty and her lover, Frank Moulton, after convincing Hatty's maid that she should tell the truth.

QUIZ 26
"THE ADVENTURE OF THE BERYL CORONET"

Published in the Strand *in May 1892*

"The Adventure of the Beryl Coronet" received admirable reviews, even though it was considered by many critics as one of the least favorite in the collection. Conan Doyle's flurry of enthusiasm concerning his writing of Holmes stories was beginning to wane. However, once the collection was completed and published in book form, the reviews were excellent. The book was dedicated to Joseph Bell, the doctor used as a model for Sherlock Holmes. Dr. Bell reviewed Conan Doyle's book for *Bookman Magazine* and had this to say: "He [Conan Doyle] has had the wit to devise excellent plots and interesting complications. He tells them in honest Saxon-English with directness and pith; and, above all his other merits, his stories are absolutely free from padding." The following quiz contains ten multiple choice questions.

Story Date: 1881 to 1890

1. How much money does the prestigious client want to borrow from Mr. Holder's bank?
   A. 1,000 pounds
   B. 27,500 pounds
   C. 50,000 pounds
   D. 18,000 pounds

2. How many beryls are in the coronet?
   A. 39
   B. 21
   C. 99
   D. 7

3. Who does Mr. Holder tell about keeping the coronet in his dressing bureau?
   A. Mr. Holder's boss, the bank president
   B. His son, Arthur, and his niece, Mary
   C. His client
   D. The bank security guard who has been an employee for over thirty years

4. Besides catching Arthur with the coronet in his possession, what other reason does Mr. Holder have for suspecting his son of stealing three beryls from the coronet?
   A. He suspects Arthur of needing money to pay a blackmailer.
   B. Arthur had been arrested for stealing when he was in boarding school.
   C. Arthur has considerable gambling debts.
   D. Arthur spoke of needing a fortune to win the woman he loves.

5. What request does Arthur make of his father before his father turns him over to the police?

   A. Arthur wishes to spend five minutes alone with Mary.
   B. Arthur asks if he could take a certain book with him to the police station.
   C. Arthur pleads to his father that he not tell Mary of the arrest until the morning.
   D. Arthur requests that his father allow him to leave the house for five minutes.

6. Why does Mary turn down Arthur's marriage proposal?

   A. Mary knows that Arthur is the thief.
   B. Mary is under the spell of Sir George Burnwell.
   C. Mary will not marry Arthur because he is broke.
   D. Mary is not romantically interested in Arthur; she thinks of him as a brother.

7. What does Mary do when the truth is revealed?

   A. Mary leaves her uncle a note saying that she is leaving forever.
   B. Mary tries to kill herself by taking arsenic.
   C. Mary ends her relationship with Sir George Burnwell.
   D. Mary wants to turn herself in to the police.

8. Why does Arthur run after the thief?

   A. He knows that if the coronet is missing his father will suspect him.
   B. Arthur wants to protect his father from losing his job.
   C. Arthur knows the thief and plans to blackmail him.
   D. Arthur is trying to protect the woman he loves.

9. How does Holmes know that Sir George was at the Holder household the night of the robbery?

   A. There is blood on the snow outside the window, and Sir George recently cut his hand.

B. While waiting outside the window for his accomplice to pass him the coronet, Sir George smokes a cigarette. Upon investigating, Holmes finds the butt and realizes that it is the same unusual brand that Sir George smokes.

C. Holmes purchases a pair of Sir George's shoes from Sir George's valet and matches them to the tracks that were left in the snow.

D. Holmes finds a key in the snow and remembers that Sir George's key ring is empty of keys.

10. Why does Mr. Holder suspect his maid, Lucy Parr, of stealing the beryls?

A. Lucy has been in his service for only a short time, and she has many admirers. While sneaking out to see a beau, she may have overheard Mr. Holder mention that he had brought the coronet home.

B. Lucy was wandering around the house and gazing out the windows during the night that the beryls were stolen. Her excuse is that she enjoys watching the moon.

C. Lucy asked for a considerable raise and was angry when Mr. Holder turned her down.

D. Lucy's boyfriend will not marry her until he makes his fortune.

QUIZ 27
"THE ADVENTURE OF THE COPPER BEECHES"

Published in the Strand *in June 1892*

Conan Doyle's mother, Mary Doyle, was a great influence in her son's life. He often consulted her on important matters, especially those that required career decisions. Mary Doyle had an intuitive insight to the needs of her son and often steered him in the right direction. At one point when Conan Doyle was threatening to write his last Sherlock Holmes story, Mary Doyle encouraged him to persevere and write a story with a Gothic flair. The result was "The Adventure of the Copper Beeches," a story listed as one of his readership's favorites. This quiz contains ten short-answer questions about the story in which Holmes professes, "There has been some villainy here."

Story Date: 1890s

1. What is the name of the agency where Miss Violet Hunter registers her services as a governess?

2. What was the initial offer Jephro Rucastle made to Miss Hunter?

3. What strange request does he make of her if she accepts the position?

4. How much time has passed before Holmes receives an urgent summons from Miss Hunter?

5. Where does Miss Hunter arrange to meet Holmes?

6. How many theories does Holmes have concerning Miss Hunter's predicament?

7. To where was Mr. Rucastle's daughter reported to have moved?

TRIVIA FACTS : DID YOU KNOW THAT . . .

1. Who did Conan Doyle use as the model for "the woman"? One theory is that opera singer Irene Adler, Holmes's nemesis in "A Scandal in Bohemia," was based on Ludmilla Huble, a singer and actress from Vienna. However, many Sherlockians believe that Adler was modeled after New Jersey–born entertainer, Lilly Langtree.

2. Holmes illustrator Sidney Paget used Queen Victoria's grandson, Kaiser Wilhelm, as the model for the King of Bohemia in Conan Doyle's story "A Scandal in Bohemia."

8. How does Miss Hunter know that a man is watching her from the road?

9. What keeps intruders away from the Rucastle house at night?

10. What is Mr. Rucastle's excuse for having the secret room in the deserted wing of the house?

Robert Downey, Jr. and Jude Law as Sherlock Holmes and Dr. Watson in the
Guy Ritchie film *Sherlock Holmes* 2009

FOUR

THE SECOND COLLECTION:
MEMOIRS OF SHERLOCK HOLMES

*"Because I made a blunder, my dear Watson—
which is, I am afraid, a more common occurrence
than anyone would think who only knew me
through your memoirs."*
—SHERLOCK HOLMES

FROM FAILURE COMES SUCCESS, from misunderstanding comes clarity, and from theory comes fact. In the first story in this collection, making the wrong assumption forces Holmes to reevaluate the case of a missing racehorse, Silver Blaze, which eventually places Holmes on the right track, so to speak. Together again at Baker Street, Holmes and Watson unravel puzzles, solve riddles, and discover lost government secrets. From the stories in this collection, "Silver Blaze," "The Yellow Face," "The Stockbroker's Clerk," "The *Gloria Scott*," "The Musgrave Ritual," "The Reigate Squires," "The Crooked Man," "The Resident Patient," "The Greek Interpreter," "The Naval Treaty," and "The Final Problem," more is learned of Watson's school days, of Holmes's very first case, of his older brother, and finally of Holmes's apparent demise at the hands of Professor Moriarty.

Memoirs of Sherlock Holmes, published in 1894, initially was to contain twelve stories, including "The Adventure of the Cardboard Box." However, when this story was first published in the *Strand Magazine* in 1893, it received a disapproving reaction because of the subject of adultery. The tale was edited from the book, only to appear twenty-three years later in the book *His Last Bow* during a time when moral standards had apparently relaxed. Of the eleven short stories in this collection, Conan Doyle listed seven as his favorites.

Quiz 28
"SILVER BLAZE"

Published in the Strand *in December 1892 and in* Harper's *in February 1893*

Early in 1892, Conan Doyle was enjoying being a writer; he was working on a historical novel entitled *The Refugees*, when the *Strand Magazine* approached him about writing another collection of Sherlock Holmes short stories. This request disrupted his peace of mind as he shouted to his mother, "They have been bothering me for more Sherlock Holmes tales. Under pressure I offered to do a dozen for a thousand pounds, but I sincerely hope that they won't accept it now." The magazine eagerly accepted, and Conan Doyle wove into his writing schedule time to create eleven new Holmes stories, the first of which was "Silver Blaze." The following quiz contains ten short-answer questions about a mystery deserving of Holmes's "strongest black tobacco."

Story Date: 1881 to 1891

1. Why does Holmes not immediately rush off to Dartmoor when he receives a telegram from Colonel Ross asking for assistance in locating the missing racehorse?

2. What did the well-dressed, mysterious man, whom the maid encountered on her way to bringing the stableboy his supper, have in his hand?

3. When the authorities found the body of trainer John Straker, what item, which was subsequently identified by the maid as belonging to the stranger, did the trainer have in his hand?

4. What damaging evidence leads to the arrest of Fitzroy Simpson?

5. After being misled by the newspaper report, which clue put Holmes back on track?

6. What are the two items found in John Straker's pockets that led Holmes to developing his theory?

7. Where does Holmes discover Silver Blaze?

8. When Holmes returns to London to follow up on his theory, what does he take with him?

9. What question does Holmes ask the stableboy as the carriage door is opened for the detective?

10. Why does Colonel Ross not recognize his horse in the race?

QUIZ 29
"THE YELLOW FACE"

Published in the Strand *and in* Harper's *in February 1893*

According to notes from Conan Doyle's diary dated 1892, "The Yellow Face" was initially called "The Livid Face." It is unclear as to why the title was changed. Character Grant Munro does, however, report having seen a "yellow livid face" in the window. "The Yellow Face" is, after all, more reflective of the person whom the title describes. The following quiz contains ten true/false statements about one of the few Holmes investigations that Watson describes as a failure.

Story Date: 1880s

1. Holmes knows Grant Munro's name before he introduces himself because Holmes notices the name in the lining of his coat.

2. Grant Munro is a country doctor.

3. Munro's wife told him that her first husband and child had died of yellow fever.

4. Munro first became suspicious about his wife's activities when she asked him for 100 pounds and would not tell him why she wanted the money.

5. Munro was suspicious about his new neighbors because he saw a woman who looked very much like his wife living in the cottage.

6. Mrs. Munro told her husband that she left the house in the middle of the night because she had a headache.

7. Munro becomes angry with his wife when he discovers her coat hanging in the cottage next door.

8. Holmes theorizes that Mrs. Munro's husband is not really dead and that he has returned and is blackmailing her.

9. In order to conceal the face of the child, Mrs. Munro covers it with a mask.

10. When Mr. Munro discovers his wife's secret, he is repulsed and leaves her.

Quiz 30
"THE STOCK-BROKER'S CLERK"

Published in the Strand *and in* Harper's *in March 1893*

In "The Stock-broker's Clerk" Holmes is perhaps at his best at deductive reasoning. Having not seen his dear friend Dr. Watson for almost three months (Watson was busy setting up his medical practice and settling down in his marriage), Holmes visits Dr. Watson and uses deductive reasoning to catch up on lost time. Here are ten multiple choice questions about a tale with a plot similar to "The Red-Headed League," written almost two years earlier.

Story Date: June in the late 1880s

1. How does Sherlock Holmes know that Dr. Watson has a summer cold?

   A. Holmes notices that Dr. Watson's nose is red, there are medicine bottles on the side table, and the room is very warm.

   B. Holmes notices that Watson's new slippers are slightly scorched. The only reasonable explanation, according to Holmes, is that Watson was warming his feet by the fire, which is rarely done in the summer, unless one is sick.

   C. Holmes smells vapor rub and detects a hoarseness in Watson's voice.

   D. Dr. Watson has a history of having summer colds, during which time he loses his appetite. Holmes notices his untouched breakfast.

2. How does Holmes know that Dr. Watson's medical practice, which he just purchased from a retired doctor, is more lucrative than the practice next door?

   A. The sign post in front is decoratively designed while the neighboring doctor's is very plain.

   B. The curb in front is chipped and scarred, indicating that more carriages have arrived at this location.

   C. The steps to Dr. Watson's office are worn down more than the steps leading to the other doctor's office.

   D. The door knocker is very worn and smooth compared to the one next door.

3. What does Pinner require of Pycroft if he agrees to take the job?

   A. Pinner does not want Pycroft to notify his prospective employer of his decision not to accept his offer.

   B. Pycroft is to tell no one about his new job.

   C. Pinner wants Pycroft to write an insulting letter to Mawson, declining the offer for the new position.

   D. Pinner wants Pycroft to decline the new position with Mawson, giving the reason that the job was too difficult.

4. What first causes Pycroft to become suspicious concerning the new company for which he now works?

   A. When he arrives for his first appointment, no one is there to meet him.

B. He is told that all transactions are made with cash.

C. He is told that once he enters the office, he may not leave under any circumstances, until dismissed at the end of the day.

D. When Pycroft enters the office, he notices that the room is very austere, lacking carpet, curtains, tables, and other employees.

5. What is Pycroft's first duty for his new employer?

A. Pycroft is assigned the task of marking off all the hardware sellers and their addresses listed in the Paris directory.

B. He is told to take an inventory of all the stock in the warehouse.

C. Pycroft is to act as receptionist to all deliveries, writing down the names and addresses of each person arriving at the office.

D. Pycroft is to answer all of Mr. Harry Pinner's correspondence.

6. When does Pycroft become suspicious about his new employers, suspecting that the two brothers are really the same man?

A. Pycroft notices a severe scar on the hands of both men.

B. Pycroft notices a sliver of brown pigment in the left blue eye of each man.

C. Each man is missing a tiny portion of his right earlobe.

D. Each man has a gold filling in the second tooth in the upper left jaw.

7. How do Holmes and Watson arrange an interview with Mr. Pinner?

A. They pose as landlords who arrive to inspect the office of their new tenant.

B. They arrive with Pycroft seeking employment.

THE SHERLOCK HOLMES QUIZ BOOK

C. They arrive disguised as plumbers to fix the drain.

D. They pretend to be interested investors.

8. On which two "fairly obvious" points does Holmes deduce the solution to this mystery?

   A. The 500 pounds per year salary offered to Pycroft, and the name of Pinner's company

   B. Arthur Pinner's black beard and the fact that Pinner quizzed Pycroft on the status of the stock market

   C. Pinner makes Pycroft write a declaration of service concerning his new job, and he requires that Pycroft not arrive at Mawson's office on Monday morning as expected.

   D. The alleged row Pinner had with the manager of Mawson's office and the 100 pounds advance Pinner gave to Pycroft

9. What does Henry Pinner do when he discovers that his brother was caught robbing the stock-broking company?

   A. Mr. Pinner leaves town on the first train.

   B. Mr. Pinner has a nervous breakdown and confesses immediately.

   C. Mr. Pinner claims that he is innocent of his brother's scam, and was used as a dupe.

   D. Mr. Pinner tries to hang himself.

10. How does Henry Pinner learn of his brother's arrest?

   A. He sees the police rushing into the building and suspects the worst.

   B. His brother manages to send a note via a messenger before the police handcuff him.

   C. On his way to the office, Mr. Pinner overhears two men talking about the arrest.

   D. He reads about his brother's arrest in an early edition of the *Evening Standard*.

QUIZ 31
"THE *GLORIA SCOTT*"

Published in the Strand *and in* Harper's *in April 1893*

Even though Conan Doyle presents us with a young, college-age Holmes in this story, the detective's skills are as sharp as Holmes in later years. Most writers who create a serial character develop that character over time and, in doing so, allow the reader and character to bond. However, the magic of Sherlock Holmes was present in the very first story. Perhaps fans appreciated the consistency and predictability of Holmes, taking comfort in the fact that he, in all his detective glory, remains forever a mainstay in literature. The following quiz contains ten short-answer questions about a case Holmes allowed Watson to pursue one winter's night.

Story Date: 1870s

1. Who is the visitor who causes Mr. Trevor to drink until he passes out?

2. Why does Holmes's friend, Victor Trevor, invite him for a second visit just two months after his first visit?

3. What puzzle does Holmes solve which eventually leads him to discover Mr. Trevor's secret?

4. How do Holmes and Victor Trevor find out the true story about Mr. Trevor's past?

5. What crime did Mr. Trevor commit when he was a young man?

6. Who led the mutiny on the *Gloria Scott*?

7. How did Mr. Trevor escape from the *Gloria Scott*?

8. What happened to the *Gloria Scott* after Mr. Trevor escaped?

9. Who was the only survivor that Trevor and Evans rescued?

10. What did Trevor, Evans, and Hudson tell the rescue ship's captain?

QUIZ 32
"THE MUSGRAVE RITUAL"

Published in the Strand *in May 1893*

Conan Doyle wrote "The Musgrave Ritual" while traveling by train with his first wife, Louise, on their way to Boulogne, France. Louise Doyle's health had begun to deteriorate, and Conan Doyle decided to take her on a short holiday away from the blustery winter of Britain.

The story begins with Watson complaining of Holmes's untidy habits and the fact that he keeps records of his early cases in a large tin box. These habits mirror those of the author, who was just as much a pack rat concerning his papers and files as his fictional character. Louise Doyle often complained about her husband's unwillingness to throw anything away, and the scene at the beginning of the story could have easily taken place in the Doyle household. The following quiz contains ten true/false statements.

Story Date: 1879

1. Holmes and Reginald Musgrave met in college.

2. Brunton, the butler, was a midshipman in the navy before he became employed by the Musgraves.

3. According to Musgrave, Brunton's only shortcoming was his tendency to bet on the horses.

4. Musgrave fired Brunton because he was too forward with the female staff.

5. The Musgrave Ritual, having lost meaning and significance over the centuries, is a series of questions and answers passed down from generation to generation.

6. Brunton broke his engagement to Rachel Howells, the second housemaid.

7. By studying the spelling in the document, Holmes determines that the Musgrave Ritual was drawn up during the time of King Henry VIII.

8. In calculating the site of the ritual from the catechism, Holmes is off track on his projection because he reads the message backward.

9. Holmes and Musgrave realize that Brunton must be in the cellar because his cigarette case was found nearby.

10. Holmes deduces that Brunton was locked in the cellar by his ex-lover, Rachel Howells.

QUIZ 33
"THE REIGATE SQUIRES"

Published in the Strand *and in* Harper's *in June 1893*

In the story of "The Reigate Squires" (the American title was "The Reigate Puzzle"), Holmes's tendency to overwork has affected his physical health. Watson recalls how Holmes "had broken down under the strain of an investigation which had extended over two months, during which period he had never worked less than fifteen hours a day and had more than once, as he assured me, kept to his task for five days at a stretch." This habit of overworking to near collapse and exhaustion was also reminiscent of the author. Below are ten multiple choice questions.

Story Date: April 1887

1. Where was Holmes convalescing when Dr. Watson received a letter that he had been ill?

   A. On the Devonshire Coast
   B. In Lyons, France, at the Hotel Dulong
   C. The Langham Hotel in the West End
   D. In a little village in the Scottish Highlands

2. What is found in William Kirwin's hand when his body is discovered?

   A. A piece of a note
   B. A button from a jacket
   C. A piece of a map
   D. A train ticket stub

3. While Holmes is writing an advertisement asking for information about the burglary, how does he trick Alec Cunningham into giving him a writing sample?

   A. Holmes asks him to write down his address so the paper will know who to bill for the ad.
   B. Holmes writes down the wrong time, and Cunningham corrects it.
   C. Holmes begins to write the ad, but because of his recent illness, he claims that his handwriting is still a bit shaky.
   D. Holmes says that since Cunningham was at the scene of the crime, he would be more articulate in composing the ad.

4. What does Holmes do to create a distraction so that he can search the pockets of Alec Cunningham's dressing gown?

A. Holmes pretends to faint, sending everyone scurrying for a brandy bottle.

B. Holmes claims that he saw someone running across the lawn.

C. Holmes claims that he smells smoke coming from the study.

D. He pretends to accidentally knock over a bowl of oranges.

5. What does Holmes deduce from the note?

A. It is written by a person of foreign origin.

B. It is written by a woman.

C. It is written by two different people.

D. It is written by someone who has had very little education.

6. How many other deductions does Holmes glean from the note?

A. Seven

B. Twelve

C. Sixteen

D. Twenty-three

7. Who witnessed the robbery at Mr. Acton's house?

A. William Kirwin

B. Annie Morrison

C. Colonel Hayter

D. Mr. Acton

8. How does Holmes know that Kirwin was not shot at close range?

A. There were no powder burns on Kirwin's clothes.

B. The wound was such that the gun could not have been close to the body.

C. The buckshot was scattered across the entire torso.

D. Kirwin placed his arms in front of his body as if to shield himself.

9. What were the thieves looking for when they broke into Mr. Acton's house?

A. Mr. Acton's will
B. A paper claiming that Mr. Acton owned half of the neighboring estate
C. Letters of blackmail
D. A damaging newspaper article

10. What piece of this puzzle does Holmes choose to ignore, feeling that since the criminals have been apprehended, this information was not necessary?

A. The real owner of the estate
B. The nature of the relationships of Annie Morrison, Alec Cunningham, and William Kirwin
C. The meaning of the note
D. The reason for Kirwin's murder

QUIZ 34
"THE CROOKED MAN"

Published in the Strand *in July 1893*

At the time Conan Doyle wrote "The Crooked Man," his younger brother, Innes, was a subaltern in the Royal Artillery Regiment stationed at Aldershot, the largest military camp in England. This small bit of personal trivia found its way into this story; Colonel James Barclay, commanding officer of the Irish regiment of the Royal Mallows at Aldershot, was found murdered in his home. This quiz contains ten short-answer questions about a tale of lost love, betrayal, and revenge.

Story Date: 1888 to 1889

1. What was unusual about Colonel Barclay's behavior?
2. How long had the colonel and Mrs. Barclay been married?
3. Where had Mrs. Barclay been right before the colonel's murder?
4. What stranger's name does Mrs. Barclay shout while arguing with her husband?

5. What is the apparent cause of the colonel's death?

6. Who enters the colonel's study along with the intruder?

7. Who gives Holmes the details about what happened on the way home from the meeting of the Guild of St. George?

8. Why does Mrs. Barclay turn against her husband?

9. What caused Colonel Barclay's death?

10. Holmes reproaches himself for not using his astute sense of reasoning to deduce that the name "David," uttered by Mrs. Barclay, was made in reference to which famous book?

TRIVIA FACTS : DID YOU KNOW THAT . . .

1. When Conan Doyle's first Sherlock Holmes stories appeared in *Beeton's Christmas Annual*, illustrator D. H. Friston portrayed Holmes as an overweight and effeminate dandy.

2. When *A Study in Scarlet* was published in book form in 1888, Conan Doyle's father, Charles Doyle, drew the illustrations. The tall, fair-haired Holmes resembled a younger Charles Doyle wearing a beard.

3. Illustrator Sidney Paget, who gave the public its immortal images of Sherlock Holmes and Dr. Watson, used his brother Walter as a model for Holmes and Conan Doyle as a model for Dr. Watson. This image of Sherlock Holmes was sexier and more appealing and resulted in thousands of young women reading the exploits of this dashing detective.

4. Shortly after the Walter Paget image of Holmes was published, Walter Paget attended a performance at the Covent Gardens Opera House where a woman saw him and shouted, "There goes Sherlock Holmes!" As a result, more eyes were on Paget than on the stage. This was only the first of many similar incidents that eventually caused Paget to regret sitting as a model for Holmes.

"THE RESIDENT PATIENT"

Published in the Strand *in August 1893*

The criminal activities of the infamous bank robber Adam Worth must have held great interest for Conan Doyle. Worth's clever plotting succeeded in allowing him access to bank vaults in the United States, making him extremely wealthy. Details of his crimes have appeared in several Sherlock Holmes stories, including "The Resident Patient." In this tale, Holmes makes reference to the bank robber when he speaks of the "Worthingdon" bank gang. This quiz contains ten multiple choice questions.

Story Date: October in the late 1800s

1. In what type of medicine does Dr. Trevelyan specialize?

    A. He specializes in nervous diseases, especially catalepsy.
    B. Dr. Trevelyan is a heart specialist.
    C. He is a dermatologist.
    D. He specializes in tropical diseases.

2. What arrangement did Mr. Blessington make with Dr. Trevelyan concerning his practice?

    A. Mr. Blessington purchased all of Dr. Trevelyan's supplies, while Dr. Trevelyan agreed to treat whomever Mr. Blessington requested, no questions asked.
    B. Mr. Blessington guaranteed Dr. Trevelyan a full appointment book, under the condition that Mr. Blessington make all of the appointments.
    C. Mr. Blessington paid Dr. Trevelyan's expenses and kept one-fourth of all the money collected.
    D. Mr. Blessington paid Dr. Trevelyan's rent, and Dr. Trevelyan agreed to treat only people afflicted with the same medical condition as Mr. Blessington.

3. How did Mr. Blessington conclude each day?

    A. He came into Dr. Trevelyan's office for an
       examination.
    B. He asked Dr. Trevelyan for an oral report of the
       condition of all of his patients.
    C. Mr. Blessington counted the money Dr. Trevelyan
       collected for the day.
    D. Mr. Blessington thoroughly examined the financial
       books.

4. Why is Mr. Blessington paranoid of being burgled?

    A. Mr. Blessington's entire collection of Chinese
       pottery had been stolen.
    B. Mr. Blessington is paranoid and distrustful of
       everyone.
    C. His best friend had been killed during a robbery.
    D. He doesn't trust banks, and he keeps everything he
       owns in a box in his room.

5. Who do the intruders say they are when they make an
   appointment to visit Dr. Trevelyan?

    A. A Russian nobleman and his son who are seeking
       medical attention
    B. A brother and a nephew of Mr. Blessington
    C. Two new doctors who want Dr. Trevelyan's advice
       about a complex case
    D. They are from Mr. Blessington's church, and it
       was recommended by a church member that they
       consult Dr. Trevelyan.

6. How does Mr. Blessington know that someone has
   been in his room?

    A. The door is left ajar.
    B. He smells the residue of cigarette smoke.
    C. Someone has left his vanity drawer open and has
       spilled his cologne.
    D. He notices footprints in the carpet.

7. What initial clue leads Holmes to realize that Blessington's apparent suicide was really a murder?

    A. There are several different cigar ends and holders left in Blessington's room, indicating the presence of other men.

    B. Blessington is hanging from the lamp fixture, but the box from which he apparently jumped is pushed too far from the body.

    C. Upon close examination of the body, Holmes finds a needle puncture behind the ear.

    D. Holmes ascertains that he had died before he was hanged.

8. Why does Blessington keep a rope under his bed?

    A. He is superstitious and believes that it will keep him from having nightmares.

    B. He is afraid of fires, and he wants to be prepared for a window escape if necessary.

    C. He uses it to raise and lower necessities when he is ill and refuses to let anyone in the house.

    D. He believes that his bed often moves in the middle of the night, and so he ties it to the radiator.

9. Which recently hired employee lets the killers in and out of Blessington's house?

    A. The cook

    B. The downstairs maid

    C. The page

    D. The coachman

10. How does Holmes deduce that Mr. Blessington is lying about not knowing who his intruders are?

    A. Mr. Blessington does not look Holmes in the eye while Holmes questions him.

    B. Holmes sees the fear in Mr. Blessington's eyes and speculates that Mr. Blessington knows who the intruders are.

C. Mr. Blessington is fidgeting while Holmes questions him.

D. Mr. Blessington is too evasive when Holmes questions him.

QUIZ 36
"THE GREEK INTERPRETER"

Published in the Strand *and in* Harper's *in September 1893*

In this story, Holmes reveals to Watson that he has an older brother who "has better powers of observation than I [Holmes]." Conan Doyle gives his readers a detailed picture of Holmes's brother, down to the exact time he enters and leaves his club every day. But why did Conan Doyle include detailed statistics about Mycroft if he was to appear in only one other story? Conan Doyle may have realized that two high-profile characters were a bit too much to contend with. Mycroft is briefly mentioned in two other stories, but he remains loyal and supportive of his younger brother, whom he clearly trusts more than anyone. The following quiz contains ten short-answer questions.

Story Date: 1880s

1. Who brought this case to Holmes's attention?

2. What nervous habit does Harold Latimer, the kidnapper, have?

3. How does Mr. Melas communicate with the kidnapped victim without the captors knowing?

4. How much is Mr. Melas paid for interpreting for the kidnappers?

5. Who answers Mycroft's ad about the missing Greek lady?

6. How do the kidnappers try to dispose of Mr. Melas and Paul Kratides?

7. Why is Sophie kidnapped?

8. How do the kidnappers disguise Paul Kratides so that his sister does not recognize him?

9. What happens to the two men who kidnap Sophie?

10. How do the kidnappers try to force Paul Kratides to sign the paper, giving them what they want?

QUIZ 37
"THE NAVAL TREATY"

Published in Harper's *in October and in the* Strand *in October and November 1893*

"The Naval Treaty" was based on a case in London in which a man named Charles Marvin had been accused of selling secret government documents to the yellow press. He had worked as a clerk in the foreign office and had used his position to gain the information. This quiz about a true-to-life story contains ten true/false statements.

Story Date: 1880s
1. Watson met Perry Phelps when they were in India.
2. Phelps's nickname in school was "Tadpole."
3. Phelps received his assignment to the foreign office from a recommendation by a college professor.
4. Phelps was given the important assignment of copying a secret treaty between England and Italy.
5. After Phelps suffered a mental and physical breakdown, he was sent to a sanitarium to recover.
6. Holmes deduces ten clues after listening to Phelps's story.
7. Holmes enlists the help of Scotland Yard detective Inspector Lestrade.
8. When the commissioner's wife failed to bring Phelps his coffee, he went to see what had detained her, and in doing so, he left the treaty unguarded.

9. Holmes received a slight flesh wound when he and the villain wrestled with a pistol.

10. The stolen papers were in Phelps's room the entire time.

QUIZ 38
"THE FINAL PROBLEM"

Published in the Strand *and in* McClure's *in December 1893*

After the publication of "The Final Problem" in which Holmes apparently died in a tumble over Reichenbach Falls while fighting with his archenemy, Professor Moriarty, Sherlock Holmes fans were in shock. To many dedicated readers, Sherlock Holmes was a real person. They waited anxiously for the next Holmes installment to hit the stands. No more Holmes was unthinkable.

To mourn the loss of one of the greatest literary characters in publishing history, Londoners wore crepe bands around their hats. And in their prolonged grief, they protested at the magazine office and even went as far as sending threatening letters to Conan Doyle. Even though the writer was tired of his creation and anxious to move his literary career to a higher level, the public was not willing to accept the fate of their most cherished and beloved detective. They would have to wait almost eight years, however, for the next Holmes story, *The Hound of the Baskervilles*, set in a time before Holmes's accident, and another two years before Conan Doyle finally resurrected his immortal detective. The following quiz contains ten multiple choice questions.

Story Date: April 1891

1. What compels Watson to write and publish the facts surrounding Holmes's tragic accident?

   A. In revealing the incident, the newspapers report the facts incorrectly.

   B. Ugly rumors surface, and Watson is adamant about setting the record straight.

   C. Letters from Moriarty's brother publicly defend the notorious professor, and Watson is compelled to write an account on behalf of Holmes.

THE SHERLOCK HOLMES QUIZ BOOK

D. Scotland Yard wants an accurate account of the incident, and they request that Watson summarize the event.

2. How does Holmes describe Professor Moriarty's genius?
   A. "He is the Socrates of evil."
   B. "He is the Sherlock Holmes of intellect."
   C. "He is the Brutus of betrayal."
   D. "He is the Napoleon of crime."

3. What are Moriarty's first words to Holmes?
   A. "You have less frontal development than I should have expected."
   B. "This situation is becoming an impossible one."
   C. "You must stand clear, Mr. Holmes, or be trodden underfoot."
   D. "I tell you that you will never beat me."

4. How many attempts had Moriarty made on Holmes's life?
   A. Three
   B. Six
   C. Five
   D. Four

5. How many days does Holmes have to wait before the police arrest Moriarty and his gang?
   A. Seven
   B. Ten
   C. Four
   D. Three

6. How is Holmes disguised when he rendezvous with Watson in their carriage on the train?
   A. Holmes is dressed as a country squire with a heavy beard.
   B. Holmes is disguised as an Italian priest.
   C. Holmes is disguised as an elderly woman.
   D. Holmes is dressed in Arab garb.

7. Who is the person who takes Watson to the station?

   A. Inspector Lestrade
   B. Billy, Holmes's page
   C. Mercer, an employee of Holmes
   D. Mycroft, Holmes's brother

8. What disturbing message does Holmes receive from the London police while in Strasbourg?

   A. Moriarty has escaped.
   B. His apartment on Baker Street has burned down.
   C. Moriarty made an attempt on Mycroft's life.
   D. All charges on Moriarty were dropped, due to lack of evidence.

9. How does Moriarty lure Watson away from Holmes, leaving him alone at Reichenbach Falls?

   A. Watson receives a message that his wife is ill and that she requests that he return to England.
   B. The hotel sends a message for Watson to attend to an Englishwoman who is very ill and who refuses to see a foreign doctor.
   C. An avalanche buried several skiers, and all available doctors are urged to attend to the victims.
   D. The hotel summons Dr. Watson to assist a young woman who is having a difficult labor.

10. With Moriarty hot on his trail, and knowing that he might not survive the pursuit, how does Holmes manage to send Watson a message after his apparent fatal accident?

   A. Mycroft delivers the message to Watson after he returns to England.
   B. Watson discovers the message in Holmes's desk when going through his papers.
   C. Holmes slips the message into his silver cigarette case, which Watson finds at the falls.
   D. Watson finds Holmes's message in his mail. Holmes posted it on the morning of the accident.

CHARACTERS ACCORDING TO WATSON—PART 2

He was a tall man, he was a small man, he was an aged man, he was a large man, and beyond these noticeable traits, he was secretive, fierce, eccentric, and cunning, and he found his way into several Sherlock Holmes stories. The twenty characters in this quiz appear in the last three collections of short stories: *The Return of Sherlock Holmes, His Last Bow,* and *The Case Book of Sherlock Holmes,* as well as in the novels *The Hound of the Baskervilles* and *The Valley of Fear.* Name the characters and the story or novel in which each appears.

1. "The cheek was lovely but it was paled with emotion, the eyes were bright, but it was the brightness of fever, the sensitive mouth was tight and drawn in an effort after self-command. Terror—not beauty—was what sprang first to the eye as our fair visitor stood framed for an instant in the open door."

2. "In the dim light of a foggy November day the sick room was a gloomy spot, but it was that gaunt, wasted face staring at me from the bed which sent a chill to my heart. His eyes had the brightness of fever, there was a hectic flush upon either cheek, and dark crusts clung to his lips; the thin hands upon the coverlet twitched incessantly, his voice was croaking and spasmodic."

3. "He was a tall and stately person, scrupulously dressed, with a drawn, thin face, and a nose which was grotesquely curved and long. His complexion was of a dead pallor, which was more startling by contrast with a long, dwindling beard of vivid red, which flowed down over his white waistcoat, with his watch-chain gleaming through its fringe."

4. "He was a very tall young man, golden-moustached, blue-eyed, with a skin which had been burned by

tropical suns, and a springy step, which showed that the huge frame was as active as it was strong."

5. "Heavily built and massive, there was a suggestion of uncouth physical inertia in the figure, but above this unwieldy frame there was perched a head so masterful in its brow, so alert in its steel-gray, deep-set eyes, so firm in its lips, and so subtle in its play of expression, that after the first glance one forgot the gross body and remembered only the dominant mind."

6. "It is hardly necessary to describe him for many will remember that large, bluff, honest personality, that broad, clean-shaven face, and, above all, the pleasant, mellow voice. Frankness shone from his gray Irish eyes, and good humour played round his mobile, smiling lips. His lucent top-hat, his dark frock-coat, indeed, every detail, from the pearl pin in the black satin cravat to the lavender spats over the varnished shoes, spoke for the meticulous care in dress for which he was famous."

7. "The nocturnal visitor was a young man, frail and thin, with a black moustache, which intensified the deadly pallor of his face. He could not have been much above twenty years of age. I have never seen any human being who appeared to be in such a pitiable fright, for his teeth were visibly chattering, and he was shaking in every limb."

8. "proved to be a very tall, loose-jointed, round-backed person, gaunt and bald, some sixty-odd years of age. He had a cadaverous face, with the dull dead skin of a man to whom exercise was unknown. Large round spectacles and a small projecting goat's beard combined with his stooping attitude to give him an expression of peering curiosity. The general effect, however, was amiable, though eccentric."

9. "Her eyes and hair were of the same rich hazel colour, and her cheeks, though considerably freckled, were

flushed with exquisite bloom of the brunette, the dainty pink which lurks at the heart of the sulphur rose."

10. "I saw a great yellow face, coarse-grained and greasy, with heavy, double-chin, and two sullen, menacing gray eyes which glared at me from under tufted and sandy brows. A high bald head had a small velvet smoking-cap poised coquettishly upon one side of its pink curve. The skull was of enormous capacity, and yet as I looked down I saw to my amazement that the figure of the man was small and frail, twisted in the shoulders and back like one who has suffered from rickets in his childhood."

11. " an enormous young man, sixteen stone of solid bone and muscle, who spanned the doorway with the broad shoulders, and looked from one of us to the other with a comely face which was haggard with anxiety."

12. "He was a terrible figure, huge in stature and fierce in manner. A large stable-lantern which he held in front of him shone upward upon a strong, heavily moustached face and angry eyes, which glared round him into every recess of the vault, finally fixing themselves with a deadly stare upon my companion and myself."

13. "He was flaxen-haired and handsome, in a washed-out negative fashion, with frightened blue eyes, and a clean-shaven face, with a weak, sensitive mouth. His age may have been twenty-seven, his dress and bearing that of a gentleman. From the pocket of his light summer overcoat protruded the bundle of indorsed papers which proclaimed his profession."

14. "The heavy, white face was seamed with lines of trouble, the hanging pouches under his closed eyes were leaden in colour, the loose mouth drooped dolorously at the corners, the rolling chins were unshaven. Collar and shirt bore the grime of a long journey, and the hair bristled unkempt from a well-shaped head."

15. "and we looked up to find a queer little old man, jerking and twitching in the doorway. He was dressed in rusty black, with a very broadbrimmed top-hat and a loose white necktie—the whole effect being that of a very rustic parson or of an undertaker's mute. Yet, in spite of his shabby and even absurd appearance, his voice had a sharp crackle, and his manner a quick intensity which commanded attention."

16. "He was a tall, handsome, swarthy fellow, clad in a suit of gray flannel, with a Panama hat, a bristling black beard, and a great, aggressive hooked nose, and flourishing a cane as he walked. He swaggered up the path as if the place belonged to him, and we heard his loud, confident peal at the bell."

17. "She rose from a settee as we entered: tall, queenly, a perfect figure, a lovely mask-like face, with two wonderful Spanish eyes which looked murder at both of us."

18. "He seemed to me like a man who was literally bowed down by care. His back was curved as though he carried a heavy burden. Yet he was not the weakling that I had first imagined, for his shoulders and chest have the framework of a giant, though his figure tapers away into a pair of spindled legs."

19. "I have seldom seen a more remarkable-looking person. It was a gaunt, aquiline face which was turned towards us, with piercing dark eyes, which lurked in deep hollows under overhung and tufted brows. His hair and beard were white, save that the latter was curiously stained with yellow around his mouth. A cigarette glowed amid the tangle of white hair, and the air of the room was fetid with stale tobacco smoke."

20. "He was certainly a remarkably handsome man. His European reputation for beauty was fully deserved. In figure he was not more than of middle size, but

was built upon graceful and active lines. His face was swarthy, almost Oriental, with large, dark, languorous eyes which might easily hold an irresistible fascination for women. His hair and moustache were raven black, the latter short, pointed, and carefully waxed. His features were regular and pleasing, save only his straight, thin-lipped mouth."

Robert Downey, Jr. and Rachel Adams as Sherlock Holmes and Irene Adler in the Guy Ritchie *Sherlock Holmes* 2009

FIVE

THE THIRD COLLECTION:
THE RETURN OF SHERLOCK HOLMES

"Holmes!" I cried. "It is really you?
Can it indeed be that you are alive?"
DR. JOHN WATSON

When Sherlock Holmes tumbled over the cliff in Switzerland, Conan Doyle fully intended to leave him in the abyss of Reichenbach Falls. The author was determined to make a clean break with his fictional detective, even if it meant a financial sacrifice. In spite of the public's outcry to resurrect Holmes, Conan Doyle did not give in, but instead became even more adamant about pursuing what he believed to be a more serious literary career, writing historical novels, political essays, and books on spiritualism.

Writing the last few Holmes stories had become an arduous task for Conan Doyle. His personal life was fraught with emotional pain and uncertainty. It was evident that his wife would not recover from her illness, which rendered her an invalid. He had recently made a courageous but frightening choice to set aside his medical practice and make a living solely as a writer. Surrounded by so much uncertainty, this tenacious decision to put an end to his Sherlock Holmes stories was one aspect of his life that he could control. As Sherlock Holmes fans continued to take to the street in protest, Conan Doyle dug in his heels and set about putting his life in order.

Fortunately for all concerned, Conan Doyle's method of eliminating Sherlock Holmes made it fairly easy to resurrect the detective ten years later when he finally had a change of heart. Had Holmes died by gunshot, stabbing, or being run down by a hansom, Conan Doyle would have had to stretch the bounds of imagination to bring Holmes back to life. Was this an intentional ploy, leaving a loophole just in case he changed his mind about writing additional Holmes stories? There is no direct indication of this foreshadowing in any of the numerous Conan Doyle biographies. But by sparing his readers a lifeless Sherlock Holmes body in "The Final Problem," Conan Doyle was able to reintroduce the Great Detective.

In his conversation with Watson, Holmes explains how he was able to save himself from the deadly grasp of Professor Moriarty by engaging in a form of Japanese wrestling called baritsu. Surviving the fall and the struggle, Holmes disappears and lays low, traveling, studying, and honing his skills. After a hiatus of three years, he feels that it is time to return to Baker Street even in the face of danger, for Colonel Sebastian Moran is waiting to avenge the death of his former crime boss, Professor Moriarty. Once Watson recovers from his swoon, the detecting duo pick up where they left off three years earlier without so much as missing a beat. The murder of the Honourable Ronald Adair is solved, Colonel Moran is put away, and it is not long before John Hector McFarlane, while standing in Holmes's room on Baker Street, is arrested for the murder of Jonas Oldacre of Lower Norwood. Holmes knows, of course, that McFarlane is innocent, and the adventures resume.

This collection includes "The Adventure of the Empty House," "The Adventure of the Norwood Builder," "The Adventure of the Dancing Men," "The Adventure of the Solitary Cyclist," "The Adventure of the Priory School," "The Adventure of Black Peter," "The Adventure of Charles Augustus Milverton," "The Adventure of the Six Napoleons," "The Adventure of the Three Students," "The Adventure of the Golden Pince-Nez," "The Adventure of the Missing Three-Quarter," "The Adventure of the Abbey Grange," and "The Adventure of the Second Stain."

QUIZ 40
"THE ADVENTURE OF THE EMPTY HOUSE"

Published in Collier's *in September 1903 and in the* Strand *in October 1903*

Although reluctant to resurrect the Great Detective, Conan Doyle could not turn down the lucrative offer made to him by his

American publisher, *Collier's*. In typical British form and in a style characteristic of the author, Conan Doyle announced, "I might add that I have finished the first one, called 'The Adventure of the Empty House.' The plot, by the way, was given to me by Jean [his wife]; and it is a rare good one. You will find that Holmes was never dead, and that he is now very much alive." Conan Doyle was quite anxious about the reception for this first story after the Great Hiatus. He wanted to prove to his fans that he could still spin a great Holmes tale. This quiz contains ten short-answer questions about the first in a new series of Sherlock Holmes stories.

Story Date: April 1894

1. What was the time and date on which Ronald Adair was murdered?

2. What vice did Ronald Adair have which apparently led to his murder?

3. How is Holmes disguised when he bumps into Dr. Watson in front of the Adair house?

4. What is the title of the book that the old man drops when Watson bumps into him?

5. How does Holmes know that Moriarty's gang is watching his rooms?

6. Who moves the bust around, making it appear to be alive?

7. Why does Holmes place the wax figure in his window?

8. Why did Adair have piles of money in front of him on his desk?

9. What happens to the wax figure of Holmes's head?

10. What happened to the air gun after Moran's arrest?

"THE ADVENTURE OF THE NORWOOD BUILDER"

Published in Collier's *in October 1903 and in the* Strand *in November 1903*

Always in touch with the latest scientific developments, and possibly even preceding them, Conan Doyle never hesitated in using such information in his stories. In "The Norwood Builder," Conan Doyle puts Holmes on the right track in solving the mystery when the detective examines a bloody thumbprint left on a wall. In the year in which this story was written, Scotland Yard had arrested a thief after he left his bloody thumbprint on the safe he had robbed. Later that year another thief was arrested when he lost his finger by snagging his wedding ring on a spike. The police matched the print of the finger to one in their criminal file and were able to apprehend the suspect. This quiz contains ten true/false statements.

Story Date: 1894 or 1895

1. John Hector McFarlane is arrested for the murder of Jonas Oldacre because his wallet and identification were found near the dead body.

2. McFarlane is arrested in Holmes's apartment while pleading for the detective's help.

3. Oldacre changed his will and bequeathed McFarlane 5,000 pounds.

4. Holmes feels that he will fail in solving this mystery, but he strongly believes that the solution depends upon the housekeeper's testimony.

5. On the night Oldacre was murdered, McFarlane spent the night in a country inn because it was too late to return home.

6. Inspector Lestrade finds a witness who saw McFarlane leave the Oldacre house on the night of the murder.

7. Holmes discovers a hidden room in Oldacre's house, which puts Holmes on the right track in proving McFarlane's innocence.

8. Holmes flushes the murderer from his hiding place by announcing in a loud voice that he is about to take target practice on the wall in the corridor.

9. Because Oldacre was being blackmailed, he conceived the scam as a way to elude his blackmailers.

10. Once caught, the murderer tries to pass off the affair as a joke.

QUIZ 42
"THE ADVENTURE OF THE DANCING MEN"

Published in Collier's *and in the* Strand *in December 1903*

By the time Conan Doyle published *The Return of Sherlock Holmes*, his American readers were as anxious for more Holmes stories as the British. To satisfy his American publisher and readership, Conan Doyle set the background for this well-calculated story in the United States. Conan Doyle was rather pleased with this tale and ranked it as number three on his list of favorite Sherlock Holmes cases. The following quiz contains ten multiple choice questions.

Story Date: 1898
1. After noticing several obvious clues, what does Holmes predict that Watson is about to do concerning his investments?

    A. Watson is not considering investing in diamond mines in India.
    B. He is not considering investing in South African securities.
    C. He has just sold several shares of stock and is planning to invest in a new shipping company.

D. He is wondering if it is too late to invest in his friend's dairy business in Kenya.

2. How long had the Cubitt family been residing at Riding Thorpe in the county of Norfolk?

   A. The Cubitt family had purchased the estate two years earlier.
   B. The Cubitts had been at Riding Thorpe since the turn of the century.
   C. The family had owned the estate for five centuries.
   D. The family had purchased the estate right after the French Revolution.

3. What promise did Mr. Cubitt have to make to his wife before she would marry him?

   A. Mrs. Cubitt insisted that her husband leave half of his estate to her family.
   B. Mr. Cubitt must never refer to her maiden name.
   C. Mrs. Cubitt insisted that Mr. Cubitt never ask about her past.
   D. Mr. Cubitt would have to promise never to inquire about her father.

4. How did Mrs. Cubitt react when her husband showed her the drawing of the dancing figures?

   A. Mrs. Cubitt fainted.
   B. Mrs. Cubitt was furious and stormed out of the house.
   C. She hurried off to church and remained there for the rest of the afternoon.
   D. She rushed to town and sent a telegram.

5. What did Mrs. Cubitt suggest that she and her husband do when the strange messages began to appear more frequently?

   A. Mrs. Cubitt suggested that they contact Sherlock Holmes.
   B. She suggested that they burn all of the messages.

C. She suggested that she and her husband take a trip and get away for a while.

D. Mrs. Cubitt suggested that they pray together every evening until the messages stop arriving.

6. Where did most of the messages appear?

A. On the sundial in the garden

B. On the second step of the front entrance

C. On the door of the stable

D. On the windowsill in the breakfast room

7. What problem faces Holmes when he arrives at Riding Thorpe to begin his investigation?

A. Mr. and Mrs. Cubitt have both been shot. Mr. Cubitt is dead, and his wife is in serious condition.

B. Mrs. Cubitt has left her husband.

C. Mr. Cubitt has shot the person responsible for writing the messages.

D. Mrs. Cubitt was arrested for a crime she committed before she met her husband.

8. What key piece of evidence does Holmes discover while studying the scene of the crime?

A. The gun found in the room did not fire the shots.

B. A third shot had been fired.

C. One victim was shot at close range, the other from a distance.

D. Both victims had been shot with the same bullet.

9. How does Holmes lure the murderer back to the scene of the crime?

A. Holmes writes him a letter using the code of the dancing men and asks him to come for a visit.

B. Holmes advertises in the newspaper that a reward will be given if anyone can decipher the code.

C. Holmes sends a newspaper boy to the village to tell everyone that Mrs. Cubitt has died.

D. Holmes closes up the Cubitt house, making it look as if it is abandoned.

10. Who invented the code of the dancing men?

    A. Elsie Cubitt
    B. Elsie's father, Mr. Patrick
    C. The man who was pursuing Elsie Cubitt
    D. It was an old prison code that her father learned
       when he was in jail.

QUIZ 43
"THE ADVENTURE OF
THE SOLITARY CYCLIST"

Published in Collier's *in December 1903 and
in the* Strand *in January 1904*

At the beginning of this story, Holmes is too busy to begin working on Violet Smith's case; he is currently involved with a complicated problem concerning tobacco millionaire John Vincent
Harden. Irritated at the intrusion, but not wanting to turn down
Miss Smith's plea for assistance, Holmes sends Watson to carry
out the initial investigation. Apparently, when Conan Doyle first
submitted this story to the *Strand*, editor Herbert Greenhough
Smith felt that Holmes did not play an active enough role in the
mystery. Conan Doyle had to revise the story before publication.
As a result, Holmes appears in the middle of the story to severely
chastise Watson for his poor investigative skills and then proceeds
to solve the mystery himself, as usual. The following quiz contains
ten short-answer questions.

Story Date: 1895

1. On what day does Violet Smith appear at Holmes's
   doorstep requesting help?

2. How does Holmes know that Violet Smith is a
   musician?

3. How did Miss Smith come to be employed by Mr.
   Carruthers?

4. Why is Holmes convinced that Miss Smith knows the identity of the cyclist?

5. Why did Mr. Carruthers forbid Mr. Woodley to visit his home?

6. How does Holmes gain information about the cyclist?

7. Why does Miss Smith quit her job with Mr. Carruthers?

8. Why does Watson fear that the situation may turn tragic?

9. Why does Mr. Woodley believe that he has the right to marry Miss Smith?

10. Who does Woodley find to help him carry out his scheme?

QUIZ 44
"THE ADVENTURE OF THE PRIORY SCHOOL"

Published in Collier's *in January 1904 and in the* Strand *in February 1904*

In several of the stories published in the collection *The Return of Sherlock Holmes,* Conan Doyle draws on his school days at Hodder prep school and at Edinburgh University. Hodder was used for the setting of "The Priory School." Also, the founder of the Priory School, Thorneycroft Huxtable, was probably based on Hodder's head teacher, Father Edward Ignatius Purbrick.

This quiz contains ten true/false statements.

Story Date: Early 1900s

1. Holmes reads the newspaper and discovers that the son of the Duke of Holdernesse has been abducted.

2. The Duke of Holdernesse offers a 10,000 pound reward for the return of his son.

3. Lord Saltire was enrolled in school just two weeks before he disappeared.

4. Holmes knows that the bicycle tracks found in the soil were not made by Mr. Heidegger's bicycle, because the tire impression was of a different type of tire than that found on the teacher's bicycle.

5. The Duke believes that his estranged wife arranged for the boy's abduction.

6. Lord Saltire's cap is found near a mire in Lower Gill Moor.

7. Lord Saltire is found in an upstairs room of the Fighting Cock public house.

8. When the Duke realizes that Holmes has discovered the truth, His Grace offers the detective 12,000 pounds to keep the situation quiet.

9. No one was ever arrested for the abduction.

10. When the Duke discovers who the kidnapper is, he refuses to prosecute because the unstable man is the son of a close friend.

QUIZ 45
"THE ADVENTURE OF BLACK PETER"

Published in Collier's *in February 1904 and in the* Strand *in 1904*

While writing "The Adventure of Black Peter," Conan Doyle drew from his experience in 1880 when, as a young man uncertain of his direction in life, he signed on as a surgeon aboard a whaling ship, the *Hope*. Ignoring the advice of friends and relatives who tried to discourage this decision, Conan Doyle accepted the offer without hesitation. He spent seven months with a company of seafaring men who loved to spin a good yarn. What better experience for a budding young author? In his autobiography, Conan Doyle often reflected on this experience as one of the most enjoyable and satisfying times in his life. The following quiz contains ten multiple choice questions.

Story Date: July 1895

1. Who is the police inspector who calls upon Holmes for assistance in solving the gruesome murder of Peter Carey?

    A. Inspector Lestrade
    B. Inspector Hopkins
    C. Inspector Gregson
    D. Inspector Jones

2. In what activity was Holmes engaged at the beginning of the story, claiming that it was good exercise?

    A. Fencing with a master who disliked him
    B. Sparring with a boxer who was training for a world match
    C. Stabbing a pig's carcass with a harpoon
    D. Cycling while blindfolded, allowing his sixth sense to guide him

---

TRIVIA FACTS : DID YOU KNOW THAT . . .

1. The idea of ending Holmes's life in a tumble over Reichenbach Falls was conceived when Conan Doyle and his wife visited the falls while vacationing in Switzerland.

2. Conan Doyle considered refusing King Edward VII's offer of knighthood because he believed that the award was in honor of his talent as the creator of Sherlock Holmes. Finally realizing that the honor was due to his contributions to the Boer War efforts, Conan Doyle accepted knighthood on behalf of the British soldiers.

3. In 1903 Collier's, Conan Doyle's American publisher, offered him $45,000 for thirteen more Holmes stories.

---

3. Rather than sleep in his comfortable home with his family, where did Black Peter Carey spend his evenings?

   A. Black Peter spent his nights in a small hut decorated like a ship.
   B. Black Peter would get drunk every night at the local pub, pass out, and sleep under the table.
   C. No matter what the weather, Black Peter slept outside on his cot.
   D. Black Peter slept in the cold barn with the sheep.

4. What was the name of Black Peter's ship?

   A. *Black Sea*
   B. *Dark Moon*
   C. *Serpent*
   D. *Sea Unicorn*

5. What evidence suggests that Black Peter had an appointment on the night of his murder?

   A. In his hand is a note with a date and time.
   B. His daughter heard voices coming from his hut.
   C. There is a bottle of rum and two glasses on the table.
   D. His door was unlocked and there was no sign of a forced entry.

6. Why does John Hopley Neligan search Black Peter's residence?

   A. Neligan is searching for a logbook.
   B. He is searching for letters written to Black Peter by his father.
   C. He is searching for Black Peter's will.
   D. He is searching for a photo proving that Black Peter and his father were acquaintances.

7. How does Holmes know that Neligan did not kill Black Peter?

A. Neligan does not have the nerve to attack a man as strong and vicious as Black Peter.

B. Neligan is not physically strong enough to stab Black Peter in the manner in which he was killed.

C. Holmes did not find Neligan's footprints around the scene of the crime.

D. Neligan is left-handed, and the killer stabbed Black Peter with his right hand.

8. What was the killer's initial intention when he called upon Black Peter on the night he was murdered?

A. The man intended to blackmail Black Peter.

B. He planned to get Black Peter drunk and search his trunk.

C. He wanted to frighten Black Peter into confessing his crime.

D. He wanted see how Black Peter prospered as a result of the man he murdered.

9. How does Holmes know that the tobacco pouch with the initials P. C. was not Black Peter's?

A. The tobacco in the pouch did not match the tobacco in Black Peter's pipe.

B. Black Peter seldom smoked, and there was not a pipe in his hut.

C. Black Peter smoked cigarettes, and the pouch contained pipe tobacco.

D. Black Peter Carey's first name was not really Peter.

10. What do Holmes and Watson do as soon as the case is solved?

A. They leave for Norway.

B. They attend a violin recital.

C. They head to Holmes's favorite tobacco shop for more shag.

D. They take a hansom to the British Museum to view a maritime exhibit.

QUIZ 46
"THE ADVENTURE OF CHARLES AUGUSTUS MILVERTON"

*Published in Collier's in March 1904 and
in the* Strand *in April 1904*

In developing the character of the notorious blackmailer, Charles August Milverton, there is some indication that Conan Doyle used loan shark Henry Padwick as a model. The suave Padwick was known to attract his lady victims with merely a smile. As Conan Doyle describes Milverton, "With a smiling face and a heart of marble, he will squeeze and squeeze until he has drained them [victims] dry." This fiery tale of greed and redemption is analyzed in ten short-answer questions.

Story Date: Late 1800s, exact date uncertain

1. Why does Lady Eva Blackwell contact Holmes?

2. How does Holmes gain entrance to Milverton's house?

3. What scandalous evidence does Milverton have that would ruin Lady Blackwell?

4. How does Holmes plan to foil Milverton's attempt at blackmail?

5. At what time does Milverton retire to bed most evenings?

6. Why is Milverton still awake past his usual bedtime on the night Holmes and Watson arrive?

7. Where were Holmes and Watson when Milverton was murdered?

8. What does Holmes do before he and Watson flee Milverton's house?

9. How does Holmes confirm the identity of the mysterious lady who shot Milverton?

10. Why does Inspector Lestrade believe that two criminals are responsible for Milverton's murder?

THE SHERLOCK HOLMES QUIZ BOOK

"THE ADVENTURE OF THE SIX NAPOLEONS"

Published in Collier's *in April 1904 and in the* Strand *in May 1904*

The story of "The Six Napoleons" presents an element of Sherlock Holmes's character that is rare, indeed. Conan Doyle gives his detective—a man of steel nerves, stern conviction, and unsurpassed confidence—a shy moment when, at the conclusion of the story, Holmes receives an earnest barrage of compliments from Inspector Lestrade. Holmes's initial reaction is one of embarrassment, as Watson describes: "and as he [Holmes] turned away, it seemed to me that he was more nearly moved by the softer human emotions than I had ever see him." But his shyness quickly evaporates as "[a] moment later he was the cold and practical thinker once more." The following quiz contains ten true/false statements.

Story Date: 1900

1. The Napoleon bust is stolen from Morse Hudson's shop on Kensington Road.

2. The famous French sculptor, Divine, created plaster casts of the bust of Napoleon.

3. Dr. Watson believes that the person who is smashing the Napoleon sculptures suffers from a condition called "idée fixe" (fixed idea), resulting in obsessive delusions.

4. The theft of the fourth bust is more serious because the thief left a threatening letter.

5. After each of the busts is stolen, the thief smashes them in a well-lighted area.

6. Finding a name and address in the coat pocket of the dead man put Holmes on the right track.

7. When Holmes visits the manufacturer of the busts, the manager of the company informs Holmes that the cousin of the man in the photograph works for him.

8. Holmes anticipates the thief's next victim, and Holmes, Watson, and Inspector Lestrade set up a stakeout and catch him.

9. When Holmes manages to purchase the last of the six Napoleon busts, he scrapes the gloss off the back, revealing a secret code engraved in the plaster.

10. Holmes is able to solve the crime with the help of a lead from a member of the Mafia.

QUIZ 48
"THE ADVENTURE OF THE THREE STUDENTS"

Published in the Strand *in June 1904 and in* Collier's *in September 1904*

Life at the College of St. Luke's in "The Adventure of the Three Students" was reminiscent of Conan Doyle's life at Edinburgh University. But the theme of this story probably stemmed from an incident at Hodder prep school, when the son of an Italian count ran away about the time a test was discovered missing. This quiz contains ten multiple choice questions about Holmes going head-to-head with the brilliant minds of young academics.

Story Date: 1895

1. On what subject is the scholarship examination that was to be administered at the College of St. Luke?

   A. Binomial equations
   B. Greek translations
   C. Human anatomy
   D. History of theology

2. How did the student gain access to Mr. Soames's study in order to see the exam?

   A. Mr. Soames's servant, Bannister, left the key in the door when he carried out the tea service.

B. The student broke a lock on the window and entered the study.

C. The student sneaked into the study and hid behind the drapery when Mr. Bannister went in to open the windows.

D. The student picked the lock and entered from the connecting room.

3. How did Mr. Soames know that someone had entered his study and copied the test?

A. Mr. Soames noticed an ink smudge on the paper.

B. He noticed the imprint of the person's writing on the blotting paper.

C. His inkwell was empty, and his chair and lamp had been rearranged.

D. The papers on his desk were rearranged.

4. Why does Holmes suspect that Bannister knows something about the crime?

A. While Holmes is interviewing Bannister, the butler does not look him in the eye; instead, his eyes dart around the room.

B. When Bannister describes how he almost fainted, Holmes discovers that the butler crossed the room and sat down in a chair positioned in an inconvenient location.

C. Bannister responds to Holmes's questions too quickly; his answers are too short and definite.

D. His story about forgetting the key seems too far-fetched for Holmes to believe.

5. What evidence does Holmes find in Soames's bedroom and sitting room?

A. Clumps of black clay

B. Blades of dry grass

C. Several burrs embedded in the rug

D. Tiny, brownish pebbles

6. How long has Bannister been an employee of Mr. Soames?
   A. Six months
   B. Two years
   C. Ten years
   D. Twenty-five years

7. What information does Holmes request that eventually leads him to discover the identity of the cheating student?
   A. Holmes requests the height of each suspect.
   B. Holmes asks to view the suspects' dorm rooms.
   C. Holmes asks for the names of the suspects' girlfriends.
   D. Holmes wants to find out if the suspects are engaged in sports.

8. How did Bannister know who had entered into Mr. Soames's study to copy the test?
   A. Bannister recognized the student's gloves left in the chair.
   B. Bannister recognized the sweet scent of the student's tobacco.
   C. Bannister recognized the muffler that the student had dropped.
   D. Bannister caught a glimpse of the student's threadbare coat as he dashed from the room.

9. Why does Bannister attempt to cover for the guilty student?
   A. The guilty student knows about a scandalous incident in Bannister's past.
   B. Bannister knew that the student was forced into the dishonest task in order to cover for a classmate.
   C. Bannister had been the loyal butler of the student's father and felt obliged to look after the son while at school.
   D. Bannister plans to blackmail the student.

10. What happens to the student after he confesses to the crime?

   A. He is expelled and asked to take leave of the college immediately.

   B. He breaks down sobbing and explains that without the scholarship he could not afford to continue his education.

   C. He laughs and proclaims his action a noble deed, as he believes the school's policy of awarding scholarships is unethical.

   D. He joins the Rhodesian Police and leaves for Africa.

QUIZ 49
"THE ADVENTURE OF THE GOLDEN PINCE-NEZ"

Published in the Strand *in July 1904 and in* Collier's *in October 1904*

While Conan Doyle and his first wife, Louise, were traveling in Egypt in 1896, he eagerly wanted to visit a famous Coptic monastery located in the desert outside of Cairo. He and his friend, Colonel Henry Lewis, rented a coach and hired a driver who managed to lose his way a few hours into the trip. As evening fell, the travelers found themselves lost in the desert. Relying on skills learned at sea, Conan Doyle used the stars to determine their location and set his baffled driver in the right direction. They arrived at the monastery the next day around noon. However, Conan Doyle had to again step out of his role as tourist and attend to the sick abbot who was too ill to show them around. When the author returned to Cairo, he sent medication for the ailing abbot. Facts about the monastery found their way into "The Adventure of Golden Pince-Nez." This quiz contains ten short-answer questions about the story in which Holmes chain-smokes his way to the solution.

Story Date: November 1894

1. Why is Inspector Stanley Hopkins perplexed over the apparent murder of Willoughby Smith?

2. What position did Mr. Smith hold in Professor Coram's household?

3. Who heard Mr. Smith's scream and then subsequently discovered him dying in the professor's study?

4. How did Mr. Smith die?

5. What were Mr. Smith's last words?

6. What evidence is found in the dead man's hand?

TRIVIA FACTS : DID YOU KNOW THAT . . .

1. Conan Doyle's idea for the cryptic messages in "The Adventure of the Dancing Men" developed while he was staying at the Hill House Hotel in Norfolk. The hotel owner's young son entertained himself by writing his name using sketches of dancing men.

2. In writing the stories which would appear in the collection entitled *The Return of Sherlock Holmes*, Conan Doyle, satisfied with the first three stories but slightly disappointed in the fourth, wrote, "I've got three bullseyes and an outer." The fourth story was "The Adventure of the Solitary Cyclist."

3. In 1914 the distraught wife of Joseph Caillaux, minister of finance of France, walked into the *Figaro* newspaper office and confronted editor Gaston Calmette about critical articles he had written about her husband. Rather than offer to retract them, he threatened to publish love letters that her husband had written to her while he was still married to his first wife. Mme. Caillaux pulled out a gun and shot him dead. This true story occurred almost ten years after Conan Doyle published "The Adventure of Charles Augustus Milverton," a story with a plot almost identical to the Caillaux case.

7. What clue leads Holmes to believe that a portion of the professor's bookcase opens to a secret room?

8. What clue convinces Holmes that the professor is hiding someone?

9. Why does Holmes believe that the person who committed the murder is still in the house?

10. How does Anna Coram escape punishment for her crimes?

Quiz 50
"THE ADVENTURE OF THE MISSING THREE-QUARTER"

Published in the Strand *in August 1904 and in* Collier's *in November 1904*

If writing was Conan Doyle's first passion, then sports was his second. He played sports, wrote about sports, and invented new sports, and it seems apropos that he should include sports in his Sherlock Holmes stories. In fact, Holmes shares Conan Doyle's interest in boxing. In "The Adventure of the Missing Three-Quarter," Holmes must find the missing player before the big game. The following quiz contains ten true/false statements.

Story Date: December 1896

1. Godfrey Staunton received a surprise visit from his uncle on the night Staunton disappeared.

2. In order to learn who Godfrey Staunton is, Holmes looks through volume "S" of his commonplace book.

3. Lord Mount-James is relieved and hopeful when he discovers that Holmes has been hired to locate his nephew.

4. Holmes tries to find out who sent the message to Staunton by stealing a glance at the receipts in the telegram office while Watson distracts the clerk.

5. Holmes connects Dr. Leslie Armstrong to Godfrey Staunton when he finds a receipt for thirteen guineas that Staunton paid to Dr. Armstrong.

6. Holmes compares Dr. Armstrong to the notorious Professor Moriarty.

7. Holmes uses the bloodhound, Pompey, to follow Dr. Armstrong by allowing the dog to sniff the doctor's boots.

8. When Holmes enters Godfrey Staunton's room, he finds a dead woman.

9. Godfrey Staunton kept his marriage secret because married men could not play on the Cambridge rugby team.

10. Cambridge won the rugby match even without their star three-quarter.

QUIZ 51
"THE ADVENTURE OF THE ABBEY GRANGE"

Published in the Strand *in September 1904 and in* Collier's *in December 1904*

In "The Adventure of the Abbey Grange," Conan Doyle again draws on his experience from seven months at sea as a surgeon on a whaling ship in 1880. Holmes, also knowledgeable about maritime practices, is able to solve the mystery. This story is best remembered, however, for the famous Holmes quote, "Come, Watson, come! The game is afoot." The following quiz contains ten multiple choice questions.

Story Date: January 1897

1. How was Sir Eustace Brackenstall murdered?

    A. Sir Eustace was shot in the back at close range.
    B. He was struck on the head with a poker.

C. He died from over a dozen stab wounds.

D. He was pushed from his upstairs balcony onto the flagstones below.

2. Who saw the murderers outside, near the lodge gate, about an hour before the murder took place?

A. Lady Brackenstall's maid, Theresa Wright

B. Lady Brackenstall

C. The butler

D. Sir Eustace

3. Which of the three facts below is not one of the reasons that Holmes doubts Lady Brackenstall's story?

A. The burglars did not kill Lady Brackenstall even though she could identify them.

B. They pulled down the bell cord to bind Lady Brackenstall, unconcerned that the bell would alert the servants.

C. An elderly man could not have struck such a violent blow.

D. Of the three glasses of wine, only one contained traces of beeswing.

4. Which clue leads Holmes to suspect that the wine was opened by a pocket screw rather than a household corkscrew?

A. The wine bottle contained deep scratches along the lip of the bottle.

B. Bits of cork floated in the bottle.

C. The household corkscrew was brand new and had never been used.

D. The pocket screw is short and had to be inserted three times in order to remove the cork. A household corkscrew is long and only one insertion is necessary.

5. Whom does Inspector Hopkins believe to be responsible for the crime?

A. The Randall gang, which is operating in the area
B. Lady Brackenstall and her maid
C. Petty thieves who had not planned to kill anyone
D. A lover from Lady Brackenstall's past

6. What is one clue that leads Holmes to suspect that a sailor is involved in the crime?

   A. The knots on the cord that is used to tie up Lady Brackenstall are commonly used by sailors.
   B. A knife, typical of one used on a ship, is used to cut the bell cord.
   C. A button from a sailor's coat is found near the body.
   D. Holmes discovers clumps of briny sand outside the window of the dining room.

7. Why does Lady Brackenstall's maid, Theresa, hate Sir Eustace?

   A. Sir Eustace would often get drunk and make a pass at her.
   B. Sir Eustace was very tight and accused the servants of pilfering.
   C. Sir Eustace was forcing Theresa to work for very meager wages, because he knew that she was dedicated to Lady Brackenstall and would not leave her service.
   D. Sir Eustace physically abused Lady Brackenstall.

8. According to Holmes, what is peculiar about the chair in the dining room?

   A. The blood stain on the chair appeared to have been there for a long time.
   B. Lady Brackenstall says that Sir Eustace was struck after she sat down in the chair. If that were true, there would not be blood stains on the chair.
   C. The dining chair does not match the other chairs in the room.
   D. There are scuff marks on the chair, as if someone had stood on it.

9. Why did Lady Brackenstall decide not to marry Jack Croker?

   A. Lady Brackenstall was already promised to marry Sir Eustace.
   B. Even though she loved Croker, she felt that he was below her station.
   C. Lady Brackenstall enjoyed Croker's comradeship and company, but she was not in love with him.
   D. She did not like to be alone, and she knew that Croker would be away at sea most of the time.

10. How does Holmes justify letting the person responsible for killing Sir Eustace go free?

   A. Sir Eustace was a violent man, and he got what he deserved.
   B. The man only has six months to live.
   C. Because of Sir Eustace, the man had already spent several years in prison for a crime that he didn't commit.
   D. Holmes and Watson set up a mock trail, in which Holmes acts as judge and Watson as jury. The man is found not guilty.

QUIZ 52
"THE ADVENTURE OF THE SECOND STAIN"

Published in the Strand *in December 1904 and in* Collier's *in January 1905*

The theme for the story of "The Adventure of the Second Stain" reflected Conan Doyle's involvement in the Boer War less than five years earlier. The character of Lord Bellinger was based on Lord Salisbury, and the Honorable Trelawney Hope was modeled after Joseph Chamberlain. Holmes is hired to find a lost document that, if not recovered, could lead to a great war in Europe. Conan Doyle subtly suggests that the situation in the story reflected England's atrocious involvement with South Africa around the turn of the century. The following quiz contains ten short-answer questions about how Holmes casually thwarted a world war and put a prime minister in his place.

Story Date: Autumn in the mid-1880s

1. At what time does Trelawney Hope, secretary for European affairs, discover the missing letter?

2. How long was the dispatch box containing the letter left unguarded?

3. Who visits Holmes the morning after the letter was discovered missing, pleading for information about the incident?

4. Who accompanies Hope when he visits Holmes to request assistance?

5. Why is Holmes certain that the missing letter has not fallen into the wrong hands?

6. How does Holmes come to suspect Lucas above the other two agents?

7. Upon investigating Lucas's murder, how does Holmes know that the constable on duty let someone view the scene of the crime?

TRIVIA FACTS : DID YOU KNOW THAT . . .

1. When Conan Doyle killed off Sherlock Holmes in a story published in 1893, many fans mourned his apparent death by wearing crepe bands round their hats.

2. The famous dictum spoken by Holmes in "The Adventure of the Abbey Grange," "The game is afoot," was first spoken in Shakespeare's *Henry V.*

THE SHERLOCK HOLMES QUIZ BOOK

8. What secret was Lucas using to blackmail Lady Hilda?

9. How does Lady Hilda gain access to the dispatch-box?

10. What did Lady Hilda see as she rushed from Lucas's house?

Jude Law, Noomi Rapace, Robert Downey, Jr. as Dr. Watson, Madam Simza
Heron, and Sherlock Holmes in the Guy Ritchie film *A Game of Shadows* 2011

SIX

THE FOURTH COLLECTION:
HIS LAST BOW

"As impassive as ever to the casual observer,
there were none the less a subdued eagerness and
suggestion of tension in his brightened eyes and brisker
manner which assured me that the game was afoot."
—DR. JOHN WATSON

IN THIS PENULTIMATE COLLECTION of eight Sherlock Holmes stories, Conan Doyle presents his readers with a variety of cases. Murder, espionage, abduction, and revenge are at the heart of "The Adventure of Wisteria Lodge," "The Adventure of the Cardboard Box," "The Adventure of the Red Circle," "The Adventure of the Bruce-Partington Plans," "The Adventure of the Dying Detective," "The Disappearance of the Lady Frances Carfax," "The Adventure of the Devil's Foot," and "His Last Bow."

In the last story of the collection, "His Last Bow," Conan Doyle makes a subtle attempt once more to end his Sherlock Holmes detective series. Having learned his lesson after his first attempt twenty-four years earlier, Conan Doyle planned to have the Great Detective fade away in the ominous cloud which reflects the theme of the story. As Holmes tells Watson, "Stand with me here upon the terrace, for it may be the last quiet talk that we shall ever have. . . . There's an east wind coming, Watson . . . and a good many of us may wither before its blast." The story concludes with Holmes saving England from a fascist government and then quietly retiring to the country, bringing a peaceful end to his long career. But the retirement is only temporary, and seven years later, the game is again afoot as Conan Doyle gives it one last shot.

The mood of the last story in this collection reflects Conan Doyle's melancholy frame of mind concerning the trauma of World War I. The east wind, a wind that has never blown over England before, symbolizes England's conflict with Germany and the feeling of impending doom that blanketed all of Europe. At this time in Conan Doyle's life, his interest in spiritualism deepened as he sought to grasp a lifeline in a difficult, changing world.

QUIZ 53
"THE ADVENTURE OF WISTERIA LODGE"

Published in Collier's *in August 1908 and in the* Strand *in September 1908*

The theme of "The Adventure of Wisteria Lodge" involves a Central American tyrant who flees to Barcelona with his family and a shipload of treasure in order to escape the uprising against him. His tentacles of terror, however, continue to reach his enemies in Britain and in Europe. This Sherlock Holmes story is based on a real dictator, José Santos Zelaya, the president of Nicaragua, who fled to New York when his country revolted against him. The following quiz contains ten short-answer questions.

Story Date: 1894

1. In the beginning of the story, what word does Holmes ask Dr. Watson to define? (This word set the tone for the story.)

2. What evidence do the police have that leads them to suspect that John Scott Eccles was linked to the death of Aloysius García?

3. When was the last time John Scott Eccles talked to anyone before he fell asleep?

4. What did Mr. Scott Eccles find the morning he awoke at Wisteria Lodge?

5. What is the name of the inspector from Surrey Constabulary who earned Holmes's respect for his ability to detect and decipher clues?

6. Which religion does Holmes research in order to understand certain events in this case?

7. What unusual fact does Holmes start with in forming his hypothesis?

8. Who sent the message to Mr. García the night Mr. Scott Eccles stayed at his house?

9. Why did Mr. García ask Mr. Scott Eccles to visit him?

10. Who gives Holmes the inside scoop on the Henderson household?

Quiz 54
"THE ADVENTURE OF THE CARDBOARD BOX"

Published in the Strand *and in* Harper's *in January 1893*

In 1888 Jack the Ripper was terrorizing the Whitechapel district in London. Stories of his hideous murders were told and retold as he managed to elude Scotland Yard and remain forever a mystery. In taunting his pursuers, Jack the Ripper threatened to send the ears of his victims to Scotland Yard. A few years later when Conan Doyle wrote "The Adventure of the Cardboard Box," he used this gruesome act, for in the cardboard box were two severed human ears. The following quiz contains ten true/false statements about this case, which involves love, hate, deception, and, finally, murder.

Story Date: August, in the late 1800s

1. Miss Cushing's mysterious package was delivered by a young boy on a bicycle.

2. Miss Cushing buried the contents of the package in her backyard.

3. Holmes detects that the string that bound the package is peculiar because it is stained with blood.

4. Inspector Lestrade suspects that the package was meant to frighten Miss Cushing out of her home.

5. The names of the three Cushing sisters are Susan, Mary, and Sarah.

6. Holmes realizes that the victim is related to Miss Cushing, because their ears are almost identical in shape.

7. Sarah Cushing hated her brother-in-law, Jim Browner, because he was a womanizer who abused his wife.

8. Jim Browner caught his wife, Mary, with her lover when he returned home after his ship put into port unexpectedly.

9. When Sarah realized what Browner had done, she tried to kill him.

10. Holmes detects the odor of coffee from the paper used to wrap the package.

QUIZ 55
"THE ADVENTURE OF THE RED CIRCLE"

Published in the Strand *in March and April 1911*

It is quite possible, considering the plethora of news articles on the subject, that the story "The Adventure of the Red Circle" was partly based on the Italian organized crime ring called the Black Hand. Several members of the organization were captured, and events of the trial were reported almost daily. The following quiz contains ten multiple choice questions.

Story Date: September 1902

1. How much money did Mrs. Warren's new tenant offer to pay her for the room if she promised to give him his own key and to leave him undisturbed?

    A. The tenant offered her an entire year's rent.
    B. Five pounds a week for a fortnight
    C. He offered to pay four times the going rate.
    D. Fifty pounds

2. How did her strange lodger communicate what was needed to Mrs. Warren?

    A. The lodger would leave a clue outside the door; for example, if the lodger needed water, an empty glass would be placed outside the door.
    B. The lodger would leave Mrs. Warren a simple riddle.

C. By printing one word on a piece of paper, the lodger communicated what was needed.

D. The lodger would draw a picture of the item needed.

3. Why does Holmes believe that the person is a foreigner?

    A. The method of communicating with Mrs. Warren leads Holmes to this conclusion.

    B. The type of food that the lodger requested

    C. The type of clothes the lodger sets out to be cleaned

    D. The type of tobacco the lodger smokes

4. In which journal does Holmes find a message meant to communicate with the mysterious lodger?

    A. *Times*

    B. *Daily Gazette*

    C. *Strand*

    D. *Herald*

5. How does Holmes get a glance at Mrs. Warren's lodger?

    A. Holmes hides behind a door and watches in a mirror as the lodger retrieves a tray left by Mrs. Warren.

    B. Holmes climbs a tree near the lodger's window and is able to briefly glimpse at the lodger.

    C. Holmes goes into the adjoining room and peers through a crack in the wall.

    D. Holmes looks through the keyhole.

6. In which language is the candlelight message sent?

    A. French

    B. Spanish

    C. Greek

    D. Italian

7. From which case does Holmes connect Mr. Leverton of the Pinkerton's American Detective Agency?

    A. A famous kidnapping case associated with an American general

    B. The Long Island cave mystery

C. The Gold Rush embezzlement mystery

D. The Reading Railroad extortion case

8. How does Emilia Lucca respond when she realizes that her husband killed Giuseppe Gorgiano?

A. Mrs. Lucca is overjoyed.

B. She faints.

C. She pleads for mercy on his behalf.

D. She swears that it must have been an accident.

9. To where did Gennaro and Emilia Lucca flee when they left Italy?

A. Brooklyn

B. London

C. Paris

D. Athens

10. What caused Gennaro Lucca to attack Gorgiano?

A. He found out that Gorgiano was blackmailing Emilia Lucca.

B. Gorgiano had insulted Emilia Lucca.

C. Gorgiano had insinuated that Emilia had had an affair.

D. Gorgiano grabbed Emilia and tried to make love to her.

QUIZ 56
"THE ADVENTURE OF THE BRUCE-PARTINGTON PLANS"

Published in the Strand *and in* Collier's *in December 1908*

Conan Doyle became close friends with King Edward VII (Sherlock Holmes stories were the only fiction that the King cared to read) and Prime Minister Herbert Asquith. The theme of "The Adventure of the Bruce-Partington Plans" involved the theft of submarine plans which could eventually lead to war. At the time, Britain was concerned because Germany's naval force surpassed hers, and the government was making plans to remedy the shortfall.

Since the subject of submarine warfare had not yet been revealed to the public, there was some speculation that Conan Doyle may have received information for this story from his friends in higher places. This quiz contains ten short-answer questions.

Story Date: November 1895

1. On a dreary day in November 1895, who presents Holmes with an intriguing investigation?

2. Where is Arthur Cadogan West's body found?

3. What is the first clue that leads Holmes to suspect foul play?

4. Where was Cadogan West apparently going on the evening of his death?

5. Why does Holmes believe that Cadogan West did not die from a train accident?

6. Why is Cadogan West's death important enough for Mycroft to leave his home and visit Holmes in person?

7. When Holmes pays a visit to Sir James Walter, the official guardian of the secret paper, what does Holmes find?

8. Who gives Holmes important information as to the emotional state of Cadogan West the night that he died?

9. What information leads Holmes to locate the man responsible for the caper?

10. Why does Holmes focus his investigation on Hugo Oberstein?

QUIZ 57
"THE ADVENTURE OF THE DYING DETECTIVE"

Published in Collier's *in November 1913*

In describing the apparent fatal condition of his detective, Conan Doyle draws on his experience as a doctor to make Holmes's symptoms severe enough to convince Dr. Watson that the situation is serious. There is also only one person in the world who can save Holmes, if indeed it is not already too late—and that person is not his lifelong friend Dr. Watson. The following quiz contains ten true/false statements.

Story Date: Late 1890s

1. Holmes tells Watson that he has contracted a contagious, fatal disease from Sumatra.

TRIVIA FACTS : DID YOU KNOW THAT . . .

1. In 1956, Captain Thomas O'Rourke and his wife Bobbye appeared on NBC's game show *The $64,000 Question*. Millions of Americans watched as the O'Rourkes tackled Sherlock Holmes trivia questions that would stop a runaway hansom. When the dust cleared, each had won $32,000, answering all questions correctly.

2. In 1903 Conan Doyle discovered a new hobby which quickly became a daring new passion—motoring. He purchased a twelve-horsepower Wolseley, along with a travelling coat, cap, and goggles. When taking his mother for a drive around her home in Yorkshire, he soon discovered that, although she enjoyed the experience, she did not share his enthusiasm, as proven by her desire to knit a sweater rather than take in the view. Their adventure ended when they collided with a horse-drawn cart carrying a load of turnips. Conan Doyle crawled from the vegetable mound to find his mother sitting on top, knitting needles clacking away.

3. In 1894 when Conan Doyle first visited the United States, Major J. B. Pond, a Civil War hero who arranged for Conan Doyle's speaking tour, greeted the author as soon as he stepped off the ship with, "Dr. Conan Doyle, I presume?"

4. In 1894 Bram Stoker, author of *Dracula*, staged Conan Doyle's one-act play, *Waterloo*. The story is about a ninety-year-old veteran who recalls his experiences in the Napoleonic Wars. The play was a tremendous success, proving quite lucrative for the young author.

THE SHERLOCK HOLMES QUIZ BOOK

2. Holmes refuses to allow Watson to examine and treat him for fear that Watson will become exposed to the disease.

3. Watson recommends that Holmes check into a hospital immediately.

4. Holmes claims that the only person who can save him is a planter from Sumatra named Culverton Smith.

5. Smith holds a grudge against Holmes for having him arrested several years before.

6. During Holmes's apparent delirium, he begins ranting about the proliferation of oysters.

7. Holmes pretends that he is dying, thus tricking Smith into confessing.

8. Holmes instructs Watson to hide behind the curtain before Smith enters the apartment so that Holmes has a witness to Smith's confession.

9. Watson realizes that Holmes is not really ill when Holmes asks for a match and cigarette.

10. The curtains are opened as a signal for Inspector Morton to make the arrest.

QUIZ 58
"THE DISAPPEARANCE OF LADY FRANCES CARFAX"

Published in the Strand *in December 1911*

In the first decade of the twentieth century, while Kingsley Doyle, Conan Doyle's son, was studying medicine in Lausanne, he reported to his father the strange disappearance of a lady from a hotel. No one was able to account for her sudden departure, but foul play was suspected due to her leaving several unpaid bills. Bringing Sherlock Holmes in to investigate such an occurrence made for a perfect detective story. This quiz contains ten multiple choice questions.

Story Date: Late 1800s

1. How does Holmes deduce that Watson has been to a Turkish bath?

   A. Watson's hair is still damp above his collar.

   B. Holmes detects the smell of massage oil.

   C. Watson's boots have been fastened with an elaborate double bow, and since they are fairly new boots, it is unlikely that Watson has been to a shoe repair shop.

   D. Watson is standing a bit taller and walks with ease, indicating that he has had a bath and massage.

2. Why does Miss Dobney become concerned and contact Holmes to locate Lady Frances Carfax?

   A. Lady Frances Carfax was scheduled to visit three days ago and has not yet arrived.

   B. Lady Frances mentioned that she was terribly frightened about something.

   C. Lady Frances has written to Miss Dobney every second week for four years, and five weeks have gone by without Miss Dobney receiving a letter.

   D. Miss Dobney suspects that Lady Frances was becoming unstable.

3. What suspicious fact does Holmes uncover before he sends Watson to investigate?

   A. Before Lady Frances disappeared, she paid her maid, Miss Marie Devine, fifty pounds.

   B. Before she disappeared, she withdrew all of her money from her bank account.

   C. Lady Frances deposited 2,000 pounds into her account.

   D. Lady Frances instructed her lawyers that she planned to change her will.

4. After Watson's initial investigation and report to Holmes, what question does Holmes telegraph to Watson?

   A. Holmes wants to know how long Marie Devine has been in service to Lady Frances.

B. Holmes wants to know what type of carriage Dr. Shlessinger uses.

C. Holmes wants to know in which month Lady Frances was born.

D. Holmes wants a description of Dr. Shlessinger's left ear.

5. What reason did Marie Devine give for Lady Frances giving her the money?

   A. Marie wants to send money to her destitute sister.

   B. Marie says that it is a wedding gift.

   C. Marie claims that the bonus is a gift for her dedication and service.

   D. Marie claims that when she gave her resignation, Lady Frances offered Marie money to stay.

6. How is Holmes disguised when he rescues Watson from an attack?

   A. Holmes is disguised as a French *ouvrier* from a cabaret. He is wearing a blue blouse.

   B. Holmes is disguised as a drunk.

   C. Holmes is wearing a nun's habit.

   D. Holmes is wearing his favorite elderly lady outfit.

7. Holmes realizes that he has overlooked an important clue when he remembers a comment about something "being out of the ordinary." Who makes this comment?

   A. Dr. Shlessinger

   B. The undertaker's wife

   C. Philip Green

   D. Mrs. Shlessinger

8. What is Dr. Shlessinger's reason for pawning Lady Frances's jewelry?

   A. Lady Frances asked him to do so because she needed the money and was too ashamed to pawn the jewelry herself.

   B. She gave him the jewelry as a gift and, therefore, he could do with it as he pleased.

C. He paid her hotel bill and ticket to London, after which she fled before repaying him. She left her jewelry, and he pawned it as reimbursement.

D. She gave him the jewelry as a donation to his ministry.

9. Why do the Shlessingers take Rose Spender into their apartment?

A. The Shlessingers rescued her from the streets. She was drunk and sick, and several thugs were tormenting her.

B. The Shlessingers rescued her from a workhouse infirmary.

C. Rose was recently fired from her position, and she had no family and was destitute.

D. Rose was ill and poor and did not want to die in a hospital.

10. What leads Holmes back to the Shlessingers' apartment the morning of Rose Spender's funeral?

A. Holmes realizes that the coffin is unusually large, especially since Rose was a small, frail woman.

B. Holmes has reason to believe that Rose Spender is really Lady Frances.

C. Holmes wants to gather the dead woman's clothes and ask Miss Dobney if they belonged to Lady Frances.

D. Holmes has reason to believe that the coffin will be empty.

QUIZ 59
"THE ADVENTURE OF THE DEVIL'S FOOT"

Published in the Strand *in December 1910 and in America in a magazine of the same name in February 1911*

The setting of the story "The Adventure of the Devil's Foot" was influenced by the trip Conan Doyle and his friend Fletcher

Robinson took to Cornwall in order to investigate the moor around Dartmoor for the book *The Hound of the Baskervilles*. Although the theme does not reflect any particular incident, the allure for Conan Doyle of this mysterious countryside was strong enough to provide the author with a perfect opening to one of the few Holmes stories set outside of London. This quiz concerning Holmes's odorous ordeal contains ten short-answer questions.

Story Date: March 1897

1. What tragedy occurs during their stay?
2. Why has Mortimer Tregennis recently quarreled with his siblings?
3. Who calls on Holmes shortly after the tragedy, inquiring about his theories concerning the case?
4. What second tragedy occurs while Holmes is investigating?
5. What piece of evidence does Holmes scrape into an envelope when he is investigating Mortimer Tregennis's death?
6. Why does Holmes take only half of the evidence?
7. What three pieces of evidence lead Holmes to believe that a strong poison was responsible for the deaths and insanity of the Tregennis family?
8. What type of poison is used?
9. Why did Dr. Sterndale not marry Brenda years earlier when he fell in love with her?
10. Why is Holmes suspicious of Dr. Sterndale?

QUIZ 60
"HIS LAST BOW"

Published in the Strand *and in* Collier's *in September 1917*

The ominous overtones of "His Last Bow" clearly reflect Conan Doyle's concern for clouds upon the horizon. World War I was a

TRIVIA FACTS : DID YOU KNOW THAT . . .

1. When Conan Doyle's publisher, Nelson & Son, sent him an advance bound copy of his book *The Great Boer War*, Conan Doyle demanded that they reprint the entire edition. Conan Doyle strongly objected to his picture being on the cover of the book.

2. Sports being one of his greatest interests, Conan Doyle was one of the first to introduce snow skiing to Switzerland.

3. Conan Doyle's boxing novel, *Rodney Stone*, was so well received that he was invited to referee a heavyweight boxing match between Jim Jeffries and Jack Johnson in 1909. He at first accepted the invitation, but later declined the offer.

4. In 1894 Conan Doyle, accompanied by his brother Innes, came to America for a lecture/book-signing tour. His visits to several cities, including New York and Chicago, were stressful and demanding, leaving him in a state of ill humor. But when he arrived in Boston, he had an encounter that lightened his mood. A cabby asked for a ticket to that evening's lecture instead of charging him a cab fare. The conversation went as such: "How on earth did you recognize me?" asked Conan Doyle. "If you will excuse me, your coat lapels are badly twisted downward, where they have been grasped by the pertinacious New York reporters. Your hair has the Quakerish cut of a Philadelphia barber, and your hat, battered at the brim in front, shows where you have tightly grasped it, in the struggle to stand your ground at a Chicago literary luncheon. Your right shoe has a large block of Buffalo mud just under the instep; the odor of a Utica cigar hangs about your clothing, and the overcoat itself shows the slovenly brushing of the porters of the through sleepers from Albany. The crumbs of the doughnut on the top of your waistcoat could only have come there in Springfield," deduced the cabby. Leaving Conan Doyle speechless, the cabby added, "And stenciled on the very end of your walking stick in perfectly plain lettering is the name Conan Doyle."

few years away, but global conflict had begun. One month after the story was published, Conan Doyle's son, Kingsley, died of complications after being wounded in the Somme. This quiz contains ten true/false statements about one of two Sherlock Holmes stories written in the third person.

Story Date: August 1914

1. When Von Bork communicates with his American agent, all the code names are in reference to Shakespearian plays.

2. The code for the double-lock combination to Von Bork's safe is August 1944.

3. The title of the blue book which Altamont (Holmes) delivers to Von Bork is *Engine Maintenance and Repair.*

4. Holmes and Watson drink a vintage bottle of claret to celebrate their success in overtaking Von Bork.

5. When giving Von Bork clues to his true identity, Holmes refers to the case involving Irene Adler and the King of Bohemia.

6. Von Bork pays 500 pounds for the information provided by Altamont.

7. The impending doom that threatens England and the world is World War I.

8. Altamont is traveling in a Rolls Royce when he arrives at Von Bork's.

9. Holmes causes Von Bork to lose consciousness by adding a drug to his wine.

10. Martha is the name of Von Bork's maid who is also Holmes's inside connection.

Benedict Cumberbatch as Sherlock Holmes in BBC's *Sherlock*

SEVEN

THE FINAL COLLECTION:
THE CASE BOOK OF
SHERLOCK HOLMES

"And so, reader, farewell to Sherlock Holmes!
I thank you for your past constancy, and can
but hope that some return has been made in the shape
of that distraction from the worries of life and
stimulating change of thought which can only
be found in the fairy kingdom of romance."
—ARTHUR CONAN DOYLE

CONSIDERED POSSIBLY the least creative of the Sherlock Holmes stories, this book contains a collection of amazing adventures and unbelievable happenings which, although enthralling, lack the typical deductive elements expected in any Holmes case. Nevertheless, to any die-hard Holmes fan the stories are truly enjoyable, as they show a human side of Holmes, one where humor and affection seem to spill out as fluidly as deductive reasoning. On one occasion, when asked by an intimidating figure who obviously lacked good personal hygiene if he was looking for his gun, Holmes replied, "No, for my scent-bottle, Steve." And when Watson received a bullet in his leg in the Garrideb case, Holmes reacted with such emotion that Watson proclaimed in his chronicle, "It was worth the wound—it was worth many wounds—to know the depth of loyalty and love which lay behind that cold mask." Realizing that the wound was superficial, Holmes's damp eyes dried and trembling lips turned to stone as he threatened the culprit with his life had his friend Watson been killed.

Criticized by many as not measuring up to the stories he had written in the past, Conan Doyle stoically continued to write his Sherlock Holmes tales, possibly as much for himself as for his readers. This collection includes "The Adventure of the Illustrious Client," "The Adventure of the Blanched Soldier," "The Adventure of the Mazarin Stone," "The Adventure of the Three Gables," "The

Adventure of the Sussex Vampire," "The Adventure of the Three Garridebs," "The Problem of Thor Bridge," "The Adventure of the Creeping Man," "The Adventure of the Lion's Mane," "The Adventure of the Veiled Lodger," "The Adventure of Shoscombe Old Place," and "The Adventure of the Retired Colourman."

QUIZ 61
"THE ADVENTURE OF THE ILLUSTRIOUS CLIENT"

Published in Collier's *in November 1924 and in the* Strand *in March 1925*

The dashing, notorious, and seductive villain, Baron Adelbert Gruner of the story "The Adventure of the Illustrious Client," was based on a compilation of three infamous characters who lived between the 1870s and early 1920s. These were Henri Landru, who murdered several women in 1922; Dr. Henri Girard, a toxicologist and ladies' man who murdered his victims by exposing them to pathogenic bacteria; and, probably the most influential, Henri Pineau. This murderous gigolo seduced men and women, stealing their fortunes, to become one of the wealthiest men in England. As his wealth increased, he began hobnobbing with the most influential members of London's society, possibly even members of the Royal Family. He was finally arrested and sentenced to life in prison where he died of blood poisoning. The first quiz in this collection contains ten short-answer questions about the unsavory villain of "The Adventure of the Illustrious Client" and how Holmes exposes his exploits.

Story Date: September 1902

1. Why does Holmes at first deny Sir James Damery's request to investigate the case of Baron Adelbert Gruner?

2. Where does Miss Violet de Merville meet the notorious Baron Gruner?

3. Of all his many interests and hobbies, on what subject is Baron Gruner an authority?

4. Who assists Holmes and Watson in investigating Baron Gruner?

5. Why does General de Merville wish that his daughter not marry the baron?

6. Who agrees to assist Holmes in convincing Violet de Merville that she should not marry Gruner?

7. What information does the baron's ex-mistress present Holmes that may convince Miss de Merville that she should not proceed with the marriage?

8. What does Kitty Winter use when she attacks the baron?

9. How does Baron Gruner convince Miss de Merville not to believe the horrid stories of his past?

10. How does Watson convince Gruner that Holmes is no longer a threat?

QUIZ 62
"THE ADVENTURE OF THE BLANCHED SOLDIER"

Published in Liberty *in October 1926 and in the* Strand *in November 1926*

In 1899 England was involved in the Boer War with South Africa, and Conan Doyle was anxious to pick up a rifle and serve. But due to his age, he was denied entry into the service. With strong conviction, however, he organized a group of volunteer doctors and formed a hospital group, and in April 1900 Conan Doyle arrived in South Africa where he saw firsthand the horrid conditions of the military hospitals. Upon returning to England, he wrote *The War in South Africa: Its Cause and Conduct*, a pamphlet that sold over 300,000 copies. All the earnings were donated to military pension funds and scholarships for South African students. This military conflict was a cause that Conan Doyle strongly believed in, and his efforts earned him knighthood. The Sherlock Holmes story, "The Adventure of the Blanched Soldier," was set during the time of the Boer War, and his personal experience in South Africa gave this story added depth. This quiz contains ten true/false statements.

Story Date: January 1903

1. James M. Dodd wants Holmes to locate Godfrey Emsworth because Dodd has not heard from his friend since he wrote from a military hospital in Cape Town.

2. When Dodd visited Godfrey's father, Colonel Emsworth, to inquire as to the location of his son, the colonel said that his son was convalescing in a sanitarium in Switzerland.

3. When Dodd asked Ralph, the butler, if Godfrey was dead, Ralph's response was, "I've never heard of Godfrey Emsworth."

4. Dodd is certain that Godfrey is at Tuxbury Old Hall, because Dodd saw Godfrey standing in the window the first evening of his visit.

5. Colonel Emsworth asked Dodd to leave Tuxbury Old Hall and return to London because Dodd accused the colonel of lying to him.

6. Because Holmes threatens to call the police if the colonel continues to lie about his son, the colonel tells the real story.

7. When he smells disinfectant on the butler's gloves, Holmes's suspicions are confirmed.

8. When Dodd saw Godfrey outside his window, his entire face was scarred.

9. Holmes brings Sir James Saunders, a dermatologist, to examine Godfrey.

10. Holmes postulates three theories as to why the colonel was lying about the location of his son.

THE SHERLOCK HOLMES QUIZ BOOK

"THE ADVENTURE OF THE MAZARIN STONE"

Published in the Strand *in October 1921 and in* Hearst's International *in November 1921*

"The Adventure of the Mazarin Stone" was the second Sherlock Holmes story written in the third person. Conan Doyle strayed from telling the story through Dr. Watson's narrative on account of the tale being based on a stage play entitled *The Crown Diamond: An Evening with Sherlock Holmes,* which was produced in 1921. "The Adventure of the Mazarin Stone" was considered the least favorite among the twelve stories in *The Case Book of Sherlock Holmes.* This quiz contains ten multiple choice questions.

Story Date: 1903

1. What slang term is used to describe the burglary of the Crown diamond?
   A. The big ice melt
   B. The displaced Crown
   C. The hundred-thousand-pound burglary
   D. The royal jewelry heist

2. Who requests Holmes's help in finding the stone?
   A. The Queen
   B. The prime minister and the home secretary
   C. The treasurer
   D. The director of Scotland Yard

3. What new addition, one that is significant in solving the crime, does Holmes add to his Baker Street flat?
   A. A new set of dueling pistols
   B. A new set of fireplace tools
   C. A dummy of himself, which he positions in the window
   D. A large mirror hung over the liquor cabinet

4. What kind of danger is Holmes expecting on the evening Dr. Watson comes to visit?

A. Holmes is expecting another major burglary.

B. Holmes is expecting the burglars to kidnap a high government official.

C. Holmes is expecting a death associated with the burglary.

D. Holmes is expecting to be murdered.

5. After Holmes gives Count Sylvius and Sam Merton an ultimatum to reveal the location of the diamond and go free or risk arrest and jail, what does Holmes do while the men are deciding?

A. Holmes smokes his black clay pipe.

B. Holmes gets his gazetteer off the shelf and starts making notes.

C. Holmes plays his violin.

D. Holmes cleans his pistol.

6. How much time does Holmes give Count Sylvius to make his decision?

A. Half an hour, the time it takes to play "Barcarole" on the violin

B. Thirteen minutes, the amount of time that his luck will run out

C. Five minutes, not much time for the count to react

D. Twenty minutes, one for every year of jail time for stealing such an expensive item

7. What lie does Count Sylvius plan to tell Holmes concerning the location of the diamond?

A. The count plans to tell Holmes that the diamond is in Liverpool.

B. He will tell Holmes that he will never find it because it has been cut into a dozen pieces and sold.

C. He plans to tell Holmes that the diamond is on the bottom of the Thames.

D. The count plans to send Holmes a message telling him that the diamond is in a barrel of wine on a ship on its way to America.

8. Where is Holmes when the count reveals to Merton the location of the jewel?

   A. Holmes is sitting in the chair that was previously occupied by the dummy.

   B. Holmes is hiding behind the bedroom door.

   C. Holmes is in the hall, having sneaked back in while the men were talking.

   D. Holmes is behind the liquor cabinet.

9. What is the sound the two men hear coming from Holmes's bedroom?

   A. A musician Holmes has hired to play the violin

   B. Holmes playing a recording of a violin on the gramophone

   C. Holmes has opened the window, and a street musician is heard playing the violin.

   D. Holmes is playing the violin.

10. What joke does Holmes play on Lord Cantlemere?

   A. Holmes uses his dummy to answer the door.

   B. Holmes shows Lord Cantlemere a paste replica of the diamond, which is set in a ring on Holmes's finger.

   C. Holmes places the diamond among fruit in a fruit bowl.

   D. Holmes slips the diamond in Lord Cantlemere's pocket without his knowing it and then accuses him of stealing it.

QUIZ 64
"THE ADVENTURE OF THE THREE GABLES"

Published in Liberty *in September 1926 and in the* Strand *in October 1926*

This story about the theft of a manuscript may have been loosely based on the true story of Oscar Slater, a man who was accused of stealing documents which included an insurance policy and the will of Marion Gilchrist of Glasgow in 1909. The woman was murdered during the robbery, and Slater was sentenced to eighteen years of hard labor for the crime. Conan Doyle believed that Slater was innocent and had the case reopened, but to no avail; the guilty verdict remained. New evidence surfaced in 1927, and Slater was finally released thanks to the efforts of the creator of Sherlock Holmes. This quiz contains ten short-answer questions.

Story Date: exact date uncertain

1. How much money would Mary Maberley have made if she had sold her home?

<hr>

TRIVIA FACTS : DID YOU KNOW THAT . . .

1. In the mid 1920s Conan Doyle purchased a second home solely for the purpose of having a private, secluded place in which to conduct his séances. However, word spread quickly concerning the goings-on in Bignell House. As a result, mail carriers refused to deliver mail to the address, leaders of a gypsy troop living nearby warned their members against looking at the house, and evil spirits, believed to come from the house, were exorcised by a priest.

2. In 1926 mystery writer Agatha Christie disappeared; her locked car was found in a ditch with the motor still running. Ten days later she was found in a hotel at the Harrogate Spa in northern England. A journalist named Ritchie-Calder believed that Christie had planned to commit suicide, staging the incident to appear as if her husband and his mistress had murdered her. When Conan Doyle was knighted, he had been appointed deputy lieutenant of Surrey, a position he retired from in 1921. However, he was consulted on the Christie case, and in turn consulted a medium who told him that Christie was alive and would surface on the following Wednesday. This prediction came true. This incident resembles Conan Doyle's story "The Problem of Thor Bridge."

2. What does Mrs. Maberley plan to do with the profit from the sale of her home?

3. What odd demand does the potential buyer specify in the purchase of the house?

4. How do the burglars prevent Mrs. Maberley from interfering with their search of the room?

5. What does Mrs. Maberley manage to retrieve from the burglars before they flee?

6. Why does Holmes deduce that the manuscript is Douglas Maberley's true story?

7. Whom does Holmes visit for information in solving this case?

8. How does Holmes convince Isadora Klein to receive him?

9. What does Isadora Klein do with the rest of the manuscript?

10. What deal does Holmes make with Isadora Klein?

QUIZ 65
"THE ADVENTURE OF THE SUSSEX VAMPIRE"

Published in the Strand *and in* Hearst's International *in January 1924*

Conan Doyle's theme for "The Adventure of the Sussex Vampire" was influenced by friend and fellow writer Bram Stoker, author of *Dracula*. However, there is some speculation that the story may have in part been based on a true account of a girl named Constance Kent, who was accused of murdering her infant half brother and her governess. She was acquitted for lack of evidence and spent the rest of her life in a convent. Years later, possibly wanting to clear her conscience before she met her maker, Kent confessed to the crimes. This quiz contains ten true/false statements about a bloodsucking tale that was convincing enough to make the most skeptical characters believe in vampires (all except Holmes, that is).

Story Date: November 1896

1. Robert Ferguson and Dr. Watson knew one another in medical school.

2. Ferguson needs Holmes's assistance because he believes that his wife has become deranged and is endangering his two sons.

3. Ferguson is embarrassed by his speculations and tells Holmes that he is requesting help on behalf of a friend.

4. In spite of her problems, Mr. Ferguson's second wife is loving and devoted to her husband's son by his first marriage.

5. Because of his suspicions, Mr. Ferguson sends his wife away to stay with relatives.

6. Holmes begins to develop his theory when he notices an encyclopedia of poisons on the bookshelf.

7. Holmes's theory is almost confirmed when he gathers information about the ailment of the family dog.

8. Holmes gets a clear picture of the emotional condition of Ferguson's oldest son while watching him play in the garden.

9. Mrs. Ferguson keeps the truth from her husband because she does not want to hurt him.

10. Holmes recommends that Jack Ferguson spend a year in a private boys' school where he can be around boys of his own age.

QUIZ 66
"THE ADVENTURE OF THE THREE GARRIDEBS"

Published in Collier's *in October 1924 and in the* Strand *January 1925*

When Conan Doyle was offered knighthood he told his mother that he did not approve of royal titles and that the title he valued most was that of "Doctor." It was a matter of principle not to accept knighthood. To his pleading mother he remarked, "I tell you, Ma'am, I can't do it! As a matter of principle!" His mother retorted, "If you wish to show your principles by an insult to the king, no doubt you can't." As in so many instances, his mother's good sense won out, and he was knighted on August 19, 1902. However, if he was not allowed to refuse the title in real life, he could do so in fiction. For this adventure there are ten multiple choice questions.

Story Date: June 1902

1. When Watson begins to tell his story about the three Garridebs, what incident does he recall happening at about the same time?

   A. Holmes was recovering from the flu.
   B. Holmes speaking for the first time about his possible retirement
   C. He and Holmes were still adjusting to Holmes's return after his absence.
   D. Holmes's refusal of knighthood

2. 2. How does Holmes know that the American John Garrideb has lived in England for an extended period of time?

   A. John Garrideb uses many English colloquialisms.
   B. Garrideb is very knowledgeable about London and the surrounding area.
   C. His entire wardrobe is English.
   D. His American accent is only slightly detectable.

3. How does Holmes know that John Garrideb is lying about being from Kansas?

   A. John Garrideb has a Chicago accent.
   B. Holmes mentions an old friend who lived in Topeka, and John Garrideb says that he also knows the man. However, Holmes just fabricated the character.

C. John Garrideb refers to Wichita as the capital of Kansas.

D. He misspells the word "Kansas" when writing down his apparent benefactor's address.

4. How does Holmes know that John Garrideb placed the Birmingham newspaper ad himself, and that Howard Garrideb was merely a creation of John Garrideb?

A. In placing the ad, John Garrideb uses the American spellings for three of the words.

B. Holmes finds a receipt for the ad in John Garrideb's coat pocket.

C. Holmes hires one of his assistants to follow Garrideb.

D. Holmes finds the address of the Birmingham newspaper on Garrideb's blotting pad.

5. Where does John Garrideb send Nathan Garrideb in order to get him away from his apartment?

A. John Garrideb sends Nathan Garrideb tickets to view an archaeological exhibit at the British Museum.

B. To an antique auction advertising rare books

C. To interview a man named Howard Garrideb

D. He sends him to a recital performed by students who study and play ancient musical instruments.

6. What does Nathan Garrideb collect?

A. Butterflies, flint instruments, and plaster skulls of ancient man

B. Impressionist art, Spanish tapestries, and relics belonging to saints

C. First edition books, carved wooden walking sticks, and Pygmy blow darts

D. Horseshoes, chess sets, and Egyptian papyri

7. What happens to Dr. Watson when he and Holmes corner Killer Evans?

A. Evans slashes Watson with a knife while trying to escape.

B. Watson tumbles down two flights of stairs during their attempt to subdue Evans.

C. Evans clubs Watson with one of Nathan Garrideb's antique cudgels.

D. Evans shoots Watson in the thigh.

8. Why was John Garrideb sent to prison in 1895?

A. Garrideb was convicted of swindling a client out of several thousand dollars.

B. He was caught trying to bribe a judge in a murder case.

C. He shot and killed a man over cards.

D. He was convicted of perjury.

9. What excuse does Holmes give Nathan Garrideb for gaining access to his apartment while he is gone?

A. Holmes asks to study his collections.

B. Holmes offers to wait for John Garrideb to return with more information.

C. Holmes tells Nathan Garrideb that his collections may be in danger of being stolen.

D. Holmes tells Garrideb that he has purchased several items for his collection which will be delivered while Garrideb is away.

10. What happens to Nathan Garrideb when he finds out that he will not receive his expected reward?

A. He donates his collections to a museum and leaves for the continent.

B. He never recovers from the shock and is placed in a nursing home.

C. He shuts himself up in his apartment, and no one ever sees him in public again.

D. He refuses to believe that he was the victim of a scam and vows to continue the search for more Garridebs.

"THE PROBLEM OF THOR BRIDGE"

Published in the Strand *in February and March 1922*

In 1924 an apparent murder occurred near Conan Doyle's home in Crowborough. Norman Thorne was arrested for killing his girlfriend, chopping up her body, and burying it in the chicken coop. He proclaimed his innocence all the way to the gallows. While Thorne admitted cutting up the body and burying it, he claimed that the woman had hanged herself because she was jealous of another woman whom he had been seeing. He theorized that his girlfriend planned revenge for his deception by committing suicide and making it appear as if a murder had been committed, hoping that Thorne would be arrested.

If this indeed was her plan, it worked. Conan Doyle used this theme in the story "The Problem of Thor Bridge." Here are ten short-answer questions about this cleverly plotted mystery.

Story Date: Late 1900

1. Why is Miss Dunbar, the governess of J. Neil Gibson's children, arrested?
2. Why does Marlow Bates rush in to visit Holmes before the arrival of J. Neil Gibson, Mr. Bates's employer?
3. Why does Holmes initially refuse to accept Mr. Gibson as a client?
4. Why did Miss Dunbar decide to stay with the Gibson family even after Mr. Gibson made advances toward her?
5. Why did the police arrest Miss Dunbar?
6. Why is Holmes concerned about the note found in Mrs. Gibson's hand?
7. Why is Holmes suspicious about the location of the murder weapon?
8. What does Holmes find on the bridge that causes him concern?

9. Who planted the damaging evidence that led to Miss Dunbar's arrest?

10. What does Holmes purchase from the village shop in order to set up a demonstration of the murder and subsequently clear Miss Dunbar?

QUIZ 68
"THE ADVENTURE OF THE CREEPING MAN"

Published in the Strand *and in* Hearst's International *in March 1923*

Conan Doyle often included Robert Louis Stevenson on his list of favorite authors. It is quite possible that Stevenson's story "The Strange Case of Dr. Jekyll and Mr. Hyde" could have been the influence for "The Adventure of the Creeping Man." The following quiz contains ten true/false statements.

Story Date: September 1903

1. Miss Presbury, Professor Presbury's daughter, requests that Holmes investigate her father's odd behavior.

2. Holmes considers the diary dates to be the most important evidence.

3. When Professor Presbury left home for a fortnight he traveled to Prague.

4. After the professor returned from his trip, he informed his assistant that he would no longer be allowed to open any of the professor's mail.

5. Mr. Bennett provides Holmes with a detailed diary of the professor's odd behavior, which allows Holmes to develop a theory.

6. The professor's daughter wakes up in the middle of the night and sees her father climbing trees in the garden.

7. Mr. Bennett obtains from the professor's blotting paper the address of the man in London who is sending the professor the mysterious packages.

8. The situation comes to a climax when the professor falls out of a tree and almost kills himself.

9. Holmes suspects that the professor's odd behavior stems from the fact that Professor Morphy's daughter refused to marry Professor Presbury.

10. Because of this case, Holmes proposes to write a monograph on how people and other primates behave the same in certain situations.

QUIZ 69
"THE ADVENTURE OF THE LION'S MANE"

Published in Liberty *in November 1926 and in the* Strand *in December 1926*

Like his creator, Sherlock Holmes kept a collection of reference books and files which he used to help prove and substantiate his theories in solving mysteries. In the case of "The Adventure of the Lion's Mane," Holmes refers to a book written by an English writer, Reverend John G. Wood, who published a collection of essays in 1874 entitled *Out of Doors: A Selection of Original Articles on Practical Natural History*. The following quiz contains ten multiple choice questions about how the aged Holmes, still mentally sharp, reveals the true cause of Fitzroy McPherson's death.

Story Date: 1907

1. Even though Fitzroy McPherson was a natural athlete, what incident had weakened his heart?

    A. A war injury
    B. He had typhoid.
    C. He had malaria.
    D. He had rheumatic fever.

TRIVIA FACTS : DID YOU KNOW THAT . . .

1. Conan Doyle and Harry Houdini were close friends and had attended a séance in which Conan Doyle's wife, Jean, acted as the medium. Lady Doyle claimed to have contacted Houdini's deceased mother. The magician was skeptical of the event and later published an article questioning Lady Doyle's spiritual powers.

2. In 1913 Conan Doyle supported many causes, calling for reforms that would eventually make England a more modern, progressive country, thus giving her a strategic advantage in the event of war. He wrote several letters to the press urging the government to construct a tunnel under the English Channel. According to Conan Doyle, this passage between England and France would prevent a blockade during war, allowing a continuous flow of food and supplies to and from the continent. He fought for the Divorce Reform Association, which supported giving incompatible couples the right to divorce on that ground alone, and he tried to ban the practice of using bird feathers to decorate women's apparel.

2. Who discovers McPherson dying on the beach and hears his last words?

    A. Holmes

    B. Murdoch, the mathematical coach

    C. His fiancée, Miss Bellamy

    D. Watson

3. What did Fitzroy McPherson do for a living?

    A. He was the swimming coach at a nearby college.

    B. He was a schoolmaster at a private boys school.

    C. He was a private tutor.

    D. He was a science teacher at an athletic and training school.

4. What clue leads Holmes to believe that McPherson fell while scrambling up the beach trail?

    A. There are slide marks above where his body is found.

    B. If McPherson fell down the hill, he would be covered with cuts and scrapes.

    C. All of McPherson's belongings are still on the beach.

    D. Holmes finds an open handprint with fingers pointed up toward the incline.

5. Why does Holmes believe that McPherson had not had his swim?

    A. His towel is still dry.

    B. His hair is not out of place.

    C. His swimming trunks are not wet.

    D. He swims for an hour each morning, and it was too early for him to have completed his exercise.

6. What four items did Holmes find in McPherson's pockets?

    A. Three shells, two shillings, cigarettes, and a match book

    B. A handkerchief, a large knife, a folding card-case, and a note from his lover

    C. A book of poetry, a wedding ring, a marriage license, and a picture of a woman

    D. A letter from his mother, a pocket watch and chain, a button from his shirt, and a receipt from his tailor

7. Why is Ian Murdoch a suspect in the apparent murder of McPherson?

    A. Murdoch was jealous of McPherson's success and was very vocal about his feelings.

    B. McPherson threatened to expose a sinister incident from Murdoch's past.

    C. Murdoch lost his girlfriend to McPherson.

    D. Witnesses overheard them quarreling, and Murdoch swore that he would kill McPherson.

8. What mysterious incident happens to McPherson's dog?

   A. The dog dies in exactly the same place where McPherson's body is found.

   B. It disappears the day McPherson dies.

   C. When the dog was found on Murdoch's front porch, it would not leave.

   D. The dog attacks Murdoch.

9. Why did McPherson and Miss Bellamy keep their engagement secret?

   A. His job required that he remain single.

   B. Miss Bellamy's father was against the marriage.

   C. Murdoch was still angry over losing Miss Bellamy to another man.

   D. McPherson's old, dying uncle may have disinherited him if he knew that he was getting married.

10. What confirms Holmes's theory as to why McPherson died and why Murdoch was attacked?

    A. Holmes consults with a marine biologist.

    B. Holmes remembers a book written by a man who had experienced a similar incident.

    C. He remembers a newspaper article about other swimmers near the area who died from the same conditions.

    D. He waits near the area where both men were attacked and finds the culprit.

QUIZ 70
"THE ADVENTURE OF THE VEILED LODGER"

Published in Liberty *in January 1927 and in the* Strand *in February 1927*

When Conan Doyle submitted "The Adventure of the Veiled Lodger" for publication, his editor requested another story instead because he claimed that Holmes was not at his best in this case. Rather than exercise his powers of deduction, the Great Detective simply listens to the confession of a guilt-ridden woman, after which he recalls and surmises the tragedy as he remembers. Conan Doyle refused his editor's request, and the story was published. The following quiz contains ten short-answer questions.

Story Date: exact date uncertain

1. Who requests that Holmes take Mrs. Ronder's case?

2. Why does Mrs. Ronder want to make a confession years after the tragedy?

3. What name does Mrs. Ronder write on a piece to paper to entice Holmes to take her case?

4. What was the name of the lion that mauled Mrs. Ronder?

5. Why was the lion fed only by Mr. and Mrs. Ronder?

6. What two facts lead Holmes to believe that another man was involved on that tragic night?

7. Why had Mrs. Ronder turned against her lover?

8. How did Leonardo make Mr. Ronder's attack look as if it was caused by the lion?

9. What does Holmes fear when Mrs. Ronder tells him that the case is closed?

10. What does Mrs. Ronder send Holmes two days after her confession?

QUIZ 71
"THE ADVENTURE OF SHOSCOMBE OLD PLACE"

Published in Liberty *in March 1927 and in the* Strand *in April 1927*

In 1910 Hawley Harvey Crippen was on trial for murdering his wife and burying her in the cellar. After the murder he attempted to flee England on the SS *Montrose*, along with his mistress, who had dressed up as Crippen's son for the ocean journey. Scotland Yard discovered the wife's body and, using the new telegraph system, wired the captain of the ship with instructions to arrest Crippen. Conan Doyle attended Crippen's trial, and seventeen years later used the true story as fodder for another Holmes tale. The following quiz contains ten true/false statements about how Holmes, Watson, and their canine assistant solve the mystery.

Story Date: exact date uncertain

1. Holmes used a powerful hand lens to determine that the tiny brown blobs on a tweed coat were glue.

2. Shoscombe Old Place is famous for its purebred racehorses and spaniels.

3. Sir Robert Norberton plans to increase his odds of winning the Derby by giving his horse a heavy stimulant.

4. John Mason believes that Sir Robert has gone mad because he spends all his time in the stable with his horse, even sleeping there.

5. Holmes becomes suspicious when he hears that Sir Robert and Lady Beatrice's relationship changed drastically.

6. Holmes starts an investigation into Sir Robert's financial situation and his interest in horse racing.

7. Mason finds the remains of a dog in the heating furnace.

8. Holmes and Watson are disguised as hunters when they arrive to investigate.

9. Holmes tries to prove that the person riding in the carriage is not Lady Beatrice by using her dog to either greet or attack the person in question.

10. Sir Robert attempts to cover up his sister's death because he is financially dependent upon her and, in the event of her death, the estate reverts to her husband's brother.

"THE ADVENTURE OF THE RETIRED COLOURMAN"

Published in Liberty *in December 1926 and in the* Strand *in January 1927*

In Michael Coren's insightful biography, *Conan Doyle*, he mentions that "The Adventure of the Retired Colourman" is the only story in the entire Holmes series that contains a reference to the mind-challenging game of chess. It would seem, given Holmes's calculating mind and Conan Doyle's knowledge of the game from a very young age, that he would have included chess as one of Holmes's hobbies. When discovering that Josiah Amberley was a proficient chess player, Holmes tells Watson that the ability to play chess well was "one mark of a scheming mind." The quiz for this final story contains ten multiple choice questions.

Story Date: 1898

1. Where does Josiah Amberley claim to have been on the night his wife and lover apparently ran off together?

    A. Amberley claims to have been at his club playing cards.
    B. At the Haymarket Theatre attending a play
    C. Visiting his brother in Sussex
    D. Attending a political meeting

2. When Watson visits Amberley, what is he doing to try to distract himself from the fact that his wife has left him?

    A. Amberley is planting fruit trees in the orchard.
    B. He has started to write a novel in which he plans to tell his story.
    C. He is painting the passageway in his house.
    D. He is burning all of his wife's belongings.

3. Besides losing his wife, from what other loss does Amberley suffer?

A. Amberley's wife also took the family dog.

B. She took his valuable collection of Mayan pottery.

C. She took his two most valuable bottles of wine.

D. His wife took seven thousand pounds worth of cash and securities.

4. What is Amberley's one hobby in life (he often engaged in this activity with Dr. Ray Ernest, the man who apparently stole his wife)?

A. Playing chess

B. Playing rugby

C. Playing croquet

D. Hunting grouse

5. What one-word message is Dr. Watson supposed to use when he telephones Holmes in the event that Mr. Amberley changes his mind and does not visit the vicarage?

A. Bolt

B. Revenge

C. Falsehood

D. Masquerade

6. Who else is investigating this case?

A. A private investigator hired by Mrs. Amberley's family

B. A private detective from America

C. A private detective hired by the family of Dr. Ray Ernest, the man who disappeared with Amberley's wife

D. Mrs. Amberley's banker

7. What question does Holmes ask Mr. Amberley when he returns to London after his wild goose chase?

A. "Was this your first murder?"

B. "What did you do with the bodies?"

C. "Whose murder would you rather be tried for first?"

D. "Do you sleep well?"

8. What information does Holmes discover that refutes Amberley's alibi that he was at the theatre?

    A. Holmes checked the box-office chart at the theatre and discovered that Amberley did not attend the play.

    B. The leading lady had lost her voice, and her understudy performed in her place.

    C. A fire broke out backstage during the performance, and the rest of the play was canceled.

    D. The play was canceled because the leading man became ill.

9. What is the first clue that Holmes notices?

    A. The smell of decaying flesh

    B. The smell of his wife's perfume, which he claims would not go away

---

TRIVIA FACTS : DID YOU KNOW THAT . . .

1. Conan Doyle's brother-in-law E. E. Hornung, husband of Connie Doyle and the creator of the fictional amateur thief Raffles, took the name from Conan Doyle's title character in the play *The Doings of Raffles Haw.*

2. Conan Doyle would write when the inspiration hit, undisturbed by any activity around him. For example, he could write while involved in conversation with family and friends and even with his young children sitting on his lap or crawling over his desk.

3. In 1922 Conan Doyle traveled to America for a series of speaking engagements about his beliefs in spiritualism. His speeches, complete with slides, were so moving and convincing that his lectures created hysteria. According to Conan Doyle biographer Charles Higham, after Conan Doyle presented seven programs in New York, speaking about how wonderful life is on the other side, several people committed suicide in order to experience this wonderment.

C. The smell of mildew

D. The strong smell of paint

10. What does Amberley do when Holmes confronts him with the crime?

    A. He bolts from the house, crashing through the window.

    B. He tells Holmes that he is "ready to take his medicine."

    C. He attempts suicide by swallowing a poison pill.

    D. He shouts, "I would gladly do it again!"

Benedict Cumberbatch and Martin Freeman as Sherlock Holmes and
John Watson in BBC's *Sherlock*

EIGHT

MORE SHERLOCK HOLMES

"there can be no grave for Sherlock Holmes
or Watson . . . Shall they not always live in
Baker Street? Are they not there this instant as
one writes? . . .Outside, the hansoms rattle through
the rain, and Moriarty plans his latest devilry.
Within, the sea-coal flames upon the hearth, and
Holmes and Watson take their well-won ease . . .
So they still live for all that love them well:
in a romantic chamber of the heart: in a nostalgic
country of the mind: where it is always 1895."
—VINCENT STARRETT

What do Shakespearian actor Basil Rathbone; co-star of the original "Star Trek" Leonard Nimoy; English comedian John Cleese, co-creator of "Monty Python's Flying Circus"; Tony Award–winning actor Frank Langella; and James Bond actor Roger Moore have in common? Along with dozens of other actors, they have portrayed the Great Detective in movies based upon either Conan Doyle's original Sherlock Holmes stories or the many spinoffs created by other writers.

"It has been claimed that Sherlock Holmes is the most popular fictional character ever created . . . it is probably no exaggeration to state that more has been written about Sherlock Holmes than any other imaginary person. *The World Bibliography of Sherlock Holmes and Dr. Watson* lists 6,221 [published] items and that tally is far from complete." Marvin Kay, author of *The Game Is Afoot: Parodies, Pastiches, and Ponderings of Sherlock Holmes*, is one of myriad writers, politicians, and members of the Baker Street Irregulars who have analyzed, philosophized about, and immortalized Sherlock Holmes. William S. Baring-Gould, Dorothy Sayers, Rex Stout, Anthony Boucher, Ellery Queen, Isaac Asimov, and hundreds more have published essays, articles, and reference books about the Great Detective, each adding their own style of wit, humor, and insightful deductions. Writers have postulated over the date of Holmes's birth, his attitude concerning women, his relationship with Dr. Watson, his experiences during the Great Hiatus, and even which university he attended. Anthologies, scrapbooks, encyclopedias, biographies, and photograph collections have turned the world of Sherlock Holmes inside out, dissecting his every nuance and adding to his popularity.

Although a century has passed since the Victorian era, when Holmes was working his magic, Conan Doyle's stories have not lost their appeal. The hansoms and dogcarts no longer clatter through the streets of London carrying cloaked passengers on foggy nights, and gaslights no longer illuminate the streets, but readers have only to open the pages of the canon to be transported back in time, joining Holmes and Watson as they pursue justice and unravel the complexities of life.

QUIZ 73
SHERLOCK HOLMES ON THE BIG SCREEN

Basil Rathbone became one of the most recognized Sherlock Holmes actors of all time, starring in over a dozen Holmes films and radio programs. However, after a few years he became impatient with fans asking him for Sherlock Holmes's autograph rather than his own. In 1946 when his radio and film contracts had expired, he chose not to re-sign, hoping to remove the typecast image of Sherlock Holmes. But the Holmes image was difficult to shake, and later he yielded to requests to appear in character on *The Bob Hope Show* and *The Milton Berle Show*. Then, in 1950, he donned the familiar cap and cape and starred in the play *Sherlock Holmes* written by his wife Ouida. The big screen quiz contains ten short-answer questions about Sherlock Holmes films and the actors who starred in them.

1. Who played Sherlock Holmes in more films than any other actor?

2. Which two actors, considered the most famous Holmes and Watson team, appeared in fourteen feature films made in America?

3. Who played Sherlock Holmes in the 1922 film *Sherlock Holmes*, produced by Goldwyn Pictures (U.S.)?

4. What was the name of the 1976 Sherlock Holmes film starring the following actors: Nicol Williamson as Holmes, Robert Duvall as Dr. Watson, Alan Arkin as Sigmund Freud, Laurence Olivier as Moriarty, and Vanessa Redgrave as Lola Devereaux?

5. What is the name of the first Sherlock Holmes film produced in 1903 and displayed on Mutascope machines? Thomas Edison owned the production company called American Mutascope and Biograph Co. The production lasted only thirty seconds.

6. Which actor played the following characters in these three different Sherlock Holmes films: Sir Henry Baskerville in *The Hound of the Baskervilles*, produced by Hammer Films (U.K.) in 1959; Sherlock Holmes in the German/Italian production of *Sherlock Holmes und das Halsband des Todes* (*Sherlock Holmes and the Necklace of Death*) in 1962; and Mycroft Holmes in *The Private Life of Sherlock Holmes*, produced in the United States in 1970 by Mirisch/United Artists?

7. What was the name of the Sherlock Holmes spoof filmed by 20th Century-Fox in 1975, starring Gene Wilder as Sigerson Holmes and Madeline Kahn as Bessie Bellwood?

8. Who played Sherlock Holmes and Dr. Watson in the 1990 Orion film production of *Without a Clue*?

9. What was the name of the 1977 Canadian film produced by Avco/Embassy, starring Peter Cook as Holmes and Dudley Moore as Dr. Watson?

10. What well-known British actor, considered one of the most popular Sherlock Holmes, starred in the 1959 Hammer Films (U.K.) production of *The Hound of the Baskerville*s? He also appeared as Holmes in several TV productions.

Quiz 74
SHERLOCK HOLMES OVER THE WIRE

In immortalizing Sherlock Holmes, creator Conan Doyle also paved the way to fame for several actors who portrayed Dr. John Watson. English actor Nigel Bruce is best known for his role as Sherlock Holmes's sidekick, having starred in fifteen Holmes movies and over 200 radio episodes between 1939 and 1947. He first appeared as Dr. Watson in 20th Century-Fox's production of *The Hound of the Baskervilles*, a performance considered by critics as one of his best. However, in subsequent films, Bruce's Dr. Watson evolved into a clumsy, inept individual who, more times than not, tried the patience of his friend Sherlock Holmes. Nevertheless, the public enjoyed his performances as he became the quintessential Dr. Watson. In his autobiography, Basil Rathbone said this about Bruce: "There is no question in my mind that Nigel Bruce was the ideal Watson, not only of his time, but possibly of and for all time." The following quiz contains ten short-answer questions about Sherlock Holmes on radio.

1. Which distinguished American stage actor ended his long acting career on the radio as the first person to play Sherlock Holmes over the wire in 1930?

2. Who starred as Sherlock Holmes in the 1938 Mercury Theatre radio program?

3. Which actors starred as Holmes and Watson in the long-running Sherlock Holmes radio series which aired in the United States between 1939 and 1946?

4. Concerning question number three, which Holmes story was their first episode?

5. Also concerning question number three, what was the title of their last episode, which aired on May 27, 1946?

6. Which two knighted actors played Holmes in the following British radio broadcasts: "The Adventure of

the Speckled Band" (1945) and "The Adventures of Sherlock Holmes" (1954)?

7. Which American actress/writer was responsible for NBC adapting Conan Doyle's Sherlock Holmes stories for radio? She also wrote all of the Holmes episodes between 1930 and 1943.

8. After over 200 episodes, Basil Rathbone retired from his role as Holmes on American radio in 1946. Who replaced him?

9. Which English actor played Holmes between 1958 and 1962 in the British broadcast of the following three Conan Doyle novels: *The Hound of the Baskervilles, The Valley of Fear,* and *A Study in Scarlet*?

10. Who hosted the anthology series *The CBS Radio Mystery Theatre*, an hour-long program which adapted *A Study in Scarlet, The Sign of Four, The Hound of the Baskervilles,* and other Holmes stories?

QUIZ 75
SHERLOCK HOLMES ON STAGE

Early in his writing career, Broadway producer Charles Frogman approached Conan Doyle with the idea of writing a Sherlock Holmes play. But, it was not until 1898 that Conan Doyle brought the idea to fruition by writing a five-act play which he sent to Frogman. Not wanting to upset Conan Doyle, but realizing that the play needed work, Frogman tactfully suggested that American actor and playwright William Gillette make a few revisions. Gillette revamped the entire play using story facts and plot lines from "A Scandal in Bohemia" and "The Final Problem." Wishing to add an element of romance to the play, Gillette telegraphed Conan Doyle, asking, "MAY I MARRY HOLMES?" Conan Doyle's response: "YOU MAY MARRY HIM, OR MURDER HIM, OR DO WHAT YOU LIKE WITH HIM." William Gillette played Holmes in the production, which was a smashing success, forever linking the actor with the character

Sherlock Holmes. He would eventually play Holmes more than 1,300 times during his career. This quiz on Holmes's stage presence contains ten short-answer questions.

1. What is the title of the earliest known Sherlock Holmes play? It was staged in 1893 and starred Charles Brookfield and Seymour Hicks.

2. Which actor played the part of Justin Playfair/Sherlock Holmes in the London staging of the play *They Might Be Giants*, a story about a judge who believed that he was Sherlock Holmes?

3. Who is the stage actor who, in portraying Holmes, created the phrase that was never actually written by Conan Doyle, "This is elementary, my dear Watson"? And which actor later shortened it to "Elementary, my dear Watson"?

4. Which Conan Doyle biographer wrote the Holmes plays *The Adventure of the Conk-Singleton Papers*, staged in 1948, and *The Adventure of the Paradol Chamber*, staged in 1949?

5. What is the name of the 1985 Holmes play written by Hugh Leonard in which Jack the Ripper makes an appearance?

6. What is the name of the Sherlock Holmes children's musical first performed at the Goodman Theatre in Chicago in 1971? It starred Michael Kerns as Holmes and Donald Livesay as Watson.

7. Who is the Tony Award–winning actor who also played Holmes in Gillette's play *Sherlock Holmes* in 1977? The play was aired on the cable TV network Home Box Office in 1981. This actor, best known for his role of Dracula in the 1979 film of the same name, had performed in several other Sherlock Holmes stage productions before 1977.

8. Which English actor starred on stage in *The Return of Sherlock Holmes* in 1923? This actor also played Holmes forty-seven times in a British film series between 1921 and 1923.

9. Which American actor played Holmes in a 1975–1976 version of Gillette's play *Sherlock Holmes*? This logical actor also referred to Holmes as his ancestor in the science fiction movie *Star Trek VI*.

TRIVIA FACTS : DID YOU KNOW THAT . . .

1. In 1893 Conan Doyle and *Peter Pan* author James M. Barrie were commissioned to write an operetta for the producers of the Savoy Theatre, the theatre where all Gilbert and Sullivan productions were staged. The result was the unsuccessful musical comedy *Jane Annie*. Evidently, the operetta could not stand up to audiences used to the quality of work produced by Gilbert and Sullivan but, because there were no other productions with which to replace it, the show ran for seven weeks.

2. In 1899 Conan Doyle and American actor William Gillette wrote a four-act play entitled *Sherlock Holmes*, which premiered in Buffalo, New York, on October 23, 1899, starring Gillette as Holmes. While touring, Gillette lost his copy of the play in a fire at a San Francisco hotel. Conan Doyle had also lost his original script, so Gillette wrote a new ending for the play that was performed in France. Conan Doyle was pleased with the new climax and later adopted it as the ending for "The Adventure of the Empty House."

3. A young Charlie Chaplin played the part of Billy, a Baker Street irregular, in the play version of *The Hound of the Baskervilles*.

4. Conan Doyle, possibly hoping to add an element of fear to the production, insisted that the starring role for his stage play *The Speckled Band* be performed by a real snake. This tactic alarmed many of the actors, causing them to appear nervous on stage. The snake's performance, however, was less than thrilling, for it just hung motionless unless prodded by a pinch on the tail. A critic described its performance as "palpably artificial."

10. What is the name of the Sherlock Holmes play written by Basil Mitchell and staged at the Lyric Theatre in London in 1933? In this story, Holmes has a daughter named Shirley whose goal is to become the first female detective at Scotland Yard. The play appeared on Broadway between 1936 and 1937.

QUIZ 76
SHERLOCK HOLMES ON TV

Almost a hundred years after Arthur Conan Doyle put pen to paper and created his Great Detective, English actor Jeremy Brett began his long television career as the quintessential Sherlock Holmes. Brett's portrayal of Holmes on the Granada Television (U.K.) series is considered by fans and critics alike as one of the best, even rivaling that of Basil Rathbone a generation before. Initially, Brett was reluctant to play the role because he felt that it had been portrayed too many times on film, TV, and stage. But eventually Brett became intrigued with the fictional character and, because of his fascination with Holmes, planned to appear in all sixty Holmes stories, a feat not yet accomplished by an actor. However, this goal was never to be reached. Brett died in his sleep in 1995 at the age of 59. He had completed forty-one episodes. In an earlier interview Brett said that Holmes at times seemed impossible to play: "Sherlock Holmes is a free spirit, you cannot pin him down—he is probably the most complicated character I've played in my life." This quiz contains ten short-answer questions about TV programs and actors who have portrayed Holmes.

1. What is the title of the first Holmes program which broadcast from Radio City in New York on November 27, 1937? It starred Louis Hector as Holmes and William Podmore as Watson.

2. What English actor/comedian played Holmes in the British broadcast of "Elementary, My Dear Watson"

in 1976 and in "The Strange Case of the End of Civilization as We Know It" in 1977?

3. Who is the British actor who played Holmes in the British television series *Sherlock Holmes* in 1968 and returned in 1984 to play the detective in the television film *The Masks of Death*?

4. What is the name of the popular U. S. children's show that teaches young people about great works of literature? One particular episode adapted *The Hound of the Baskervilles* as one of its stories.

5. Who played Dr. Watson opposite Jeremy Brett in the 1987 PBS *Mystery!* production of *The Sign of Four*?

6. Who is the British actor who played Holmes in the European television productions of *Sherlock Holmes, Incident at Victoria Falls* (1991) and *Sherlock Holmes and the Leading Lady* (1992)?

7. Which Canadian actor played Holmes opposite James Mason as Watson in the 1979 British television production of *Murder By Decree*, a story about the Jack the Ripper murders in Whitechapel?

8. What is the title of the 1998 production of a Holmes animated children's series produced by Scottish Television Enterprises Ltd. and DIC Productions? In this futuristic story, Holmes is resurrected to assist Scotland Yard in a challenging case, accompanied by a robotic version of Dr. Watson.

9. Who played Sherlock Holmes in the 1976 television film *Sherlock Holmes in New York*?

10. What is the title of the 1987 U. S. made-for-TV film in which the story is set in the present? In the film, a female Watson, descendent of Dr. Watson, travels to England to claim her inheritance, an English manor. In her exploration, she finds the body of Sherlock Holmes frozen in suspended animation.

Quiz 77
SHERLOCKIAN LITERATURE

For Sherlock Holmes fans who wish to discover the details of the Great Detective's life, William S. Baring-Gould's delightful book, *Sherlock Holmes of Baker Street: A Life of the World's First Consulting Detective*, is a Holmes biography which reads like a novel. Using a plethora of resources, the author has created the most accurate and concise parody of Holmes ever written. The following quiz asks ten questions about writers and their publications of Sherlockian lore.

1. In 1896, after Sherlock Holmes had tumbled over into Reichenbach Falls, Conan Doyle wrote a Holmes parody for Edinburgh University's magazine. What is the name of this story?

2. What is the name of the author who is currently writing Sherlock Holmes tales which feature a young female apprentice who eventually becomes Holmes's partner?

3. What is the name of the 1984 collection of science fiction stories which features Sherlock Holmes? Writers of these tales include Isaac Asimov, Philip José Farmer, Poul Anderson, and Gordon R. Dickson.

4. Which American writer wrote the Sherlock Holmes parody character of Fetlock Jones, who appeared in the tale "A Double-Barreled Detective Story," published by *Harper's Monthly Magazine* in 1902?

5. What is the name of the first Sherlock Holmes parody, written in 1892 by Robert Barr under the pen name Luke Sharp? The story appeared in the *Idler Magazine* in May of 1892.

6. What is the name of the Sherlock Holmes novel written by Loren D. Estleman in which Holmes solves the mystery of Dr. Jekyll and Mr. Hyde?

7. What is the title of the 1893 parody written by R. C. Lehmann in which the chronicler is named Cunnin Toil? It was first published in *Punch* magazine.

THE SHERLOCK HOLMES QUIZ BOOK

8. What is the name of the collection of Sherlock Holmes stories which was written by Conan Doyle's son, Adrian Conan Doyle, in collaboration with John Dickson Carr?

9. What is the name of the parody character created by Charles Harold St. John Hamilton writing under the pseudonym Peter Todd? The eighteen stories were published in *Greyfriar's Herald* in 1915 and were chronicled by a character named Jotson.

10. What is the name of the 1984 novel written by Cay Van Ash in which Sherlock Holmes encounters the notorious fictional character Dr. Fu Manchu?

TRIVIA FACTS : DID YOU KNOW THAT . . .

1. Well known for his portrayal of Sherlock Holmes in the popular British television series, Jeremy Brett had earlier played Dr. Watson opposite Charlton Heston as Holmes in the 1980 version of the Holmes play entitled *Crucifier of Blood*.

2. Nigel Bruce was perhaps the most famous Dr. Watson, starring in fifteen Sherlock Holmes films and over 200 radio broadcasts between 1939 and 1947. Friend and coactor Basil Rathbone had hoped that the aging Bruce would perform as Dr. Watson one last time in the 1953 stage production *Sherlock Holmes*, but, unfortunately, Bruce died a few weeks before the play opened.

3. In 1890 Conan Doyle wrote a three-act play which included Dr. Watson, but not Sherlock Holmes. The play, entitled *Angels of Darkness*, takes place entirely in the United States. Realizing that his readership would never approve of a story about the good doctor without the Great Detective, Conan Doyle set the play aside. *Angels of Darkness* has never been produced.

4. Christopher Lee is the only actor to play both Sherlock and Mycroft Holmes in two separate films. He played Sherlock Holmes in the 1962 German film *Sherlock Holmes und das Halsband des Todes* (*Sherlock Holmes and the Necklace of Death*) and Mycroft Holmes in the 1970 film *The Private Life of Sherlock Holmes*.

5. *The Hound of the Baskervilles* has been adapted into over three dozen feature films, TV movies, radio programs, and plays since its publication in 1901.

Lara Pulver and Benedict Cumberbatch as Irene Adler and Sherlock Holmes in BBC's *Sherlock*

NINE
SHERLOCK CONTINUES

THE FOLLOWING TWENTY-FIVE QUIZZES comprise some of the most recent Sherlock Holmes adaptations. They include the two Sherlock Holmes films starring Robert Downey, Jr., and directed by Guy Ritchie, BBC's *Sherlock* series, CBS's *Elementary* series, and HBO and Hulu's *Miss Sherlock* series. Also included are trivia facts about Robert Downey, Jr., and Jude Law, Benedict Cumberbatch, Martin Freeman, Jonny Lee Miller, and Lucy Liu. Who knows what the future of Sherlock Holmes and Dr. John Watson will have in store? One thing is for sure: The game is *always* afoot.

GUY RITCHIE'S
SHERLOCK HOLMES (2009)

The Warner Brothers' action film, *Sherlock Holmes*, directed by Guy Ritchie, was released on Christmas Day 2009. The story is set in 1890s London with Robert Downey, Jr. as Sherlock Holmes and Jude Law as Dr. John Watson. The film won two Academy Awards: Best Original Score and Best Art Direction. Box office results were over sixty-two million dollars, and lifetime gross has been over 220 million.

Cast of Main Characters:
Sherlock Holmes: Robert Downey, Jr.
Dr. John Watson: Jude Law
Irene Adler: Rachel McAdams
Mrs. Hudson: Geraldine James
Mary Morstan: Kelly Reilly
Inspector Lestrade: Eddie Marsan

QUIZ 78
SHERLOCK HOLMES (2009) FACTS

"Don't fill up on bread."
—IRENE ADLER

Guy Ritchie's film version of the exploits of Sherlock Holmes is action-packed with witty dialogue, numerous fight scenes, and strong female characters that rival their male counterparts. Here are ten short-answer questions.

1. Watson is tending to an elderly patient when they hear gunfire coming from upstairs. Watson goes to check on Holmes. What is Holmes's excuse for firing the gun indoors?

2. What does Holmes do before an attack or fight?

3. What did Holmes do to the family dog, Gladstone, to render him unconscious?

THE SHERLOCK HOLMES QUIZ BOOK

4. Holmes meets Watson's fiancée, Mary Mortson, over dinner at the Royale restaurant. Hearing about his deductive reasoning skills, she asks that he analyze her. What is her response once he finishes his analysis?

5. Why does Holmes keep Watson's checkbook locked away?

6. Lord Henry Blackwell is hanged for his ritualistic murders of five women. What happens three months later?

7. It is evident by their familiarity with each other that Irene Adler and Holmes have, on occasion, been involved romantically. Why does Irene Adler contact Holmes?

8. Why are Holmes and Watson arrested after a violent encounter in a shipyard with a huge man named Dredger?

9. When Holmes realizes that Irene is in danger, he pleads for her to flee. She refuses. What does she do to keep Holmes from following her?

10. In one of the final scenes, Mary walks into Baker Street and sees Holmes hanging from a noose. Watson cuts him down and tells Mary that Holmes is too arrogant to commit suicide. What is the reason for Holmes's antic?

QUIZ 79
SHERLOCK HOLMES (2009)
CANONICAL QUOTES

The following quiz contains seven quotes spoken by Holmes in the film that come directly from Arthur Conan Doyle's stories. Can you name the short story or novel the quote refers to?

1. "You have the grand gift of silence, Watson. It makes you quite invaluable as a companion."

2. "Crime is common, logic is rare."

3. "My mind rebels at stagnation. Give me problems, give me work."

4. "Data, data, data. I cannot make bricks without clay."

5. "One begins to twist facts to suit theories, instead of theories to suit facts."

6. "There is nothing more stimulating than a case where everything goes against you."

7. "The game is afoot."

GUY RITCHIE'S FILM
A GAME OF SHADOWS (2011)

A Game of Shadows, the sequel to *Sherlock Holmes*, brings the ever-popular Professor Moriarty and Mycroft Holmes, as well as Sebastian Moran, into the story. Holmes investigates Moriarty's plan to carry out terrorist attacks on London, as Dr. Watson and Mary plan their wedding. Watson is determined to sever his investigatory ties with Holmes and begin a peaceful domestic life. But Holmes is not ready to cut Watson loose, and the doctor is quickly drawn into the saga.

Additional characters:
Professor James Moriarty: Jared Harris
Mycroft Holmes: Stephen Fry
Sebastian Moran: Paul Anderson

Quiz 80
A GAME OF SHADOWS (2011) FACTS

"You mean there are two of you?"
—MARY (MORSTAN) WATSON

The following ten true/false statements provide tidbits from the plot without spoiling the ending, for we all know, no matter the version, pastiche, or twist on Holmes's exploits, he always survives "the fall."

1. In the first film, *Sherlock Holmes*, Irene Adler plays a significant role. In *A Game of Shadows*, she only appears early in the movie because she goes into hiding.

2. Holmes was to plan Watson's stag party the night before the wedding. When Watson arrives at the music hall, he learns that Holmes did not invite anyone.

3. Holmes throws Mary Watson, John's new bride, from a moving train. She lands in a river and is rescued by Moriarty.

4. Holmes learns that Professor Moriarty, having amassed arms and ammunition factories, plans to start a war in Europe.

5. Moriarty will direct his retaliation to Mycroft if Holmes interferes with Moriarty's plan.

6. At the stag party, Holmes encounters Madam Simza, an opera singer, and saves her from becoming another Moriarty victim.

7. Holmes steals Moriarty's account book, which contains evidence that links him to all his misdeeds.

8. Madam Simza helps Holmes decipher the code that Moriarty used to hide his connections.

9. Supposedly Moriarty uses Irene Adler to carry out his murderous plan in Paris.

10. Holmes survives the fall in Reichenbach and delivers his favorite pipe to Watson as a clue that he's still alive.

QUIZ 81
A GAME OF SHADOWS (2011) CANONICAL REFERENCES

The following quiz contains five Holmes canonical reference questions. Can you name the short story or novel the references come from?

1. One of Holmes's most famous quotes, "Come at once if convenient. If inconvenient, come all the same. S.H.," comes from a note Holmes sent Watson. In which Arthur Conan Doyle short story did this appear?

2. What two Arthur Conan Doyle short stories is *A Game of Shadows* based on?

3. Dr. Watson introduces Mary Morstan, his fiancée, to Holmes as he did in which novel?

4. Holmes disguises himself as a woman. In which Conan Doyle short story does Holmes do the same?

5. Moriarty is introduced in the second film. In which story in the canon does Holmes mention he has a brother?

BBC'S *SHERLOCK*

BBC'S *SHERLOCK* SEASON 1: THE STAGE IS SET

Season one introduces us to a modern-day Sherlock Holmes and Dr. Watson, Mrs. Hudson, along with Inspector Lestrade, Mycroft Holmes, and James Moriarty. In the first season, their relationships unfold and their lives intertwine. The stage is set for future drama.

Cast of Main Characters:
Sherlock Holmes: Benedict Cumberbatch
Dr. John Watson: Martin Freeman
Mrs. Hudson: Una Stubbs
Inspector Lestrade: Rupert Graves
Molly Hooper: Louise Brealey
Mycroft Holmes: Mark Gatiss
Professor James Moriarty: Andrew Scott
Mary Watson: Amanda Abbington

QUIZ 82
"A STUDY IN PINK"

*"The name is Sherlock Holmes and
the address is 221B Baker Street."*
—SHERLOCK HOLMES

Sherlock Holmes and Dr. John Watson become flatmates out of necessity and soon find one another indispensable. Try your hand at the following ten short-answer questions.

1. John's therapist suggests, now that he's returned from Afghanistan, he write a blog about everything that happens to him. What is his reply?

2. What's the name of Sherlock's website?

3. What does Mycroft say about bravery?

4. In what business was Mrs. Hudson's husband involved?

5. When Sherlock and John meet, Sherlock asks John if he was recently in Afghanistan or Iraq. What's his next question?

6. What does Sherlock say to John about his post-traumatic stress condition?

7. What case does Inspector Lestrade call Sherlock to help investigate?

8. Who is the serial killer's sponsor?

9. What weapon is used to kill the victims?

10. John finds Sherlock in the nick of time and rescues him. How does John know where to find Sherlock?

QUIZ 83
"THE BLIND BANKER"

"The world's run on codes and ciphers, John."
—SHERLOCK HOLMES

When Sherlock is hired by an acquaintance from his university days to investigate an office break-in, Sherlock discovers the case involves a human fly, a Chinese circus, a giant crossbow, and murder. The following seven questions have true/false answers.

1. John needs to earn extra money and takes a part-time job working in a library.

2. The name of the Chinese crime syndicate operating in London is the Lucky Spider.

3. Sherlock discovers warning messages in the form of ancient Chinese symbols spray-painted in yellow paint.

4. John is attacked and almost killed outside Soo Lin Yao's flat while Sherlock is inside gathering more information.

5. Soo Lin Yao, Chinese pottery expert at the National Antiquities Museum, tells Sherlock what the symbols mean.

6. The villains threaten to kill Sarah, John's new girlfriend, because they mistake him for Sherlock and are trying to get him to reveal the location of a valuable artifact.

7. The artifact is a thousand-year-old ivory vase, and it is sitting on the desk of the banker who hired Sherlock to investigate a break-in.

QUIZ 84
"THE GREAT GAME"

> *"If you don't stop prying, I will burn you.*
> *I will burn the heart out of you."*
> —JIM MORIARTY

Sherlock is in dire need of a case to stave off boredom. An urgent call from his brother, Mycroft, and a bombing outside of 221B Baker Street has Sherlock off and running, along with John and his new girlfriend. What are the answers to the following five short-answer questions?

1. What is Sherlock doing when John enters the flat?
2. What items are used as symbols for the puzzles Sherlock must solve in order to prevent murders?
3. Mycroft wants Sherlock to solve an important case involving a murder and the theft of the government's missile plans. The name of the case was taken from an original Conan Doyle Holmes story published in *His Last Bow* collection. What is the title of the story?
4. In the original canon, Sherlock uses his gang of street urchins to gather information. Who does modern-day Sherlock use?
5. In the BBC series *Sherlock*, what is Moriarty's cell phone ringtone?

BBC'S *SHERLOCK* SEASON 2: MORIARTY UPS THE ANTE

In season two, Sherlock meets his match when he tangles with Irene Adler. Modern technology cleverly melds with the daunting moors of Dartmoor, and the season's final episode, "The Reichenbach Fall," rivals any adaptation of the original ever written.

QUIZ 85
"THE SCANDAL IN BELGRAVIA"

"I'm not dead. Let's have dinner."
—IRENE ADLER

In the opening scene, Sherlock and John are bantering about titles John will use for his blogs about Sherlock's cases. Their wordplay, "The Belly Button Murders," "The Speckled Blonde," and "The Geek Interpreter," all reference Conan Doyle's titles, "The

Adventure of the Naval Treaty," "The Adventure of the Speckled Band," and "The Adventure of the Greek Interpreter." The following quiz contains seven short-answer questions, all focused on the seductive Irene Adler.

1. How does Sherlock become involved with Irene Adler?

2. What is Sherlock wearing when he is taken to the palace?

3. During their meeting, Sherlock tells Mycroft that sex doesn't alarm him. What is Mycroft's response?

4. In the original canon, Irene Adler is an opera singer. How is she portrayed in this modern-day version?

5. Sherlock and John attempt a ruse to get into Irene's flat. Sherlock is disguised as a clergyman as in the original Conan Doyle story, "The Scandal in Bohemia." What is Irene wearing when she walks into the room?

6. Sherlock tricks Irene into disclosing the location of her cell phone with the suggestive photos. How does she steal it back? And what does she do with his phone?

7. Irene seeks Sherlock's help in deciphering a code she stole from a Ministry of Defense. What does she do with it after Sherlock cracks the code?

QUIZ 86
"THE HOUNDS OF BASKERVILLE"

"Listen, what I said before, John, I meant it.
I don't have friends. I've just got one."
—SHERLOCK HOLMES

This episode opens with a humorous scene. Sherlock enters Baker Street covered with blood and holding a harpoon. We learn he's just taken the tube home after solving a case that required him to stab a pip carcass. But the episode ends on a disturbing note: Moriarty is released from prison, having manipulated Mycroft. In the meantime, Sherlock is going manic over quitting smoking and begs John to help him find a case. Out of desperation, Sherlock decides to accept the Baskerville case. The following quiz contains seven short-answer questions.

1. When Henry Knight was a boy, he witnessed his father being torn to pieces by a giant hound near their estate in Dartmoor. He comes to Sherlock for help because he believes the hound has returned. What is his explanation for the beast's existence?

2. How does Knight convince a reluctant Sherlock to take the case?

3. How do Sherlock and John enter the well-guarded Baskerville facility?

4. Why does Inspector Lestrade show up on the scene?

5. Where did the secret experimental project being conducted by Dr. Franklin at the Baskerville lab have its origin?

6. What was the byproduct of the chemical weapon?

7. What does Sherlock reveal to John after the case is solved?

QUIZ 87
"THE REICHENBACH FALL"

"Every fairy tale needs a good old-fashioned villain.
You need me, or you're nothing."
—JIM MORIARTY

In this episode, Sherlock becomes a celebrated hero for solving several high-profile cases. But with Moriarty's plans to bring Sherlock down, the stage is set for one of the most compelling episodes of the entire series, one that became the topic of conversation until the next season aired two years later. The following quiz contains seven short-answer questions.

TRIVIA FACTS: DID YOU KNOW THAT . . .

1. Martin Freeman (Dr. Watson) and Abigail Abbington (wife Mary Watson) were a couple for sixteen years before recently separating.

2. In 2011, Freeman won the British Academy of Film and Television Arts award for best supporting actor in *Sherlock*.

3. Freeman was nominated for an Oscar for best actor in his role as Bilbo Baggins in *The Hobbit*.

4. He appeared in more than twenty feature films between 1998-2018.

5. *"I would wear a full-length cape if I could get away with it — I do love a good swirl in the fog."* — Martin Freeman

1. What warning does John give Sherlock about his recent popularity with the press?

2. Moriarty breaks into the Tower of London, the Bank of London, and Pentonville Prison by cracking their security codes. What does he write on the glass case that holds the Crown Jewels?

3. Moriarty is arrested for the break-ins. Why is he found not guilty even though he offers no defense?

4. How does Moriarty publicly discredit Sherlock as a fraud?

5. Who does Moriarty manipulate to assist him in his grand scheme of deception?

6. Who does Sherlock turn to for help in his time of desperation?

7. Where do Moriarty and Holmes meet for their final showdown?

BBC'S *SHERLOCK* SEASON 3: HAT DETECTIVE RETURNS

Sherlock returns to London after faking his death. In this series, we meet Mary Morstan, watch Sherlock give one of the most moving best-man speeches ever made, meet an evil villain, learn of Mary's past life, and find out what we've all waited two years to know—how Sherlock survived the fall.

QUIZ 88
"THE EMPTY HEARSE"

"Oh, you bastard."
—INSPECTOR LESTRADE

John's romantic relationship with Mary Morstan tempers his grief over losing Sherlock. Sherlock returns to London and is exonerated of all slander. After a few bumpy starts, the two are together again, but life as they knew it is gone, as they will soon find out. The following quiz contains seven fill-in-the-blank statements.

1. Mycroft goes undercover to _____ (country) to bring Sherlock out of hiding because a terrorist attack is about to occur in London.

2. John is about to propose to Mary at the Landmark restaurant when Sherlock comes to the table disguised as a _____.

3. Mycroft and Sherlock are playing _____ (children's board game) while they discuss the proposed terrorist attack.

4. Sherlock anticipates _____ (number) possible outcomes occurring on the roof of the hospital.

5. Each of the outcomes mentioned in the above question has a code name. Sherlock uses the code name, _____ , to alert Mycroft.

6. John is knocked down by a _____ and fails to see what happens after Sherlock jumps from the building.

7. The terrorist attack is supposed to occur on the night of the British holiday _____.

QUIZ 89
"THE SIGN OF THREE"

"John, I am a ridiculous man, redeemed only by the warmth and consistency of your friendship."
— SHERLOCK HOLMES

In "The Sign of Three," Sherlock has mellowed. Emotions have surfaced as the friendships with Dr. Watson, Molly Hooper, and Inspector Lestrade have evolved. His acceptance of Mary Marston into their world is evident in his relaxed humor. Although he is still somewhat suspicious of her, he has learned to appreciate her insight and intellect. Try your hand at the following seven short-answer questions.

1. At the beginning of the episode, a woman comes to Holmes for help. What is her concern?

2. Sherlock and John get drunk the night before John and Mary's wedding. What game are they playing at 221B Baker Street?

3. Why does Sherlock desperately call Lestrade for help just as he is about to arrest the Waters gang for bank robbery?

4. What does Sherlock realize is about to happen while giving his speech?

5. What clues does Sherlock use to deduce who is about to become the victim?

6. What is the weapon used on both victims?

7. What surprise does Sherlock reveal to John and Mary after making three observations concerning Mary's recent behavior?

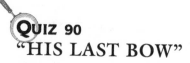

QUIZ 90
"HIS LAST BOW"

"The problems of your past are your business.
The problems of your future are my privilege."
—DR. JOHN WATSON

In the last episode of the season, Sherlock meets another nemesis, Charles Augustus Magnussen, who is based on Conan Doyle's character, Charles Augustus Milverton, a.k.a. the King of All Blackmailers. Although Sherlock thwarts Magnussen's evil blackmail scheme, Sherlock does not prevent the villain from leaving a lasting, deep scar. The following quiz contains seven true/false questions; the first three reflect the original stories of Arthur Conan Doyle.

1. The beginning of the episode opens with John searching for a friend in a crack house. He also finds Sherlock there and assumes he's using drugs again. This scenario is based on Arthur Conan Doyle's short story "The Adventure of Shoscombe Old Place."

2. Details of Mary Morstan's life are revealed. "The Adventure of the Dancing Men," an original Sherlock Holmes story, features a woman, Elsie Cubitt, who also has a sordid past life.

3. The initials on Mary's memory stick, A.G.R.A., reflect the story, "The Sign of Four," and the Agra treasure.

4. Charles Augustus Magnussen is a real estate tycoon.

5. Magnussen blackmails Lady Elizabeth Smallwood by threatening to expose the affair she is having with an underage boy.

6. The tension ramps up when Sherlock learns that Magnussen is also blackmailing Mrs. Hudson.

7. During the confrontation in Magnussen's office, Lady Smallwood shoots Sherlock.

THE SHERLOCK HOLMES QUIZ BOOK

BBC'S *SHERLOCK* SEASON 4: BE CAREFUL WHAT YOU WISH FOR

Life and death, truth and lies, victims and villains are the themes of season four, as the past comes back to haunt Sherlock and Watson in their struggles to make sense of what life has dished out.

QUIZ 91
"THE SIX THATCHERS"

"It's not a girl's name."
—JOHN AND MARY WATSON

In the first episode, we discover who Mary Watson really is. We see John weaken to temptation, and Sherlock unable to fulfill his vow to protect. This quiz offers seven short-answer questions.

1. In season three's last episode, Sherlock is exiled for killing Charles Augustus Magnussen, but only for a few minutes. Why does Mycroft rescind Sherlock's exile and bring him back immediately?

2. How does Sherlock avoid arrest for killing Magnussen?

3. What is the name of John and Mary's baby, and what do they call her?

4. While Sherlock is at the home of a cabinet minister, investigating the disappearance of his son, what does Sherlock become distracted by?

5. Sherlock discovers that several of these items have been taken and destroyed. He believes they contain a black pearl, but finds out that it is a memory stick belonging to whom?

6. Mary realizes that a former colleague blames her for a botched rescue mission and is seeking her out for revenge. To protect John, Mary disappears, but Sherlock tracks her down. Where does he find her?

7. Sherlock learns that Vivian Norbury, Lady Smallwood's secretary, is responsible for thwarting the rescue mission. What happens when Sherlock, John, Mary, and Mycroft confront Norbury?

QUIZ 92
"THE LYING DETECTIVE"

"Get out of my house, you reptile."
—MRS. HUDSON

In "The Lying Detective," John blames Sherlock for Mary's death and refuses to see him. Even though Mary has died, she reaches out to Sherlock to save her grieving husband. More is revealed in seven true/false statements.

1. Fearing she might die, Mary communicates her message to Sherlock in her diary she left for him to read.

2. With John still grieving, Rosie is being cared for by Sherlock's parents.

3. Sherlock has chosen to investigate the activities of Culverton Smith, a well-known entrepreneur and philanthropist, in order to draw John back to Baker Street.

4. As part of his strategy to carry out Mary's plan, Sherlock uses drugs and becomes out of control, causing Mrs. Hudson to subdue him by handcuffing him and putting him in the trunk of her car.

5. When Sherlock and John confront Culverton Smith, he takes them to his private lab in the basement of the hospital.

6. John learns the truth behind Sherlock's behavior and activities from Mrs. Hudson.

7. This episode is loosely based on Conan Doyle's story, "The Adventure of the Dying Detective."

"THE FINAL PROBLEM"

> *"You might want to close that window.*
> *There is an east wind coming."*
> —DR. JOHN WATSON

In the previous episode, Mycroft admits to Sherlock and John that there is a younger Holmes sibling, a sister named Eurus, who turns out to be both villain and victim. Could there be anyone more sinister than Moriarty? Seems so. Here are seven short-answer questions to contemplate.

1. What do Sherlock and John do to trick Mycroft into revealing the existence of Eurus?

2. Where has Eurus been all these years?

3. Why did Mycroft and his Uncle Rudy have Eurus committed?

4. Even though Eurus is imprisoned, Mycroft tells Sherlock and John that she is still dangerous. What is his explanation?

5. What mistake does Mycroft admit to making five years earlier, which causes them to be imprisoned by Eurus at the facility?

6. Sherlock realizes that Redbeard was not a dog. Who was Redbeard?

7. Now that Sherlock understands what caused Eurus's violent behavior, what does he do after she goes back to prison?

BBC'S "THE ABOMINABLE BRIDE"

"The Abominable Bride" is a special *Sherlock* episode set partly in the Victorian London of Arthur Conan Doyle's original stories and partly in current time. It aired on New Year's Day in 2016. More than 8.4 million viewers tuned in to watch. The title is taken from the mention of an unrecorded case in Conan Doyle's short story, "The Adventure of the Musgrave Ritual," when Holmes tells Watson about "Ricoletti of the club-foot and his abominable bride." "The Abominable Bride" won the Primetime Emmy Award for Outstanding Television Movie. Enjoy this quiz focused on this TV special. The Victorian era questions refer to Sherlock Holmes and John Watson by use of their last names. The modern-day scenes refer to them by their first names.

QUIZ 94
"THE ABOMINABLE BRIDE" FACTS

"You! You! You or me!"
—EMELIA RICOLETTI, THE ABOMINABLE BRIDE

This quiz consists of fifteen short-answer questions.

1. What is Holmes doing in the morgue when Stamford brings John Watson in to meet the Great Detective for the first time?

2. Inspector Lestrade calls Holmes in to investigate what appears to be a murder/suicide, except the suspected killer, Emelia Ricoletti, kills herself before apparently killing her husband. Holmes loses interest in the case until what happens?

3. What modern-day James Moriarty quote does Emelia Ricoletti use when she, or her ghost, reappears months after the initial case?

4. Upon meeting Watson, how does Holmes test the doctor's reflexes?

5. When John asks Mrs. Hudson if she likes the stories he's publishing in the *Strand*, what is her reply and her reason?

6. At the beginning of the episode, who is the woman dressed in a black dress and veil, waiting for Holmes and Watson to return to Baker Street?

7. Holmes and Watson visit Mycroft at the Diogenes Club and use sign language to communicate with Wilder, the concierge, since talking is not allowed unless in a private room. Watson's use of sign language is lacking. What insulting comment does he sign in reply to Wilder telling him that he enjoyed "The Blue Carbuncle?"

8. Watson makes several incorrect observations, except for one involving Hooper, the medical examiner. What is his accurate observation?

9. What is the underlying subplot, which involves Mycroft, Mary Morstan, and most of the other women in the story?

10. What does Mycroft tells Holmes about the invisible enemy that is threatening war on the country?

11. Who does Mycroft summon to assign the task of keeping an eye on Holmes and Watson during the Ricoletti case?

12. When Watson teases Holmes about his apparent interest in Lady Carmichael, what is his response?

13. Sherlock uses cocaine to stimulate his brain and tap into his problem-solving vault. What does he call this part of his brain?

14. Mary Watson sends Holmes a telegram informing him she's discovered important information regarding the Ricoletti case at a desanctified church. What do Holmes, Watson, and Mary find at this church?

15. After Holmes's futuristic discussion with Watson, what does the Great Detective see out his window of 221B Baker Street?

CBS'S *ELEMENTARY*

CBS's acclaimed *Elementary* first aired on September 27, 2012, and by the end of season seven, 154 episodes have aired. The story is set in New York City, and Dr. Watson is portrayed as a woman. Besides Holmes's and Watson's personal troubles, most of the main characters have their issues, problems, and secrets. As their backgrounds are revealed in the series, it becomes easy to sympathize with what, at first, might seem like undesirable traits or unforgivable behavior.

Cast of Main Characters:
Sherlock Holmes: Jonny Lee Miller
Dr. Joan Watson: Lucy Liu
Captain Thomas Gregson: Aidan Quinn
Detective Marcus Bell: Jon Michael Hill
Dr. Eugene Hawes: Jordon Gelber
Morland Holmes: John Noble
Professor Moriarty/Irene Adler: Natalie Dormer
Mrs. Hudson: Candis Cayne
Mycroft Holmes: Rhys Ifans

QUIZ 95
SHERLOCK HOLMES IN THE BIG APPLE

> *"I'm smarter than everyone I meet, Watson."*
> —SHERLOCK HOLMES

Try your hand at the ten-question short-answer quiz.

1. How do Sherlock Holmes and Joan Watson meet?
2. How does Sherlock describe Joan's presence in his life to his colleagues at the police force?

3. What does Sherlock do when Joan finds his violin in a closet and suggests he start playing again to relax?

4. At the end of season one, Sherlock experiences flashbacks of events that led to his addiction. What happens to cause these flashbacks?

5. What is the name of Sherlock's pet tortoise?

6. After Sherlock and Joan solve their first case together, Joan is eagerly watching the end of a baseball game on TV, rooting on her team while Sherlock impatiently wants to grab a bite to eat. It's the bottom of the 9th inning, and Sherlock correctly deduces the ending of the game, spoiling Joan's fun. Of what baseball team is Joan a fan?

7. What song is playing at the end of the pilot, symbolizing that Joan will become Sherlock's partner and not merely his sober companion?

8. How do Holmes and Captain Gregson meet?

9. How does Mrs. Hudson, Sherlock's ex-housekeeper, differ from the Mrs. Hudsons in all other portrayals?

10. Sherlock's arch-enemy, Professor Moriarty, is a female assassin in *Elementary*. Why does she manipulate Sherlock into falling in love with her?

QUIZ 96
"TREMORS"

"My experience . . . diligence is the mother of luck."
— SHERLOCK HOLMES

The first episode of season two, "Step Nine," finds Sherlock and Joan in London. They've been summoned by Scotland Yard to help solve a case, but quickly return to New York City. Mycroft Holmes plays a significant role this season. Here are seven multiple choice questions from season two.

1. What is the name of the group of cyber-activists that Sherlock and Joan are investigating in episode three?

   A. Everyone
   B. Black Cloud
   C. Number Nine
   D. Raze

2. Also in episode three, what does Joan do when she becomes frustrated with Sherlock's inability to build meaningful relationships?

   A. She plays matchmaker to find him a suitable partner.
   B. She opens an online dating account for him.

C. Joan joins an online dating site.

D. She accuses him of being too frightened to become involved with someone.

3. In episode ten, "Tremors," what drives a wedge between Sherlock and Detective Bell, resulting in Bell refusing to speak to Holmes?

   A. Holmes accuses Detective Bell of being a mediocre detective.

   B. Holmes does not tell Detective Bell about the vital evidence he discovered in solving a case.

   C. Detective Bell is shot protecting Holmes for an incident that should not have occurred.

   D. Detective Bell accuses Holmes of relapsing in his addiction recovery.

4. "Ears to You," episode seventeen, reflects which Conan Doyle short story?

   A. "The Adventure of the Cardboard Box"

   B. "The Adventure of the Lion's Mane"

   C. "The Adventure of the Engineer's Thumb"

   D. "The Adventure of the Blue Carbuncle"

5. One of the most bizarre cases involves the murder of serial killer Aaron Coville, in episode nineteen, "The Many Mouths of Aaron Coville." Sherlock and Joan discover eight suspects, all with the same wound on their skin. What is this unusual marking?

   A. A cross carved into their forehead.

   B. A burn mark on their left shoulder.

   C. The attempted removal of a tattoo.

   D. Bite marks from the same set of teeth.

6. Episode twenty-one has the exact title of one of Conan Doyle's original short stories. What is the title?

   A. "Silver Blaze"

   B. "The Adventure of the Reigate Squire"

   C. "The Man with the Twisted Lip"

   D. "The Adventure of the Copper Beeches"

7. From strain caused by her involvement with Mycroft, what does Joan decide to do in this season's last episode, "The Grand Experiment"?

    A. Joan goes into therapy.
    B. Joan decides to leave Baker Street and find her own apartment.
    C. She confides in Sherlock.
    D. She writes Mycroft a letter telling him how hurt she is.

QUIZ 97
"ENOUGH NEMESIS TO GO AROUND"

"Everything I've told you is true, more or less. I've just omitted a great deal."
—MYCROFT HOLMES

In season three, a new character enters the picture, Kitty Winter, who is Sherlock's new protégé he brought back from London. The following quiz contains seven short-answer questions.

1. In episode one, "Enough Nemesis to Go Around," in what martial art do Joan and Kitty Winter engage?

2. Episode two involves a murder related to the poisoning of several children from tainted toy beads. The title of this episode refers to which Conan Doyle short story?

3. What warning to viewers is announced at the beginning of episode four, "Bella"?

4. Why does Joan not appear in "Rip Off," episode five?

5. In episode eleven, "The Illustrious Client," what character's name is taken directly from the original Conan Doyle story of the same title?

THE SHERLOCK HOLMES QUIZ BOOK

6. What devastating occurrence happens to Joan at the end of episode thirteen, "Hemlock"?

7. In "A Controlled Descent," the last episode of season two, what happens to Sherlock, causing him to withdraw from Joan?

QUIZ 98
"A VIEW WITH A ROOM"

"You've made a mess, Sherlock. I'm here to fix it."
—MORLAND HOLMES

Season four begins with Sherlock and Joan fired from their consulting assignment with the NYPD, and Sherlock narrowly avoids arrest for assault. As the season progresses, Sherlock is determined to resume his commitment to sobriety. The following quiz offers seven true/false statements.

1. In episode two, "Evidence of Things Not Seen," Sherlock's supervisor from Scotland Yard is responsible for getting Sherlock and Joan reinstated as consulting detectives with the NYPD.

2. In episode four, "All My Exes Live in Essex," Joan challenges Detective Cortes to a boxing match to resolve their conflict.

3. In episode seven, "Miss Taken," Joan confronts her stepfather about writing a book that closely resembles the story of her and Sherlock as consulting detectives.

4. In "A View with a Room," episode twelve, Sherlock steps out of his comfort zone by promising Joan he will become more active in AA recovery.

5. The name of the episode that refers to the title of Conan Doyle's novel, *A Study in Scarlet*, is "A Study in Charlotte."

6. In episode fifteen, "Up to Heaven and Down to Hell," Paige Cowan, Captain Gregson's girlfriend, tells him that she has brain cancer.

7. In the last episode, "A Difference in Kind," Morland announces to Sherlock while they are on the rooftop of his brownstone that Sherlock is not his son.

QUIZ 99
"MOVING TARGETS"

"For the truly evil, the path back to prison is as inevitable as the sun rising in the east."
—SHERLOCK HOLMES

Season five begins with Joan reflecting on her past life as a doctor and feeling regretful that she can no longer help medical patients in times of crisis. Here are seven short-answer questions.

1. In episode one, "Folie A Deux," what does Sherlock do when he realizes Joan is struggling emotionally over leaving her medical practice?

2. What original Conan Doyle story mentions Shinwell Johnson?

3. What does Sherlock do when he realizes Shinwell is attempting to bring down his former gang?

4. Why does Kitty Winter, once Sherlock's protégé, return to New York after disappearing three years earlier?

5. What does Joan discover that Kitty is hiding?

6. In "Moving Targets," episode twenty-two, what does Shinwell do to try and gain Joan's trust?

7. Why did Aidan Quinn not appear in season five's episode, "Serves You Right to Suffer"?

TRIVIA FACTS: DID YOU KNOW . . .

1. Lucy Liu decided to enter the world of professional acting after landing the lead in *Alice in Wonderland* during her senior year at the University of Michigan.

2. Lucy Liu's hobbies include horseback riding, rock climbing, skiing, practicing Kali-Eskrima-Silat (knife and stick fighting), and playing the accordion.

3. Although born in the United States, her family spoke Mandarin Chinese at home. She did not learn English until she was five.

4. She got her big break in 1997 when cast as the merciless Ling Woo on *Ally McBeal*.

5. Lucy Liu directed at least one episode per season after season one.

6. *"You don't want to continue to do one thing and only one thing. You want to keep challenging yourself and if you do well at it, great, if you fall on your face, you tried."* — Lucy Liu

QUIZ 100
"AN INFINITE CAPACITY FOR TAKING PAINS"

"You're not going through this alone, okay?"
—JOAN WATSON

Season six begins with Sherlock fearing he will not be able to continue his career as a detective and ends with Sherlock and Joan leaving Baker Street. Try your hand at the following seven short-answer questions.

1. In episode one, "An Infinite Capacity for Taking Pains," what career-threatening diagnosis does Sherlock tell Joan he has?

2. Why does Sherlock return to England in the last episode, "Whatever Remains, However Improbable"?

3. Why does Detective Bell consider leaving the NYPD?

4. What happens to Joan after Sherlock leaves the United States to return to London?

5. What is Joan's response when Sherlock tells her she was a much better partner when they were in New York?

6. Which episode marked Jon Michael Hill's directorial debut?

7. "The Geek Interpreter," episode nineteen, is a reference to which original Conan Doyle short story?

QUIZ 101
"THE FURTHER ADVENTURES"

"As long as we're together, it doesn't matter."
—SHERLOCK HOLMES

As *Elementary* comes to a close, Sherlock and Joan experience life-changing events and decisions. The following quiz contains eleven multiple choice questions on this last and final season.

1. In episode one, "The Further Adventures," Sherlock and Joan are working as consulting detectives for Scotland Yard in London. What brings them back to New York City?

   A. Sherlock receives a call from Captain Gregson, admitting he was covering for the murderer of Michael Rowan, the man Joan was accused of killing.

   B. Joan wants to return to New York to adopt a child.

   C. Joan is worried about the failing health of her mother.

   D. Sherlock and Joan learn Captain Gregson has been shot and is in critical condition.

2. Who do Sherlock and Joan turn to in order to stop Odin Reichenbach's vigilante crime prevention organization?

A. Captain Gregson
B. Morland Holmes
C. Moriarty
D. Scotland Yard

3. We learn Sherlock has been in exile for three years, during which time he traveled, assuming different identities and solving crimes anonymously. What did he do when he was living in France?

A. He posed as a researcher for coal tar derivatives.
B. He worked in a gallery, authenticating artwork.
C. He worked as a wine merchant.
D. He lived in an ashram.

4. What signal do Sherlock and Joan agree upon to summon him back to New York City if she needs him?

A. She is to send a message through Mrs. Hudson.
B. She is to destroy his gravestone.
C. She is to send a coded text to Lestrade, a former Scotland Yard detective.
D. She is to add a code word in a blog title.

5. Why does Joan summon Sherlock back to New York City?

A. Odin Reichenbach, now in prison, has arranged to have her killed.
B. She receives a message that Morland is alive.
C. She gets a message that Moriarty is still alive.
D. Reichenbach has escaped from prison and is tracking Sherlock's movements.

6. In the last three years since Sherlock's absence, several changes occurred in Joan's life. Which of the following is *not* one of them?

A. She dyed her hair blond.
B. She adopted a child.
C. She fell in love and got married.
D. She is diagnosed with breast cancer.

7. What turn has Detective Bell's career taken?
    A. He has been promoted to captain, taking over for Captain Gregson.
    B. He works for the FBI.
    C. He has decided to go to law school.
    D. He has decided to accept a position with the United States Marshalls Service.

8. Who tells Sherlock the secret Joan has been keeping from him?
    A. Marcus Bell
    B. Rose, the nanny and guardian Joan hired to help care for her son, Arthur.
    C. Joan's stepfather
    D. Captain Gregson

9. What did Joan do during Sherlock's absence that he viewed as revenge toward himself?
    A. She started a blog documenting Sherlock's past cases.
    B. She wrote a book about Sherlock.
    C. She remodeled the brownstone.
    D. She opened her own detective agency.

10. Whose grave is Sherlock visiting toward the end of the episode?
    A. Moriarty
    B. Paige, Captain Gregson's wife
    C. Morland
    D. Shinwell Johnson

11. What does Sherlock have in his pocket when he and Joan go into Marcus Bell's office to ask for their old jobs back?
    A. A report from Joan's doctor
    B. A new contract for Bell to sign
    C. A birthday card for Bell
    D. A list of all the NYPD cases he and Joan helped solve

HBO AND HULU'S *MISS SHERLOCK*

Japan was introduced to the world of Sherlock Holmes in 1894 with the magazine publication of "The Man with the Twisted Lip." Soon after, *A Study in Scarlet* and the collection, *The Adventures of Sherlock Holmes*, were translated into Japanese and published in newspapers. Since then, several Japanese Sherlock Holmes societies were formed, including the Baritsu Chapter of the Baker Street Irregulars. Holmes was also a master of the martial art baritsu, as readers discovered in "The Adventure of the Empty House," the first story after his hiatus. Holmes attributes his self-defense skill to practicing baritsu, which he uses to defend himself while fighting Moriarty at Reichenbach Falls.

The first episode of *Miss Sherlock* aired on April 27, 2018. The setting is modern-day Tokyo. It is the first major series to cast both Holmes and Watson as female. Sherlock is a consulting detective with the Metropolitan Police. Her roommate, Dr. Wato, often referred to as Wato-san, has just returned from volunteering medical aid in a war zone. It is co-produced by HBO Asia and Hulu Japan with English subtitles.

Cast of Main Characters:
Sara "Sherlock" Shelly Futaba: Yūko Takeuchi
Dr. Wato Tachibana: Shihori Kanjiya
Kento Futaba, Sherlock's brother: Yukiyoshi Ozawa.
Ran Itô, Sherlock's landlady: Kimi Hatano

QUIZ 102
TOKYO'S *MISS SHERLOCK*

"At times, the two of them [Holmes and Watson] complete each other, but when you try to put them together, they are like repelling magnets."
—YŪKO TAKEUCHI

Learn more about this series from the following ten short-answer questions.

Jonny Lee Miller and Lucy Liu as Sherlock Holmes and Joan Watson in CBS's
Elementary

1. How do Sherlock and Wato meet?
2. What is Sherlock doing when they meet?
3. The premise for the first case is taken from which Arthur Conan Doyle story?
4. Where is Dr. Wato returning from at the start of the series?
5. Why is Dr. Wato no longer practicing medicine?
6. What instrument does Sherlock play?
7. What does Sherlock do when she is stressed or frustrated?
8. What is the name of the secret society Sherlock battles throughout the series?
9. Besides Dr. Wato being underfoot, what other issue does Sherlock find annoying about her new roommate?
10. What governmental position does Kento Futaba hold?

Lucy Liu, Aidan Quinn, and Jonny Lee Miller as Joan, Captain Gregson, and Sherlock in CBS's *Elementary*

TEN

THE MAN BEHIND THE DETECTIVE

"I have had a life which, for variety and romance,
could, I think, hardly be exceeded. I have known
what it was to be a poor man and I have known what
it was to be fairly affluent. I have sampled
every kind of human experience."
—ARTHUR CONAN DOYLE

TO STUDY THE LIFE of Arthur Conan Doyle is to study the lives of Sherlock Holmes and Dr. Watson. In-depth information can be gleaned from knowing who Conan Doyle was, how he thought, and what his talents and interests were. Knowing Conan Doyle gives Sherlock Holmes readers a better understanding of how the author created such a brilliant collection of stories about the lives and adventures of Holmes and Watson. It stands to reason that Conan Doyle's personal attributes find their way into the hearts of these characters, giving them genuineness.

Where did Conan Doyle get the ideas for his stories? How was Holmes so easily able to deduce the unknown from observing the obvious? Conan Doyle kept a collection of crime-related news stories and often used them as springboards for writing Sherlock Holmes stories. In some cases, if the story was compelling, the author would launch his own investigation. He eventually gained a reputation as an insightful criminologist, often assisting the authorities.

In one such case in 1913, a man named Henry Williams was suspected of murdering his second wife by drowning her in the bathtub, although he was acquitted. Conan Doyle smelled a rat and, with the help of a Scotland Yard detective, was able to discover enough evidence to convict him of drowning a third wife. Henry Williams, a.k.a. John Lloyd, a.k.a. George Joseph Smith, was eventually hanged.

In his book, *The Real World of Sherlock Holmes: The True Crimes Investigated by Arthur Conan Doyle*, Peter Costello describes more than two dozen cases involving murder, disappearances, and robbery in which Conan Doyle took an active part in the investigations. In fact, at the time Conan Doyle published his first Sherlock Holmes story, Jack the Ripper was terrorizing London.

This unsolved case fascinated the author, and years later he gave an American journalist an account of how, if given the chance, Holmes could have discovered the identity of this infamous killer.

QUIZ 103
SIR ARTHUR CONAN DOYLE

Creator of Sherlock Holmes, novelist, spiritualist, sportsman, and political activist, Sir Arthur Conan Doyle was a prolific writer who made numerous contributions to several facets of society during his seventy-one years. His active life is best described in his own words: "The man who goes upon occult paths does certainly have an extraordinary variety of experiences." The following quiz contains ten short-answer questions about Conan Doyle and his family.

1. When was Arthur Conan Doyle born?
2. How many children did Conan Doyle's parents, Charles Doyle and Mary Foley Doyle, have?
3. Where did Conan Doyle study medicine?
4. Who was Conan Doyle's first wife and in what year were they married?
5. Where did Conan Doyle set up his first medical practice?
6. Which family member was the greatest influence in Conan Doyle's life?
7. Who did Conan Doyle marry almost a year after his first wife's death on September 18, 1907?
8. How many children did Conan Doyle have?
9. In what year was Conan Doyle knighted?
10. Who was Conan Doyle's greatest literary influence?

TRIVIA FACTS : DID YOU KNOW THAT . . .

1. Conan Doyle stood for Parliament in 1901 and 1907 as a Unionist candidate from Edinburgh, but lost both times. His strong opinions concerning Britain's part in the Boer War and his opposition to Ireland's independence may have contributed to his unsuccessful attempt at winning the seat.

2. Long before Jurassic Park Conan Doyle's novel *The Lost World* was made into a successful motion picture in 1925, starring Wallace Beery as Professor Challenger. The film included animated creatures created by filmmaker Willis O'Brien, who later created the techniques for King Kong.

QUIZ 104
BEYOND SHERLOCK HOLMES

Although best known for his Sherlock Holmes detective stories, Conan Doyle wrote dozens of novels, nonfiction books, plays, and articles concerning his passions, political beliefs, and spiritual experiences. These publications give the reader an insight into the creator of Sherlock Holmes which cannot be found in the canon. The following quiz contains ten short-answer questions about these literary works.

1. In which book did Conan Doyle write about his time in private practice with the eccentric and sometimes cruel and unethical Dr. George Budd?

2. What is the name of Conan Doyle's book in which he defends the sighting of fairies by two young girls in Yorkshire?

3. What is the title of Conan Doyle's novel set in the seventeenth century, in which the Duke of Monmouth

battled King James II when he tried to reinstate Catholicism in England?

4. What are the names of Conan Doyle's two books based on the life of Baron de Marbot?

5. In 1891 Conan Doyle and his wife traveled to Vienna. What did he write in order to pay for this trip?

6. Which Conan Doyle historical romance is set in the fourteenth century and features a protagonist named Alleyne Edricson who fights for France and later returns to England?

7. What is the name of Conan Doyle's 1912 novel that features Professor Challenger and three companions who travel to South America where they encounter dinosaurs which have survived from ancient times?

8. What is the title of Conan Doyle's 1896 novel about the world of boxing?

9. In 1909 Conan Doyle wrote a political account of the conflict between Belgium and the Congo. His strong beliefs concerning the situation resulted in a 45,000-word book which he wrote in eight days. What is the

---

TRIVIA FACTS : DID YOU KNOW THAT . . .

1. When Conan Doyle sent Holmes over Reichenbach Falls, his final comment in his notebook was, "Killed Holmes."

2. As Conan Doyle's interest in spiritualism increased, almost to the point of being an obsession in his later life, he had the nursery of his stately mansion turned into a séance room.

3. Once Conan Doyle ceased practicing medicine and began writing full time, his work schedule increased, often beginning at 6:30 A. M. and continuing until three or four o'clock on the following morning.

---

name of this book, praised by Theodore Roosevelt and
Mark Twain?

10. What is the name of Conan Doyle's 1929 book about
explorers who travel via a diving bell deep into the
Atlantic Ocean? The cable breaks upon their descent,
and they are rescued by descendants of Atlantis.

One character may have been based on Conan Doyle's friend
Harry Houdini.

QUIZ 105
THE SPIRITUAL WORLD OF
ARTHUR CONAN DOYLE

World War I had ended, but not before it had taken its toll on the
survivors. Conan Doyle's son, Kingsley, and his younger brother,
Innes, both died of pneumonia, the former due to complications
which set in after being wounded in battle. While her son was still
recovering from the loss of his son and brother, Conan Doyle's
mother, the most influential person in his life, Mary Doyle, died at
the age of eighty. The entire world was grieving in the aftermath
of the war, and the overall atmosphere was one of questioning and
confusion.

Conan Doyle, like so many others, turned to the world of spiritualism and mystic phenomena to help explain these tragedies.
The following ten-question quiz concerns Conan Doyle's spiritual
writings, beliefs, and experiences.

1. What was the title of Conan Doyle's first book on
spiritualism published after World War I?

2. While in the United States, Conan Doyle and his
second wife Jean attended a séance in Atlantic City.
Which famous celebrity also attended the event?

3. What is the name of the spiritual journal in which
Conan Doyle wrote passionate letters about his belief in
spiritualism? The letters were inspired by spiritual leader

TRIVIA FACTS : DID YOU KNOW THAT . . .

1. When the Earl of Carnarvon, financier of the excavation of King Tut's tomb, became ill and died, Conan Doyle was convinced that he was a victim of an ancient Egyptian curse which condemns anyone who disturbs a mummy's eternal rest.

2. Even in his sixties, Conan Doyle's passion and curiosity for life seemed to escalate. On the way to and from the golf course, Conan Doyle often asked his chauffeur to drop him off on the side of the road so that he could converse with whomever happened to be walking by. On one snowy winter's day, Conan Doyle visited with a tramp, asking him about his life and eventually bonding with the old man. Later Conan Doyle arrived home barefooted because he had given his shoes to his new friend.

3. On July 7, 1930, Sir Arthur Conan Doyle died in his home with his wife by his side. Within days, spiritualists and mediums from around the world claimed that the author had made contact with them from the "other side." Joseph Dunninger, director of the Science Investigating Committee of Psychic Phenomena, claimed that a ghostly figure resembling Conan Doyle had told him that he wanted a pencil and paper because he wanted to write a book while he was there.

and member of the Society for Psychical Research, Major-General Alfred W. Drayson.

4. What was the name of Conan Doyle's collection of spiritual essays written shortly before his death?

5. As he advanced in age and became less inhibited about expressing his spiritual beliefs, no matter how profound, what did Conan Doyle do to promote and support the causes in which he believed?

6. What is the title of Conan Doyle's second spiritualistic book, which may be one of his most popular? After it was published in 1919, he enthusiastically promoted the book while on an extensive book-signing tour.

7. Conan Doyle attended a séance in London, which was conducted by a well-known medium. With whom did she claim to have made contact, causing Conan Doyle to launch an investigation as to her credibility?

8. With which science fiction author did Conan Doyle frequently correspond on the subject of spiritualism and the concept of contacting deceased individuals from the afterlife?

9. After his lecture tour through Australia in 1920, what book did Conan Doyle write about his spiritual experiences?

10. What was the name of the American organization that formed a committee, which included Harry Houdini, to investigate the mediums that Conan Doyle claimed were bona fide?

Mark Gatiss as Mycroft Holmes in BBC's *Sherlock*.

ELEVEN
CROSSWORD PUZZLES

*"The number of Napoleons plus the
number of Randall gang"*

"The kind of Pedro whence came the tiger"

*"What was done of the opposite wall in
bullet-pocks by the patriotic Holmes"*

*"Holmes found this because he was
looking for it in the mud."*

The above clues were just a few featured on the original Sherlock Holmes crossword puzzle created by Frank V. Morley, one of the founders of the original Baker Street Irregulars in 1934. In order to gain admission into the club and be able to attend the first dinner of the society, applicants had to complete the puzzle, which appeared in the *Saturday Review of Literature*. The famous dinner was held at the Christ Cella Restaurant in New York with members Rex Stout, John Bennett Shaw, and Frederic Dorr Steele.

The five crossword puzzles in this chapter feature characters, creatures, aliases, modus operandi, and story titles. Answering the trivia questions in the first nine chapters or taking a preliminary peek at the answer section will give hints to some of the clues.

PUZZLE 1
CHEMICALS, CLUES, AND DEADLY THINGS

*Indicates puzzle theme.

ACROSS

1. "The Adventure of the Priory School" (monograph)*
3. "The Adventure of the Veiled Lodger" (corrosive)*
8. "The Adventure of the Blanched Soldier" (disease)*
9. "The Red-Headed League" (reference book)
12. *The Hound of the Baskervilles* (footwear)*
14. "The Adventure of the Devil's Foot" (poison)*

15. *The Sign of Four* (slimy dinner dish)

19. "The Five Orange Pips" (organization)

20. "The Adventure of the Abbey Grange" (wine residue)*

21. "The Adventure of the Empty House" (weapon)*

DOWN

2. "The Disappearance of Lady Frances Carfax" (anesthetic)*

4. *The Sign of Four* (tar)*

5. "The Adventure of Charles Augustus Milverton" (crime)

6. "The Adventure of the Second Stain" (smear)*

7. "The Man with the Twisted Lip" (drug)*

10. "Silver Blaze" (spice)*

11. "The Adventure of the Sussex Vampire" (dart)*

13. "The Adventure of the Bruce-Partington Plans" (machine)

16. *The Sign of Four* (Andaman native)

17. "Silver Blaze" (weapon)*

18. *The Hound of the Baskervilles* (scented clue)*

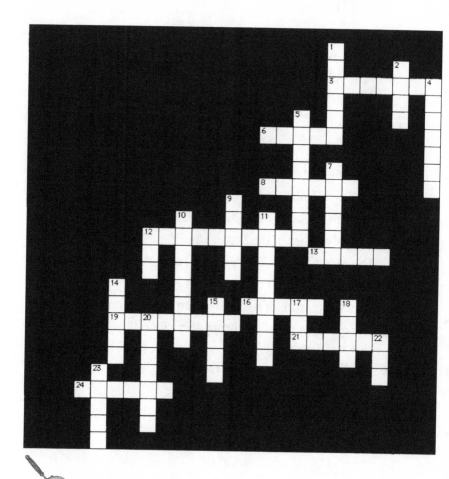

PUZZLE 2
A.K.A.

*Indicates puzzle theme.

ACROSS

3. Nickname for Perry Phelps in "The Naval Treaty"*

6. Morecroft in "The Adventure of the Three Garridebs"*

8. Holmes in "The Stock-broker's Clerk"*

12. Steve Dixie in "The Adventure of the Three Gables"*
13. The King of Bohemia in "A Scandal in Bohemia"*
16. Dr. Watson in "The Stock-broker's Clerk"*
19. James Ryder in "The Adventure of the Blue Carbuncle"*
21. Duncan Ross in "The Red-Headed League"*
24. Dr. Watson in "The Adventure of the Illustrious Client"*

DOWN

1. Dr. Shlessinger in "The Disappearance of Lady Frances Carfax"*
2. Number of Holmes novels written by Conan Doyle
4. John McMurdo in *The Valley of Fear*
5. Ted Baldwin in *The Valley of Fear*
7. One of the Beddington brothers in "The Stock-broker's Clerk"*
9. Holmes in "The Adventure of Black Peter"*
10. Device used to create carbonated water for mixing drinks
11. Don Murillo in "The Adventure of Wisteria Lodge"*
12. Initials for Holmes's fan club
14. Number of Garridebs
15. Nickname for Shinwell Johnson in "The Adventure of the Illustrious Client"*
17. Initials of notorious blackmailer
18. Collection of stolen jewels in *The Sign of Four*
20. Evans in "The *Gloria Scott*"*
22. Number of Napoleons
23. Black Peter in "The Adventure of Black Peter"*

PUZZLE 3
IN OTHER WORDS
(REWORDED TITLES)

*Indicates puzzle theme.

ACROSS

3. Last Conflict*
4. Initials for submarine schematics
5. Splotched Stripe*
10. Sacred writings

11. Vined Cottage*
12. Brassy Wood*
15. Bright Customer*
19. Crown
20. Official abbreviation for "The Musgrave Ritual"
21. Official abbreviation for "The Adventure of the Mazarin Stone"
22. Maritime Act*
24. Twisted Guy*
25. Pale Front*
26. Prancing Fellows*
27. Official abbreviation for "The Adventure of the Priory School"
28. Masked Resident*

DOWN
1. Diamond
2. Unoccupied Dwelling*
6. Builder
7. Final Bend*
8. Official abbreviation for *The Valley of Fear*
9. Official abbreviation for "The Adventure of the Golden Pince-Nez"
13. Eye Glasses*
14. Satin's Appendage*
16. Jellyfish*
17. Official abbreviation for "The Stock-broker's Clerk"
18. Bloodthirsty*
20. Official abbreviation for "The Adventure of the Missing Three-Quarter"
23. Official abbreviation for "The Adventure of the Retired Colourman"
24. Official abbreviation for "The Adventure of the Creeping Man"

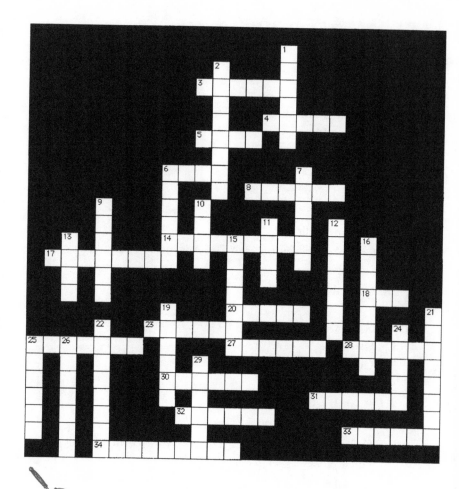

PUZZLE 4
BUTLERS, MAIDS, VALETS, ETC.

*Indicates puzzle theme.

ACROSS

3. Cook and housekeeper for the Tregennis family in "The Adventure of the Devil's Foot"

4. Sherlock Holmes's page

5. Cook at Riding Thorpe Manor in "The Adventure of the Dancing Men"
6. Don Murillo's valet in "The Adventure of Wisteria Lodge"
8. Countess Morcar's maid in "The Adventure of the Blue Carbuncle"
14. Bartholomew Sholto's housekeeper in *The Sign of Four*
17. Housemaid for the Hilton Cubitts in "The Adventure of the Dancing Men"
18. Indian butler of Bartholomew Sholto in *The Sign of Four*
20. Maid of Hatty Doran in "The Adventure of the Noble Bachelor"
23. Former gardener at High Gable in "The Adventure of Wisteria Lodge"
25. Robert Ferguson's stableboy in "The Adventure of the Sussex Vampire"
27. Holmes's first housekeeper
28. Jephro Rucastle's groom in "The Adventure of the Copper Beeches"
30. Stableboy in "The Adventure of Shoscombe Old Place"
31. John Straker's maid in "Silver Blaze"
32. Housemaid of Charles Augustus Milverton in "The Adventure of Charles Augustus Milverton"
33. Lady Frances Carfax's maid in "The Disappearance of Lady Frances Carfax"
34. Jonas Oldacre's housekeeper in "The Norwood Builder"

DOWN
1. Cunningham's coachman in "The Reigate Squires"
2. Gardener at Yoxley Old Place in "The Adventure of the Golden Pince-Nez"

6. Butler at Whitehall Terrace in "The Adventure of the Second Stain"

7. Housekeeper of Professor Coram in "The Adventure of the Golden Pince-Nez"

9. Childhood governess of Lady Frances Carfax in "The Disappearance of Lady Frances Carfax"

10. Second waiting maid in "The Adventure of the Beryl Coronet"

11. Charles McCarthy's groom in "The Boscombe Valley Mystery"

12. Maid of Mrs. Ferguson in "The Adventure of the Sussex Vampire"

13. Openshaw's servant in "The Five Orange Pips"

15. Housemaid to the Barclays in "The Crooked Man"

16. Eugenia Ronder's landlady in "The Adventure of the Veiled Lodger"

19. Von Bork's housekeeper in "His Last Bow"

21. Dr. Watson's clumsy housekeeper in "A Scandal in Bohemia"

22. Coachman for Professor Presbury in "The Adventure of the Creeping Man"

24. Housekeeper at Birlstone Manor in *The Valley of Fear*

25. Eduardo Lucas's valet in "The Adventure of the Second Stain"

26. John Turner's gamekeeper in "The Boscombe Valley Mystery"

29. Housemaid and nurse of Lady Brackenstall in "The Adventure of the Abbey Grange"

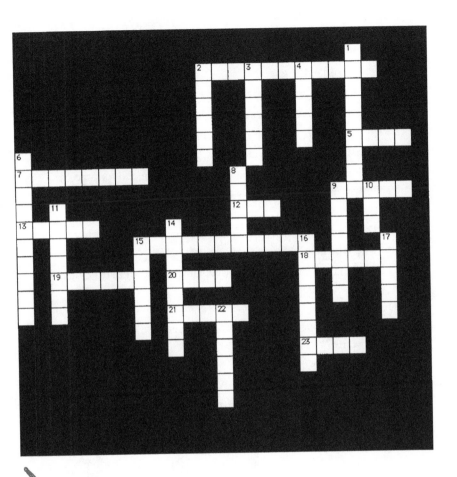

PUZZLE 5
CANINES AND OTHER CREATURES

*Indicates puzzle theme.

ACROSS

2. Victor Trevor's dog in "The *Gloria Scott*"*

5. Number of pips

7. Fitzroy McPherson's dog in "The Adventure of the Lion's Mane"*

9. Number of gables

12. Rodent featured in the unchronicled Holmes case of Matilda Briggs*

13. Animal with phosphorus eyes*

15. Chester Wilcox's dogs in *The Valley of Fear*

18. Sir Robert Norberton's racehorse in "The Adventure of Shoscombe Old Place"*

19. Part foxhound and part beagle in "The Adventure of the Missing Three-Quarter"*

20. Part spaniel and part lurcher in *The Sign of Four*

21. Christmas dinner in "The Adventure of the Blue Carbuncle"*

23. Sahara King of "The Adventure of the Veiled Lodger"*

DOWN

1. Deadly sea creature in "The Adventure of the Lion's Mane"*

2. Holmes's sport

3. Primate responsible for Professor Presbury's odd behavior in "The Adventure of the Creeping Man"

4. Watson's sport

6. One type of animal featured in "The Adventure of Shoscombe Old Place"*

8. Mastiff in "The Adventure of the Copper Beeches"*

9. Mrs. Hudson's dog in *A Study in Scarlet*

10. Wolfhound in "The Adventure of the Creeping Man"*

11. Dr. Watson's dog in *A Study in Scarlet*

14. Holmes's first London address

15. Horse owned by Colonel Ross in "Silver Blaze"*

16. Another type of animal featured in "The Adventure of Shoscombe Old Place"*

17. Pet mongoose of Henry Wood in "The Crooked Man"*

22. County where Holmes retired

ANSWERS TO QUIZZES

QUIZ 1

Easy

1. Mycroft Holmes
2. Violin
3. Professor James Moriarty
4. Irene Adler
5. Bradley's on Oxford Street
6. Mrs. Hudson
7. Chemistry

Moderate

8. "How are you? You have been in Afghanistan, I perceive."
9. Coffee
10. It is a gift from the King of Bohemia for Holmes's assistance in the case of "A Scandal in Bohemia."
11. Scotch and soda
12. Mrs. Turner
13. The agony columns
14. Seventy-five

Difficult

15. Seventeen
16. The Capital and Counties on Oxford Street
17. Coffee and curaçao
18. Two
19. "The Adventure of the Abbey Grange"
20. *Anthropological Journal*

QUIZ 2

1. Sir George Burnwell—"The Adventure of the Beryl Coronet"
2. Henderson—"The Adventure of Wisteria Lodge"
3. J. Neil Gibson—"The Problem of Thor Bridge"
4. Hudson—"The *Gloria Scott*"
5. Fitzroy Simpson—"Silver Blaze"
6. Anderson—"The Adventure of the Lion's Mane"
7. Irene Adler—"A Scandal in Bohemia"
8. Hugh Boone—"The Man with the Twisted Lip"
9. Mycroft Holmes—"The Greek Interpreter"
10. Reginald Musgrave—"The Musgrave Ritual"
11. Professor Moriarty—"The Final Problem"
12. Victor Trevor Jr.—"The *Gloria Scott*"
13. Maud Bellamy—"The Adventure of the Lion's Mane"
14. Jonathan Small—*The Sign of Four*
15. Inspector Bardle—"The Adventure of the Lion's Mane"

PART 1

1. B. Location where the body of Enoch J. Drebber was found—*A Study in Scarlet*

2. A. Hotel in Lyons, France, where Holmes was convalescing—"The Reigate Squires"

3. F. Stables owned by Colonel Ross—"Silver Blaze"

4. C. Area where Holmes hid out while conducting his investigation—*The Hound of the Baskervilles*

5. G. Residence of Hatty Doran—"The Adventure of the Noble Bachelor"

6. D. Residence of Reginald Musgrave—"The Musgrave Ritual"

7. I. Home of Major Sholto—*The Sign of Four*

8. J. Desert where John Ferrier and Lucy were rescued—*A Study in Scarlet*

9. E. Residence of Grimesby Roylott and Helen Stoner—"The Adventure of the Speckled Band"

10. H. Hotel near Reichenbach Falls where Holmes and Watson stayed—"The Final Problem"

QUIZ 3

PART 2

1. A. Inn owned by Reuben Hayes—"The Adventure of the Priory School"

2. H. Home of Josiah Amberley—"The Adventure of the Retired Colourman"

3. D. Holmes's retirement village—"The Adventure of the Lion's Mane"

4. E. Address of Inspector Stanley Hopkins—"The Adventure of Black Peter"

5. J. Murder site of Ronald Adair—"The Adventure of the Empty House"

6. B. Restaurant in the Strand frequented by Holmes and Watson—"The Adventure of the Dying Detective" and "The Adventure of the Illustrious Client"

7. G. House across the street from 221B Baker Street from which Sebastian Moran tried to shoot Holmes—"The Adventure of the Empty House"

8. C. Residence of Colonel Emsworth—"The Adventure of the Blanched Soldier"

9. I. Coastal town in Ireland where Holmes spied for the British government—"His Last Bow"

10. F. Moor near the Priory School—"The Adventure of the Priory School"

QUIZ 4

1. "The Man with the Twisted Lip"
2. "The Adventure of the Noble Bachelor"
3. "The Adventure of the Beryl Coronet"
4. "The Adventure of the Creeping Man"
5. "The Adventure of the Bruce-Partington Plans"
6. *The Valley of Fear*
7. "The Adventure of the Copper Beeches"
8. "The Problem of Thor Bridge"
9. "The Final Problem"
10. "The Adventure of the Empty House"
11. "The Boscombe Valley Mystery"
12. "The Naval Treaty"
13. *The Hound of the Baskervilles*
14. "The Adventure of the Illustrious Client"
15. "The Man with the Twisted Lip"
16. "A Case of Identity"
17. *The Sign of Four*
18. "The Disappearance of Lady Frances Carfax"
19. "The Adventure of the Three Gables"
20. "The Adventure of the Lion's Mane"

QUIZ 5

1. Considering the year Watson entered the university, he was probably born in the early 1850s.
2. University of London in 1878
3. St. Bartholomew's Hospital
4. Rugby
5. An Eley's No. 2 revolver
6. He was involved in the Afghan campaign when he was shot by a Jezail bullet at the Battle of Maiwand.
7. Arcadia mixture
8. In 1888 Watson purchased Dr. Farquhar's practice in Paddington. In 1890 he was practicing in Kensington, and in 1902 he was on Queen Anne Street.
9. July 1888
10. "The Naval Treaty"
11. "The Man with the Twisted Lip"
12. Mary Jane
13. 1914
14. The records are kept in a tin dispatch box with John H. Watson, M.D., Late Indian Army stamped on it. The box is kept in a bank vault in Cox and Co. Bank.
15. Seventeen

QUIZ 6

1. James
2. Moriarty has two brothers: an older brother who is a colonel and who is also named James, and a younger brother who is a station master in the West of England.
3. Mathematics
4. *The Dynamics of the Asteroid*
5. 700 pounds a year
6. Jean Baptiste Greuze
7. They are murdered.
8. Colonel Sebastian Moran earns 6,000 pounds a year.
9. Three
10. Dr. Watson sees Moriarty at Victoria Station.

QUIZ 7

1. Seven years
2. The Diogenes Club
3. Every day between 4:45 and 7:40 P.M.
4. He apparently is an auditor for the government.
5. Pall Mall
6. "A light, watery gray . . . , " according to Watson
7. Tortoiseshell
8. Red silk
9. No one is allowed to speak. If this rule is broken three times, the member is expelled.
10. 450 pounds a year

QUIZ 8

1. For the first and only time in Watson's life, he faints.
2. Holmes used his knowledge and skill of the Japanese system of wrestling called baritsu.
3. Holmes was gone for three years.
4. For two years, Holmes was in Tibet, then Norway, Persia, and France.
5. Holmes researched coal tar derivatives.
6. Holmes returns to his room on Baker Street at two o'clock in the afternoon.
7. Holmes learned that only one of his enemies remained in London, and he felt safe in returning.
8. Holmes's brother knew that he was still alive.
9. Sigerson
10. The villain in his first case was Professor Moriarty's Chief of Staff.

QUIZ 9

1. "The Adventure of the Solitary Cyclist" (To Bob Carruthers from Jack Woodley)
2. *The Valley of Fear* (To Sherlock Holmes from Fred Porlock)
3. "The Disappearance of Lady Frances Carfax" (To Sherlock

Holmes from the manager of the Englischer Hof)

4. "The Problem of Thor Bridge" (To Mrs. Gibson from Grace Dunbar)

5. "His Last Bow" (To Von Bork from Altamont)

6. "The Adventure of the Creeping Man" (To Watson from Holmes)

7. *The Sign of Four* (To Mary Morstan from an unknown friend)

8. "The Adventure of the Lion's Mane" (To Fitzroy McPherson from Maudie Bellamy)

9. "The Adventure of Wisteria Lodge" (To Mr. García from D)

10. "The Adventure of the Retired Colourman" (To Josiah Amberley supposedly from Elman, the Vicar)

11. "The Adventure of the Noble Bachelor" (To Hattie Doran from F. H. M.)

12. "The Five Orange Pips" (To James Calhoun from Sherlock Holmes)

13. "The Yellow Face" (To Sherlock Holmes from Grant Munro)

14. "The Five Orange Pips" (To Joseph Openshaw from unknown)

15. "The *Gloria Scott*" (To Trevor Sr. from Beddoes)

QUIZ 10

1. "The Adventure of Abbey Grange"

2. "The Adventure of Black Peter"

3. "The Adventure of the Bruce-Partington Plans"

4. "The Five Orange Pips"

5. "A Case of Identity"

6. *A Study in Scarlet*

7. "The Adventure of Charles Augustus Milverton"

8. "The Adventure of the Three Gables"

9. "The Adventure of the Engineer's Thumb"

10. "A Scandal in Bohemia"

11. "The Naval Treaty"

12. "The Reigate Squires"

13. "The Adventure of Wisteria Lodge"

14. "The Adventure of the Empty House"

15. "The Adventure of the Missing Three-Quarter"

16. "The Final Problem"

17. "The Adventure of the Copper Beeches"

18. "The Boscombe Valley Mystery"

19. *The Sign of Four*

20. "The Adventure of the Beryl Coronet"

21. "The Greek Interpreter"

22. *The Hound of the Baskervilles*

23. "The Problem of Thor Bridge"

24. "The Adventure of the Norwood Builder"

25. "The Adventure of the Devil's Foot"

26. "The Adventure of the Dancing Men"

27. "The Adventure of the Three Garridebs"

28. "The Adventure of the Solitary Cyclist"

29. "The Adventure of the Mazarin Stone"

30. "The Adventure of the Lion's Mane"

QUIZ 11

1. Alexander Holder in "The Adventure of the Beryl Coronet"

2. Mary Morstan in *The Sign of Four*

3. Sherlock Holmes in *A Study in Scarlet*

4. Mary Holder in "The Adventure of the Beryl Coronet"

5. Mary Sutherland in "A Case of Identity"

6. Annie Harrison in "The Naval Treaty"

7. Mr. Thaddeus Sholto in *The Sign of Four*

8. Inspector Lestrade in "The Boscombe Valley Mystery"

9. Dr. Grimesby Roylott in "The Adventure of the Speckled Band"

10. Dr. Percy Trevelyan in "The Resident Patient"

11. Violet Hunter in "The Adventure of the Copper Beeches"

12. Victor Hatherley in "The Adventure of the Engineer's Thumb"

13. The King of Bohemia in "A Scandal in Bohemia"

14. Jabez Wilson in "The Red-Headed League"

15. Henry Baker in "The Adventure of the Blue Carbuncle"

MAKING THE GRADE

At the end of each chapter, total the number of correct answers to determine how well you know the Great Detective, and how skilled you are at solving mysteries.

Level	Total Correct Answers
Deductive Genius	241–315
Holmes's Apprentice	161–240
Watson's Apprentice	81–160
Moriarty's Victim	0–80

QUIZ 12

PART 1

Characters

1. Inspector Tobias Gregson

2. Constable John Rance

3. A red-faced drunken man wearing a brown coat

4. A person dressed as an old woman, claiming to be Mrs.

Sawyer, mother of the woman who lost the ring

5. A group of young boys, who Holmes refers to as his "division of the detective police force," led by a boy named Wiggins

6. Arthur Charpentier, the brother of a girl to whom Drebber made advances

7. Madame Charpentier gives Gregson information concerning Drebber's activities on the evening he was murdered.

8. Stangerson was stabbed.

9. A milk boy saw a man descending the ladder which was placed at Stangerson's window.

10. Wiggins finds the cab driver and brings him to Holmes.

Clues

1. Holmes sniffs the dead man's lips and studies the soles of his boots.

2. A woman's wedding ring

3. There are two letters in the dead man's pockets—one addressed to E. J. Drebber and the other to Joseph Stangerson.

4. The man was about to sail for New York.

5. On the wall, written in blood, are the letters, RACHE.

6. Holmes gathered up a pile of gray dust.

7. Trichinopoly cigar

8. The letter "A" was not written in a fashion typical of the language which it was supposed to represent.

9. After noticing the address of the hat maker on the inside of Drebber's hat, Inspector Gregson was able to trace Drebber's address.

10. Lestrade discovered an ointment box containing gray pills.

Circumstances

1. Holmes examines the outside of the house first—the ground, pavement, and railings.

2. Holmes refers to the men as Patent leather shoes and Square-toes.

3. Holmes wants to attend a concert that afternoon.

4. Holmes plays with a half-sovereign while questioning the constable.

5. The constable saw a light coming from the abandoned house.

6. Holmes places an ad in the lost and found section of the paper, announcing that he had found a ring.

7. The *Daily Telegraph* blames the Socialists.

8. The *Standard* blames the Liberal administration.

9. The *Daily News* blames Liberalism.

10. Once Drebber perceived that he was being followed, Charpentier gave up the chase and spent the rest of the evening with a shipmate.

QUIZ 12

PART 2

1. Part two takes places in the western United States near Sierra Blanco.

2. They were all that was left of a party traveling to the West. They got lost and ran out of food and water.

3. A group of Mormons rescued the starving pair.

4. John Ferrier had won the admiration and respect of the four elders, and upon settling, they presented him with a large farm.

5. Jefferson Hope was prospecting for silver.

6. John Ferrier received a visit from Brigham Young. Young had selected two potential husbands for Lucy, Mr. Stangerson or Mr. Drebber, and Lucy had one month to decide.

7. Ferrier received a daily message reminding him how many days he had left before his daughter would have to marry one of the two men.

8. The code was "nine to seven," and the response was "seven to five."

9. A month after being forced to marry Drebber, Lucy died of grief.

10. Jefferson Hope died in jail of an aneurism.

QUIZ 13

Characters

1. Mary contacted Major Sholto, her father's friend who served in the same regiment.

2. Bartholomew is angry with his brother for revealing the treasure's existence to Miss Morstan.

3. Major Sholto hired two prize-fighters as bodyguards.

4. He had a heart attack while arguing with Major Sholto.

5. Holmes reminds McMurdo that they had once fought one another in an amateur match many years ago.

6. Mrs. Bernstone, the housekeeper, cannot get her employer to open his door or answer her pleas.

7. Holmes sends Watson after Toby, the best tracking hound in the business.

8. Inspector Jones arrests Thaddeus Sholto, the prize-fighter McMurdo, the gatekeeper, the housekeeper, and the Indian servant.

9. Holmes hires Wiggins and his street gang.

10. Watson and Jones fire their pistols at the same time.

THE SHERLOCK HOLMES QUIZ BOOK

Clues

1. The Greek "e" and the twirl of the "s" are the same.

2. While Major Sholto's sons searched the garden for the man in the window, their father's room was searched, and a note was placed upon his chest.

3. Bartholomew added up the square footage of the house and realized that four feet were unaccounted for, indicating a hidden room.

4. "The sign of the four"

5. Holmes finds an impression of a wooden stump and a boot mark.

6. Holmes finds blood on the rope, indicating that the man rubbed the skin off his hands while sliding down the rope.

7. Homes finds another footprint in the attic.

8. The victim's muscles are in a state of extreme contraction.

9. The footprint is very tiny, and the toes are distinctly divided by a wide space.

10. The person stepped in creosote.

Circumstances

1. Ten years

2. Major Sholto was about to reveal to his sons where the treasure was hidden when he saw a face in the window and then dropped dead.

3. Watson has fallen in love with Mary and is afraid that if she becomes a rich heiress, she will have no interest in him.

4. Following the scent, the dog takes Holmes to a timber-yard, where the wheels of the trolley are smeared with the same substance which the criminal stepped in.

5. *Aurora*

6. The fugitive's wooden leg stump sinks into the soil on the river bank, preventing him from escaping.

7. Jonathan Small throws the treasure overboard, piece by piece.

8. He waits twenty years to get his hands on the treasure.

9. Small was attacked by a crocodile while swimming in the Ganges River.

10. The Great Mogul, the second largest stone in existence

QUIZ 14

Characters

1. Hugo Baskerville wrote the manuscript.

2. Barrymore, the butler of Baskerville Hall

3. Holmes hires a boy named Cartwright to aid in the investigation.

4. Sherlock Holmes

5. Holmes suspects the groom of Baskerville Hall, two moorland farmers, Dr.

Mortimer, his wife, Stapleton, Stapleton's sister, Mr. Frankland, and one or two other neighbors.

6. Selden saw the stranger on the moor.

7. Holmes brings his young messenger, Cartwright.

8. Beryl Stapleton warns Sir Henry about brewing trouble.

9. Holmes notices the man's resemblance in a Baskerville family portrait.

10. Stapleton is sucked into the mire.

Clues

1. Dr. Mortimer notices that the ash from his cigar has dropped twice.

2. Sir Charles's footprints were of the toes only, indicating that he was running.

3. Holmes recognizes the "bourgeois" type used by the *Times.*

4. An unworn brown boot and a black boot are stolen from Sir Henry.

5. Watson hears a woman sobbing from somewhere in the hall.

6. Sir Charles had a rendezvous with a woman.

7. Holmes finds Watson's cigarette stub.

8. Selden wore Sir Henry's clothes, and the hound followed Sir Henry's scent.

9. Holmes detects a scent of white jessamine.

10. The incident of the convict on the moor and his relationship to the Barrymores complicates the case.

Circumstances

1. The story takes place in 1889.

2. Holmes assigns the messanger-boy, Cartwright, to search for the newspaper.

3. Holmes warns Sir Henry by quoting from the Baskerville manuscript: "avoid the moor in those hours of darkness when the powers of evil are exalted."

4. When they step from the coach, the first thing they notice is a mounted soldier holding his rifle and peering over the moor.

5. The mire on the moor is called Grimpen Mire.

6. Archeologists have found remains of a Neolithic man on the moor.

7. Stapleton invites Watson to view his butterfly collection.

8. Dr. Watson finds a note that says, "Dr. Watson has gone to Coombe Tracey."

9. The hound is kept in the tin mine.

10. Beryl Stapleton is tied up and cannot warn Sir Henry of impending danger.

QUIZ 15

PART 1

Characters

1. A man name Fred Porlock, who was an informant in Professor Moriarty's gang

2. Inspector Alec MacDonald

3. John Douglas was shot in the face with a shotgun at close range.

4. John Douglas and Cecil James Barker met in America.

5. White Mason

6. Bodymaster McGinty

7. Mrs. Douglas asks Watson if Holmes would keep confidential information from the police.

8. Holmes believes that Mrs. Douglas and Mr. Barker are lying.

9. They could have been describing Mr. Douglas.

10. Mr. Ames, the butler, allows Holmes to use the study.

Clues

1. A bloody print made from a boot

2. A card with the initials V. V. and the number 341 were found near the dead man's body.

3. The murderer stole Mr. Douglas's wedding ring.

4. If the murder was premeditated, as it appears, why then did the murderer choose a loud gun for a weapon?

5. There is a piece of plaster on Mr. Douglas's jaw, indicating that he may have cut himself shaving.

6. Holmes notices only one dumbbell under the side table. The other one is missing.

7. Mrs. Douglas smiles slightly when she is told that her husband's wedding ring is missing.

8. Holmes notices that Mrs. Douglas is not grieving, and that she has eaten a rather healthy meal.

9. Holmes finds the real murder weapon, along with a complete suit of men's clothing.

10. Holmes deduces that the initials V. V. stand for Vermissa Valley.

Circumstances

1. The moat bridge is usually lowered around sunset.

2. Mr. Douglas had a scar in the shape of a triangle inside a circle on his right forearm.

3. Since he was in his dressing gown when he was murdered, Douglas did not have his revolver with him. He always kept his revolver in his pocket.

4. Holmes is full of energy, with an excellent appetite.

5. The servants usually retire between 10:30 P.M. and 11:00 P.M.

6. The sound is muffled.

7. Holmes asks Watson if he would be afraid to sleep in the same room with a lunatic.

8. Holmes sends a message to Mr. Barker that the moat will be drained by morning.

9. February 1875

10. John Douglas was acquitted as having acted in self-defense.

QUIZ 15

PART 2

1. Jack McGinty

2. McMurdo stayed in a boarding house owned by Jacob Shafter.

3. McMurdo took a job as a bookkeeper.

4. McGinty stole public money, bribed auditors, and blackmailed citizens into paying him large sums of money.

5. McMurdo killed a man.

6. McMurdo was a counterfeiter.

7. McGinty branded McMurdo's right forearm with a circle surrounding a triangle.

8. He was arrested for the beating of James Stanger.

9. McMurdo was assigned to kill Chester Wilcox, the chief foreman of the Iron Dyke

Company, along with his family.

10. McGinty was hanged, and Baldwin was sentenced to ten years in prison.

MAKING THE GRADE

Level	Total Correct Answers
Deductive Genius	226–300
Holmes' Apprentice	151–225
Watson's Apprentice	76–150
Moriarty's Victim	0–75

QUIZ 16

1. B. Watson has gained seven and a half pounds.

2. C. He wears a black mask over his face.

3. A. A photograph of the King and Miss Adler, which proves that they had an affair

4. D. Five

5. D. Irene Adler plans to send the item(s) to the fiancée's family, the King of Scandinavia.

6. C. An ill-kept groom and a benevolent clergyman

7. A. Holmes has Watson throw a smoke rocket into her room and shout "Fire!".

8. A. She falls in love with another man and marries him.

9. D. The sovereign that she gave Holmes for assisting

her in the Church of St. Monica

10. B. The photograph that Irene Adler left behind

QUIZ 17

1. The pink-stained fish tattoo on his right wrist is of a Chinese design, and Mr. Wilson had Chinese coins dangling from his watch chain.

2. Ezekiah Hopkins is a fictitious person who is supposedly an American millionaire who founded the Red-Headed League.

3. Jabez Wilson is the owner of a small pawnbroker's business at Coburg Square.

4. Mr. Wilson was asked to copy the *Encyclopedia Britannica*, and he was required to work from 10:00 A. M. to 2:00P.M.

5. The office of a manufacturer of artificial kneecaps

6. Inspector Peter Jones whose only positive virtue, according to Holmes, is his bravery.

7. French gold, 30,000 napoleons from the Bank of France

8. The knees of Vincent Spaulding's trousers are worn, wrinkled, and stained, apparently from burrowing.

9. Mr. Merryweather, the chairman of the bank directors

10. Holmes realized that something of value was hidden in or near the pawnbroker's office, because Mr. Wilson's job of copying the encyclopedia kept him away from this location for several hours each day.

QUIZ 18

1. True

2. False—Mary's father was a plumber.

3. False—They plan to marry at St. Saviour's, near King's Cross.

4. True

5. True

6. False—Mary runs an ad in the *Chronicle*.

7. False—Mary supplements her inheritance by working as a typist.

8. True

9. False—Holmes threatens to strike Windibank with a whip.

10. False—The solution is obvious to Holmes because of Hosmer Angel's strange conduct and the fact that Angel and James Windibank were never seen together.

QUIZ 19

1. C. Both John Turner and Charles McCarthy were widowers with one teenaged child each, a daughter and a son, respectively.

2. D. William Crowder, the gamekeeper

3. B. Patience Moran

4. B. Something about a rat

5. D. A gray coat of some sort

6. C. James refused to marry Alice Turner.

7. A. Charles McCarthy was struck on the left side of his head.

8. C. The rock had been moved because there is grass growing under it.

9. D. John Turner was a member of a gang of wagon robbers.

10. B. Cooee and rat

QUIZ 20

1. John Openshaw remembers how Holmes saved Major Prendergast from a scandal concerning his cheating at cards in the Tankerville Club.

2. Elias Openshaw opened a plantation in Florida and served in the Confederate Army under Andrew Jackson.

3. Uncle Elias received a strange letter from India in March and died seven weeks later.

4. Three men received the message: John Openshaw, his father, and his uncle. Each one died shortly afterward.

5. John Openshaw gives Holmes a piece of unburned paper that he salvaged from the remains of the papers that his uncle burned.

6. "S.H. for J.O." (Sherlock Holmes for John Openshaw)

7. Holmes reviews the ship registers and files of Lloyd's and traces the activities of all the ships that docked at Pondicherry in January and February of 1883. He is then able to trace one ship back to the United States; this ship is now docked in London.

8. *Lone Star*

9. In each case, there was no sign of violence. Their deaths were made to look like suicides or accidents.

10. "A name derived from the fanciful resemblance to the sound produced by cocking a rifle."

QUIZ 21

1. False—After reading De Quincey's description of his dreams, Isa Whitney tries to induce the same effect by lacing his tobacco with laudanum.

2. True

3. False—Holmes is looking for Neville St. Clair.

4. False—Mrs. St. Clair saw her husband in the window of the Bar of Gold.

5. False—St. Clair's coat pockets are filled with 421 pennies and 270 half-pennies.

6. False—Mrs. St. Clair noticed that her husband was not wearing his collar or tie.

7. False—Mrs. St. Clair surprises Holmes by telling him that she received a letter from her husband that very day.

8. True

9. True

10. True

QUIZ 22

1. B. An old felt hat

2. C. His wife no longer loves him.

3. C. 1,000 pounds

4. B. On the banks of the Amoy River in southern China

5. A. The Hotel Cosmopolitan

6. D. Two murders, a vitriol-throwing, suicide, several robberies

7. A. It is white with a barred tail.

8. D. John Horner, the plumber who came to the Countess's dressing room to solder a grate

9. A. Henry Baker is a member of the Alpha Inn goose club, whose members contributed a few pence each week to the inn's owner in return for a goose on Christmas.

10. A. Holmes throws open the door and shouts at him to leave.

QUIZ 23

1. C. Eight

2. B. Mrs. Farintosh, from the case of the opal tiara

3. A. Helen believes that her sister died of fright and nervous shock.

4. A. She had spent the night in the room of her deceased sister and heard the strange whistle that her sister had heard a few days before she died.

5. C. A cheetah and a baboon

6. A. He started repairing the west wing of the manor, which required the wall of Miss Stoner's room to be replaced.

7. C. It is nailed to the floor.

8. B. A small shaft used for ventilation

9. D. Because of the scuff marks on the seat of the chair, Holmes knows that Dr. Roylott stood on the chair many times.

10. A. Dr. Roylott bends Holmes's fireplace poker with his bare hands.

QUIZ 24

1. Victor Hatherley is a hydraulic engineer.

2. Hatherley worked for Venner & Matheson, a firm from Greenwich.

3. Fifty guineas

4. Fuller's Earth

5. A German woman named Elise

6. Hatherley notices a metallic deposit crusted on the floor.

7. Hatherley's thumb is chopped off while he is hanging from a window sill.

8. Holmes discovers an advertisement in a newspaper about Mr. Jeremiah Hayling, a hydraulic engineer who has disappeared.

9. Dr. Becher and Elise help Hatherley escape.

10. Counterfeit coins

QUIZ 25

1. False—Hatty Doran's father became wealthy from mining gold.

2. True

3. True

4. False—Lestrade believes that Hatty Doran's body will be found in the river because he found a wedding dress, a pair of satin shoes, a bride's wreath, and a veil floating near the shore.

5. True

6. False—Hatty Doran's message was written on the back of a hotel bill.

7. False—As Hatty walked past Frank's pew, she dropped her flowers, and upon picking them up, Frank passed her a note.

8. False—Hatty believed that Frank was killed by the Apache Indians.

9. True

10. False—Holmes finds Frank by visiting the hotel where they stayed and discovering their forwarding address.

QUIZ 26

1. C. 50,000 pounds

2. A. 39

3. B. His son, Arthur, and his niece, Mary

4. C. Arthur has considerable gambling debts.

5. D. Arthur requests that his father allow him to leave the house for five minutes.

6. B. Mary is under the spell of Sir George Burnwell.

7. A. Mary leaves her uncle a note saying that she is leaving forever.

8. D. Arthur is trying to protect the woman he loves.

9. C. Holmes purchases a pair of Sir George's shoes from Sir George's valet and matches them to the tracks that were left in the snow.

10. A. Lucy has been in his service for only a short time, and she has many admirers. While sneaking out to see a beau, she may have overheard Mr.

Holder mention that he had brought the coronet home.

QUIZ 27

1. Westaway

2. 100 pounds a year

3. That Miss Hunter sit in a certain place in the room, wear an electric blue dress, and cut off her long hair

4. A fortnight

5. Black Swan Hotel at Winchester

6. Seven

7. Philadelphia

8. She spies him in the piece of mirror she holds in her hand when her back is to the window.

9. A large mastiff named Carlo

10. He says that he uses the room as a photography studio.

MAKING THE GRADE

Level	Total Correct Answers
Deductive Genius	91–120
Holmes' Apprentice	61–90
Watson's Apprentice	31–60
Moriarty's Victim	0–30

QUIZ 28

1. Holmes believes that Silver Blaze will show up because it is not possible to conceal such a popular horse in the sparsely inhabited area.

2. The man took a small white piece of paper from his waistcoat pocket.

3. John Straker held a red and black silk cravat.

4. Fitzroy Simpson had bet 5,000 pounds against Silver Blaze winning in the Wessex Cup, and an item of his clothing was found with the dead man.

5. The dish of curried mutton prepared by Mrs. Straker

6. A cataract knife and a receipt for an expensive dress

7. Silver Blaze is discovered in the neighboring stable of Mapleton.

8. A photograph of John Straker

9. Holmes asks if he has noticed anything amiss with his sheep.

10. Colonel Ross does not recognize Silver Blaze because the horse's white markings were darkened with a stain.

QUIZ 29

1. False—Holmes reads the name printed on the lining of his hat.

2. False—Grant Munro is a hops merchant.

3. True

4. True

5. False—Munro was suspicious about his neighbors because he saw a strange face in the window of the cottage.

He claimed that there was something unnatural about it.

6. False—Mrs. Munro told her husband that she needed fresh air because she felt as if she were choking.

7. False—Munro becomes angry when he discovers her photograph on the mantelpiece.

8. True

9. True

10. False—Mr. Munro lovingly accepts the situation.

QUIZ 30

1. B. Holmes notices that Watson's new slippers are slightly scorched. The only reasonable explanation, according to Holmes, is that Watson was warming his feet by the fire, which is rarely done in the summer, unless one is sick.

2. C. The steps of Dr. Watson's office are worn down more than the steps leading to the other doctor's office.

3. A. Pinner does not want Pycroft to notify his prospective employer of his decision not to accept his offer.

4. D. When Pycroft enters the office, he notices that the room is very austere, lacking carpet,

curtains, tables, and other employees.

5. A. Pycroft is assigned the task of marking off all the hardware sellers and their addresses listed in the Paris directory.

6. D. Each man has a gold filling in the second tooth in the upper left jaw.

7. B. They arrive with Pycroft, seeking employment.

8. C. Mr. Pinner makes Pycroft write a declaration of service concerning his new job, and he requires that Pycroft not arrive at Mawson's office on Monday morning as expected.

9. D. Mr. Pinner tries to hang himself.

10. D. He reads about his brother's arrest in an early edition of the *Evening Standard*.

QUIZ 31

1. A man named Hudson, who was on a ship with Mr. Trevor, thirty years ago

2. Victor's father was dying of apoplexy and nervous shock.

3. Holmes realizes that a secret code is written into the letter that caused Mr. Trevor to go mad.

4. Mr. Trevor reveals to his son, posthumously, the story of his

past in a letter that he kept in a Japanese cabinet.

5. When he was working for a London banking house, Mr. Trevor stole money to pay a debt.

6. Jack Prendergast

7. Trevor refused to take part in the mutiny, so Prendergast allowed him and a convict named Evans to board a boat and leave the *Gloria Scott*.

8. The ship exploded, either intentionally by the hands of the first mate or by a stray bullet.

9. Hudson was the only person who survived the explosion.

10. They told the captain that they were the only survivors of a passenger ship that had exploded.

QUIZ 32

1. True

2. False—Brunton was a schoolmaster before he went to work for the Musgrave family.

3. False—Brunton's only shortcoming was that he was a ladies man.

4. False—Brunton was fired when Reginald Musgrave found him going through the family papers in the library.

5. True

6. True

7. False—The Musgrave Ritual was drawn up during the time of the Norman Conquest.

8. False—Holmes miscalculates because he forgot to consider the words "and under."

9. False—Brunton's muffler is found near the cellar.

10. True

QUIZ 33

1. B. In Lyons, France, at the Hotel Dulong

2. A. A piece of a note

3. B. Holmes writes down the wrong time, and Cunningham corrects it.

4. D. He pretends to accidentally knock over a bowl of oranges.

5. C. It is written by two different people.

6. D. Twenty-three

7. A. William Kirwin

8. A. There were no powder burns on Kirwin's clothes.

9. B. A paper claiming that Mr. Acton owned half of the neighboring estate

10. B. The nature of the relationships of Annie Morrison, Alec Cunningham, and William Kirwin

QUIZ 34

1. Colonel Barclay had bouts of depression and was afraid of the dark.

2. Thirty years

3. Mrs. Barclay was attending the meeting of the Guild of St. George.

4. David

5. A blow to the back of the neck

6. A mongoose named Teddy

7. Mrs. Barclay's friend, Miss Morrison

8. Mr. Barclay was responsible for the capture and torture of the man she loved.

9. Apoplexy brought on by fright

10. The Bible

QUIZ 35

1. A. He specializes in nervous diseases, especially catalepsy.

2. C. Mr. Blessington paid Dr. Trevelyan's expenses and kept three-fourths of all the money collected.

3. D. Mr. Blessington thoroughly examined the financial books.

4. D. He doesn't trust banks, and he keeps everything he owns in a box in his room.

5. A. A Russian nobleman and his son, who are seeking medical attention

6. D. He notices footprints in the carpet.

7. A. There are several different cigar ends and holders left in Blessington's room.

8. B. He is afraid of fires, and he wants to be prepared for a window escape if necessary.

9. C. The page

10. B. Holmes sees fear in Mr. Blessington's eyes and speculates that Mr. Blessington knows who the intruders are.

QUIZ 36

1. His brother, Mycroft

2. Harold Latimer has the nervous habit of giggling when he speaks.

3. When Mr. Melas speaks to the victim, he adds short questions at the end of each statement.

4. Five sovereigns

5. J. Davenport

6. The kidnappers try to dispose of Melas and Kratides by poisoning them with carbon monoxide from burning charcoals.

7. Sophy would not cooperate with her captors.

8. They put plaster over Paul Kratides's face so that his sister will not recognize him.

9. The kidnappers were found stabbed to death in Buda-Pesth.

10. They withhold food from Paul Kratides to try to force him into signing the paper.

QUIZ 37

1. False—Watson knew Perry Phelps from school. Phelps was two classes ahead of Watson, but they were the same age.

2. True

3. False—His uncle, Lord Holdhurst, secured the position for him.

4. True

5. False—Phelps's fiancée, Miss Annie Harrison, and her brother Joseph Harrison cared for Phelps in his home.

6. False—Holmes deduces seven clues from Phelps's story.

7. False—Holmes is aided by Detective Forbes.

8. True

9. False—The villain slashed Holmes's knuckles with a knife.

10. True

QUIZ 38

1. C. Letters from Moriarty's brother, publicly defends the notorious professor, and Watson is compelled to write an account on behalf of Holmes.

2. D. "He is the Napoleon of crime."

3. A. "You have less frontal development than I should have expected."

4. A. Three

5. D. Three

6. B. Holmes is disguised as an Italian priest.

7. D. Mycroft, Holmes's brother

8. A. Moriarty has escaped.

9. B. The hotel sends a message for Watson to attend to an Englishwoman who is very ill and who refuses to see a foreign doctor.

10. C. Holmes slips the message into his silver cigarette case, which Watson finds at the falls.

QUIZ 39

1. Lady Hilda Trelawney Hope in "The Adventure of the Second Stain"

2. Sherlock Holmes in "The Adventure of the Dying Detective"

3. The Duke of Holdernesse in "The Adventure of the Priory School"

4. Captain Jack Croker in "The Adventure of the Abbey Grange"

5. Mycroft Holmes in "The Adventure of the Bruce-Partington Plans"

6. Sir James Damery in "The Adventure of the Illustrious Client"

7. John Hopley Neligan in "The Adventure of Black Peter"

8. Nathan Garrideb in "The Adventure of the Three Garridebs"

9. Laura Lyons in *The Hound of The Baskervilles*

10. Culverton Smith in "The Adventure of the Dying Detective"

11. Cyril Overton in "The Adventure of the Missing Three-Quarter"

12. Sir Robert Norberton in "The Adventure of Shoscombe Old Place"

13. John Hector McFarlane in "The Adventure of the Norwood Builder"

14. Dr. Thorneycroft Huxtable in "The Adventure of the Priory School"

15. Lord Mount-James in "The Adventure of the Missing Three-Quarter"

16. Abe Slaney in "The Adventure of the Dancing Men"

17. Isadora Klein in "The Adventure of the Three Gables"

18. Josiah Amberley in "The Adventure of the Retired Colourman"

19. Professor Coram in "The Adventure of the Golden Pince-Nez"

20. Baron Gruner in "The Adventure of the Illustrious Client"

MAKING THE GRADE

Level	Total Correct Answers
Deductive Genius	114–150
Holmes' Apprentice	76–113
Watson's Apprentice	38–75
Moriarty's Victim	0–37

QUIZ 40

1. Ronald Adair died between 10:00 and 11:20 on the night of March 30, 1894.

2. Adair was a member of three card clubs and often gambled on the games.

3. Holmes is disguised as an old, deformed man.

4. *The Origin of Tree Worship*

5. Holmes recognizes one of the gang members lurking near his apartment.

6. Mrs. Hudson changes the position of the wax figure every fifteen minutes.

7. To lure Colonel Moran into a trap

8. Holmes suspected that Adair, realizing that Moran cheated at cards that evening, was attempting to return the money he won.

9. A bullet from the air gun shattered the forehead of the wax figure.

10. The air gun was placed in the Scotland Yard Museum.

QUIZ 41

1. False—John Hector McFarlane is arrested because his walking stick was found near the body.

2. True

3. False—Oldacre left McFarlane his entire estate.

4. True

5. True

6. False—Lestrade finds McFarlane's bloody thumbprint on the wall in the hall of Oldacre's house.

7. True

8. False—Holmes shouts "Fire!" and the murderer bolts from his hiding place.

9. False—Oldacre was in financial trouble and was trying to elude his creditor.

10. True

QUIZ 42

1. B. He is not considering investing in South African securities.

2. C. The family had owned the estate for five centuries.

3. C. Mrs. Cubitt insisted that Mr. Cubitt never ask about her past.

4. A. Mrs. Cubitt fainted.

5. C. She suggested that she and her husband take a trip and get away for a while.

6. A. On the sundial in the garden

7. A. Mr. and Mrs. Cubitt have both been shot. Mr. Cubitt is dead, and his wife is in serious condition.

8. B. A third shot had been fired.

9. A. Using the code of the dancing men, Holmes writes him a letter and asks him to come for a visit.

10. B. Elsie's father, Mr. Patrick

QUIZ 43

1. Miss Smith visits Holmes on April 13, 1895.

2. Holmes knows that Miss Smith is a musician because of her spatulate finger ends.

3. Mr. Carruthers claimed that he was a friend of Miss Smith's late uncle and, upon hearing that Miss Smith was in grave financial need, Mr. Carruthers hired her as a music teacher for his ten-year-old daughter.

4. The cyclist does not allow her to get close enough to see him.

5. Mr. Woodley made inappropriate advances toward Miss Smith.

6. Holmes sends Watson to investigate the situation and report back.

7. Mr. Woodley started sneaking around Mr. Carruthers's house, concealing himself in the shrubbery.

8. Watson notices that Holmes grabs his revolver on his way to assist Miss Smith.

9. Carruthers and Woodley played cards for the right to court Miss Smith and subsequently marry her. Woodley won the card game.

10. Williamson, a defrocked clergyman

QUIZ 44

1. False—Holmes learns that the boy was abducted when he receives a frantic visit from Dr. Huxtable, the founder and principal of the Priory preparatory school.

2. False—The Duke offers 5,000 pounds to anyone who can tell him where his son is, and 1,000 pounds for the name of the man or men who abducted the boy.

3. True

4. True

5. False—The Duke believes that his son ran away to be with his mother.

6. False—The boy's cap is found in the van belonging to a group of gypsies.

7. True

8. True

9. False–The owner of the inn, Reuben Hayes, was arrested.

10. False—The Duke refuses to prosecute because the man is his illegitimate son.

QUIZ 45

1. B. Inspector Hopkins

2. C. Stabbing a pig's carcass with a harpoon

3. A. Black Peter spent his nights in a small hut decorated like a ship.

4. D. *Sea Unicorn*

5. C. There is a bottle of rum and two glasses on the table.

6. A. Neligan is searching for a logbook.

7. B. Neligan is not physically strong enough to stab Black Peter in the manner in which he was killed.

8. A. The man intended to blackmail Black Peter.

9. B. Black Peter seldom smoked, and there was not a pipe in his hut.

10. A. They leave for Norway.

QUIZ 46

1. Lady Blackwell wants Holmes to negotiate with her blackmailer.

2. Holmes disguises himself as a plumber and courts Milverton's housemaid.

3. Milverton plans to send Lady Blackwell's love letters, written to a previous lover, to her fiancé, the Earl of Dovercourt.

4. He plans to break into Milverton's safe and steal the damaging letters.

5. Milverton retires at 10:30.

6. Milverton has made an appointment to purchase letters that he will use in another blackmail attempt.

7. Holmes and Watson were behind the window curtain in Milverton's study.

8. Holmes burns all the letters that Milverton planned to use in future blackmailings.

9. He remembers seeing her picture in a shop window displaying photographs of celebrities. He and Watson return to the shop to view the photograph and confirm her identity.

10. Lestrade notices two sets of footprints (those made by Holmes and Watson).

QUIZ 47

1. False—Morse Hudson's bust of Napoleon is smashed.

2. True

3. True

4. False—This robbery is more serious because a man is murdered.

5. True

6. False—Holmes is one step closer to solving the case because of the photograph found in the dead man's pocket.

7. True

8. True

9. False—Holmes smashes the sixth bust of Napoleon.

10. False—Holmes solves the crime because of a link with a previous case.

QUIZ 48

1. B. Greek translations

2. A. Mr. Soames's servant, Bannister, left the key in the door when he carried out the tea service.

3. D. The papers on his desk were rearranged.

4. B. When Bannister describes how he almost fainted, Holmes discovers that the butler crossed the room and sat down in a chair positioned in an inconvenient location.

5. A. Clumps of black clay

6. C. Ten years

7. A. Holmes requests the height of each suspect.

8. A. Bannister recognized the student's gloves left in the chair.

9. C. Bannister had been the loyal butler of the student's father and felt obliged to look after the son while at school.

10. D. He joins the Rhodesian Police and leaves for Africa.

QUIZ 49

1. Inspector Hopkins cannot discover a motive for the murder.

2. Mr. Smith was Professor Coram's personal secretary.

3. Susan Tarlton, the maid, discovered Mr. Smith in the library.

4. He was stabbed in the carotid artery with a sealing-wax knife.

5. "The professor, it was she."

6. A golden pince-nez

7. Holmes had smoked several cigarettes in front of the bookcase and noticed later that the ashes had been disturbed, indicating that the case had swung open since the last time he was in the room.

8. The professor's consumption of food increased.

9. The murderer lost a pince-nez and could not see well enough to escape.

10. Anna commits suicide by drinking poison.

QUIZ 50

1. False—Staunton received a visit from a man of fifty with a grizzled, pale face.

2. True

3. False—Lord Mount-James is angry when he finds out that a detective has been hired and declares that he will not foot the bill.

4. False—Holmes tells the clerk at the telegraph office that he had sent a message the day before and did not include his name.

5. True

6. True

7. False—Pompey tracks Dr. Armstrong because Holmes uses a syringe to squirt aniseed over the hind wheel of the carriage. This scent is a bloodhound's favorite.

8. True

9. False—Godfrey Staunton feared that he would be disinherited if his uncle found out that he had married his landlady's daughter.

10. False—Cambridge lost the rugby match to Oxford.

QUIZ 51

1. B. He was struck on the head with a poker.

2. A. Lady Brackenstall's maid

3. C. An elderly man could not have struck such a violent blow.

4. D. The pocket screw is short and had to be inserted three times in order to remove the cork. A household corkscrew is long and only one insertion is necessary.

5. A. The Randall gang which is operating in the area

6. A. The knots on the cord that is used to tie up

THE SHERLOCK HOLMES QUIZ BOOK

Lady Brackenstall are commonly used by sailors.

7. D. Sir Eustace physically abused Lady Brackenstall.

8. B. Lady Brackenstall says that Sir Eustace was struck after she sat down in the chair. If that were true, there would not be blood stains on the chair.

9. C. Lady Brackenstall enjoyed Crocker's comradeship and company, but she was not in love with him.

10. D. Holmes and Watson set up a mock trial, in which Holmes acts as judge and Watson as jury. The man is found not guilty.

QUIZ 52

1. Trelawney Hope discovers that the letter is missing at 8:00 A. M.

2. The box was left unguarded for four hours, between 7:30 P.M. and 11:30 P.M.

3. Lady Trelawney Hope, the secretary's wife

4. The prime minister

5. If the letter were in the hands of a hostile government, there would have been news of a political uprising.

6. Lucas lived only a short distance from the Hope residence.

7. The blood stain on the rug was not directly over the stain on the floor underneath, leading Holmes to believe that someone had moved the rug. This action had to have occurred while the constable was on duty.

8. Lucas had a love letter that Lady Hilda had written to a man before she married Trelawney Hope.

9. Lady Hilda has a duplicate key to the dispatch box.

10. A madwoman rushing into the house wielding a knife

MAKING THE GRADE

Level	Total Correct Answers
Deductive Genius	61–80
Holmes' Apprentice	41–60
Watson's Apprentice	21–40
Moriarty's Victim	0–20

QUIZ 53

1. Holmes asks Watson how he would define "grotesque."

2. The police find a letter from Scott Eccles in García's pocket, stating that Scott Eccles planned to visit García on the night he was killed.

3. Scott Eccles spoke to no one after 1:00 A. M.

4. García and his household staff had disappeared.

5. Inspector Baynes

6. Voodoo

---

7. Holmes thinks that it is unusual that García would invite Scott Eccles to spend a few days at his lodge, having met him only two days prior.

8. Miss Burnet, Mr. Henderson's governess, sent the message.

9. Mr. García needed an alibi because he had planned to kill Mr. Henderson.

10. John Warner, a gardener whom Henderson fired, gives Holmes the information he needs to solve the mystery.

QUIZ 54

1. False—She received the package through the mail.

2. False—Miss Cushing put them in the outhouse.

3. False—The string is covered with tar and tied with a sailor's knot.

4. False—Inspector Lestrade suspects that it was a practical joke performed by medical students while dissecting a corpse.

5. True

6. True

7. False—She had fallen in love with him, and he spurned her.

8. True

9. False—Sarah went down with "brain symptoms of great severity."

10. True

QUIZ 55

1. B. Five pounds a week for a fortnight

2. C. By printing one word on a piece of paper, the lodger communicated what was needed.

3. A. The method of communicating with Mrs. Warren leads Holmes to this conclusion.

4. B. *Daily Gazette*

5. A. Holmes hides behind a door and watches in a mirror as the lodger retrieves a tray left by Mrs. Warren.

6. D. Italian

7. B. The Long Island cave mystery

8. A. Mrs. Lucca is overjoyed.

9. A. Brooklyn

10. D. Gorgiano grabbed Emilia and tried to make love to her.

QUIZ 56

1. His brother Mycroft

2. Arthur Cadogan West's body is found on the train track outside of Aldgate Station on the Underground system.

3. There is no train ticket found in his pocket.

4. Cadogan West was going to the theatre, as there were two tickets in his pocket to a performance at Woolwich Theatre.

5. There was no sign of blood on the tracks; therefore, the body must have been moved.

6. Found on Cadogan West's body are the British government's secret plans to build a submarine.

7. Sir James has died that morning.

8. His fiancée, Miss Violet Westbury

9. A list of suspects from Mycroft

10. The Underground trains stop a mere four feet away from the back stairs window of Oberstein's residence.

QUIZ 57

1. True

2. False—Holmes discourages Watson's medical treatment because Holmes says that Watson is only a general practitioner with limited experience and mediocre qualifications.

3. False—Watson suggests that Holmes consult Dr. Ainstree, an authority on tropical diseases.

4. True

5. False—Smith holds Holmes responsible for the death of Smith's nephew.

6. True

7. True

8. False—Holmes instructs Watson to hide behind the bed.

9. True

10. False—The gas lamp is turned up, and the room is illuminated; this is Inspector Morton's signal.

QUIZ 58

1. C. Watson's boots have been fastened with an elaborate double bow, and since they are fairly new boots, it is unlikely that Watson has been to a shoe repair shop.

2. C. Lady Frances has written to Miss Dobney every second week for four years, and five weeks have gone by without Miss Dobney receiving a letter.

3. A. Before Lady Frances disappeared, she paid her maid, Miss Marie Devine, fifty pounds.

4. D. Holmes wants a description of Dr. Shlessinger's left ear.

5. B. Marie says that it is a wedding gift.

6. A. Holmes is disguised as a French *ouvrier* from a cabaret. He is wearing a blue blouse.

7. B. The undertaker's wife

8. C. He paid her hotel bill and ticket to London, after which she fled before repaying him. She left her jewelry, and he pawned it as reimbursement.

9. B. The Shlessingers rescued her from a workhouse infirmary.

10. A. Holmes realizes that the coffin is unusually large, especially since Rose was a small, frail woman.

QUIZ 59

1. Three residents are stricken by a strange malady which killed Brenda Tregennis and left her two brothers insane.

2. They quarreled over the sale of the family's tin-mining company.

3. Dr. Leon Sterndale, the great lion hunter and explorer

4. Mortimer Tregennis is found dead in his room, apparently of the same malady that killed his family.

5. Ashes from the chimney

6. He wants to leave some for the police to discover.

7. Something was burned in each room, the rooms were stuffy, and the nature of the deaths and madness that afflicted the victims was unusual.

8. It is called Devil's-foot root, and it comes from west Africa.

9. Dr. Sterndale was already married and was not able to get a divorce.

10. Dr. Sterndale asks Holmes whom Holmes suspects killed Brenda Tregennis.

QUIZ 60

1. False—Motor-car parts are used as code names.

2. True

3. False—The title is *Practical Handbook of Bee Culture*

4. False—They drink a bottle of Imperial Tokay.

5. True

6. True

7. True

8. False—Altamont is traveling in a Ford.

9. False—Holmes uses chloroform.

10. True

MAKING THE GRADE

Level	Total Correct Answers
Deductive Genius	98–130
Holmes' Apprentice	66–97
Watson's Apprentice	33–65
Moriarty's Victim	0–32

QUIZ 61

1. Sir James is acting as an intermediary for a client who wishes to go unnamed.

2. Violet de Merville and Baron Gruner meet on a Mediterranean yachting voyage.

3. Baron Gruner has written a book on the topic of Chinese pottery.

4. Shinwell Johnson, who had once been a criminal, but had

changed his ways and began working for Holmes

5. Baron Gruner has a very shady reputation, including the fact that many believe he murdered his first wife.

6. Miss Kitty Winter, ex-mistress to the baron

7. The baron keeps a brown leatherbound book listing all the people he has ruined. The book includes photos and details of each case.

8. She throws vitriol on his face.

9. Baron Gruner claims that he has hypnotized her.

10. Holmes tells Watson to spread the word that Holmes's injuries are life-threatening.

QUIZ 62

1. True

2. False—Colonel Emsworth told Dodd that Godfrey was on a voyage around the world.

3. False—Ralph's response was "I wish to God he was!"

4. True

5. False—The colonel asked his guest to leave because Dodd was found sneaking around and peering into a small cottage in back of Tuxbury Old Hall.

6. False—Holmes writes one word on a slip of paper, and the colonel immediately tells the truth.

7. True

8. False—The skin on Godfrey's forehead appeared blanched.

9. True

10. True

QUIZ 63

1. C. The hundred-thousand-pound burglary

2. B. The prime minister and the home secretary

3. C. A dummy of himself, which he positions in the window

4. D. Holmes is expecting to be murdered.

5. C. Holmes plays his violin.

6. C. Five minutes, not much time for the count to react

7. A. The count plans to tell Holmes that the diamond is in Liverpool.

8. A. Holmes is sitting in the chair that was previously occupied by the dummy.

9. B. Holmes playing a recording of a violin on the gramophone

10. D. Holmes slips the diamond in Lord Cantlemere's pocket without his knowing it, and then accuses him of stealing it.

QUIZ 64

1. 500 pounds

2. Travel around the world

3. The buyer wants every item inside the home to remain.

4. The burglars chloroform Mrs. Maberley.

5. The last page of her son's manuscript

6. The writing was so passionate that Maberley changed points of view from "he" to "my."

7. Holmes visits Langdale Pike, the local gossip columnist.

8. Holmes sends Isadora Klein a note threatening to bring in the police if she refuses to see him.

9. She burns the manuscript.

10. Holmes will not turn her over to the police if she agrees to give Mrs. Maberley 500 pounds to travel around the world first class.

QUIZ 65

1. False—Ferguson and Watson played on opposing rugby teams.

2. True

3. True

4. False—Mrs. Ferguson began acting violently toward her stepson, striking him on two occasions.

5. False—Mr. Ferguson locks his wife in her room.

6. False—Holmes begins to develop his theory when he notices a quiver and a small bird-bow among a display of weapons.

7. True

8. False—Holmes notices Ferguson's older son's face in the window and realizes that the son is consumed with "cruel hatred."

9. True

10. False—Holmes recommends that the boy spend a year at sea.

QUIZ 66

1. D. Holmes's refusal of knighthood

2. C. His entire wardrobe is English.

3. B. Holmes mentions an old friend who lived in Topeka, and John Garrideb says that he also knows the man. However, Holmes had fabricated the character.

4. A. In placing the ad, John Garrideb uses the American spellings for three of the words.

5. C. To interview a man named Howard Garrideb

6. A. Butterflies, flint instruments, and plaster skulls of ancient man

7. D. Evans shoots Watson in the thigh.

8. C. He shot and killed a man over cards.

9. A. Holmes asks to study his collections.

10. B. He never recovers from the shock and is placed in a nursing home.

QUIZ 67

1. She is arrested for the murder of Neil Gibson's wife.

2. Marlow Bates wants to warn Holmes about Mr. Gibson's malicious nature.

3. Mr. Gibson lies to Holmes about his relationship with Miss Dunbar.

4. She felt responsible for the children, and she believed that she could influence Mr. Gibson to change his evil ways.

5. The murder weapon was found in the bottom of her wardrobe.

6. The note is very short, and there was no need for Mrs. Gibson to have it with her.

7. If Miss Dunbar were guilty, she would not hide the weapon in her room after committing the murder.

8. There is a chip out of the stonework on the lower edge of the parapet.

9. Mrs. Gibson

10. A ball of stout twine

QUIZ 68

1. False—Trevor Bennett, the professor's assistant, requests Holmes's assistance.

2. True

3. True

4. False—Mr. Bennett was not allowed to open letters marked with a cross under the stamp.

5. True

6. False—She wakes in the middle of the night and sees her father looking at her through the window, in spite of the room being on the second floor.

7. True

8. False—The professor is attacked by his dog.

9. True

10. False—Holmes plans to write a monograph on how dogs reflect the personality of their masters and the atmosphere of their masters' homes.

QUIZ 69

1. D. He had rheumatic fever.

2. A. Holmes

3. D. He was a science teacher at an athletic and training school.

4. D. Holmes finds an open handprint with fingers pointed up toward the incline.

5. A. His towel is still dry.

6. B. A handkerchief, a large knife, a folding card-case, and a note from his lover

7. C. Murdoch lost his girlfriend to McPherson.

8. A. The dog dies in exactly the same place where McPherson's body is found.

9. D. McPherson's old, dying uncle may have disinherited him if he knew that he was getting married.

10. B. Holmes remembers a book written by a man who had experienced a similar incident.

QUIZ 70

1. Mrs. Ronder's landlady, Mrs. Merrilow

2. Mrs. Ronder is dying and wants to tell her story. She is also experiencing nightmares over the incident.

3. Abbas Parva, the name of the village where the tragedy occurred

4. Sahara King

5. Mr. Ronder believed that the lion would not attack the person who fed him.

6. According to the police report, a man was shouting just at the time Mrs. Ronder was attacked, but Mr. Ronder had apparently been attacked first and killed. If that were the case, Mr. Ronder could not have been the one shouting. Holmes was also curious as to why the lion returned to its cage rather than escape.

7. He was too frightened to come to her rescue when the lion attacked.

8. Leonardo designed a club to resemble a lion's paw. It was made with five steel nails pointed outward and spaced like claws.

9. Holmes fears that Mrs. Ronder is contemplating suicide.

10. A prussic acid bottle, which contained the poison she'd planned to use to commit suicide

QUIZ 71

1. False—Holmes used a low-power microscope.

2. True

3. False—Sir Robert plans to race his prize horse, Prince, but is showing the public Prince's half brother who is slower, therefore increasing the stakes for the faster horse.

4. False—John Mason believes that his employer has gone mad because his close relationship with his sister has drastically changed, and he gives away his sister's most beloved spaniel.

5. True

6. True

7. False—Mason finds the remains of the upper section of a charred human femur.

8. False—Holmes and Watson arrive disguised as fishermen.

9. True

10. True

QUIZ 72

1. B. At the Haymarket Theatre attending a play

2. C. He is painting the passageway in his house.

3. D. His wife took seven thousand pounds worth of cash and securities.

4. A. Playing chess

5. A. Bolt

6. C. A private detective hired by the family of Dr. Ray Ernest, the man who disappeared with Amberley's wife

7. B. "What did you do with the bodies?"

8. A. Holmes checked the box-office chart at the theatre and discovered that Amberley did not attend the play.

9. D. The strong smell of paint

10. C. He attempts suicide by swallowing a poison pill.

MAKING THE GRADE

Level	Total Correct Answers
Deductive Genius	91–120
Holmes' Apprentice	61–90
Watson's Apprentice	31–60
Moriarty's Victim	0–30

QUIZ 73

1. Eille Norwood starred in forty-seven Sherlock Holmes films between 1921 and 1923.

2. Basil Rathbone as Sherlock Holmes and Nigel Bruce as Dr. Watson

3. John Barrymore

4. *The Seven-Per-Cent Solution*, produced by United Artists

5. *Sherlock Holmes Baffled*

6. All three roles were played by Christopher Lee.

7. *The Adventure of Sherlock Holmes' Smarter Brother*

8. Michael Caine played Sherlock Holmes, and Ben Kingsley played Dr. Watson.

9. *The Hound of the Baskervilles*

10. Peter Cushing

QUIZ 74

1. William Gillette

2. Orson Welles

3. Basil Rathbone as Holmes and Nigel Bruce as Dr. Watson

4. "The Sussex Vampire"

5. "The Baconian Cipher"

6. Sir Cedric Hardwicke and Sir John Gielgud, respectively

7. Edith Metier

8. Tom Conway

9. Carleton Hobbs

10. E. G. Marshall

QUIZ 75

1. *Under the Clock*
2. Harry H. Corbett
3. William Gillette and Basil Rathbone, respectively
4. John Dickson Carr
5. *The Mask of Moriarty*
6. *The Marvelous Misadventures of Sherlock Holmes: A Musical Mystery for Children*
7. Frank Langella
8. Eille Norwood
9. Leonard Nimoy
10. *The Holmeses of Baker Street*

QUIZ 76

1. "The Three Garridebs"
2. John Cleese
3. Peter Cushing
4. *Wishbone*
5. Edward Hardwicke, son of Sir Cedric Hardwicke, who played in the 1945 British radio broadcast
6. Christopher Lee
7. Christopher Plummer
8. *Sherlock Holmes in the 22nd Century*
9. Roger Moore
10. *The Return of Sherlock Holmes*

QUIZ 77

1. "The Field Bazaar"
2. Laurie King

3. *Sherlock Holmes Through Time and Space*
4. Mark Twain
5. *The Adventures of Sherlaw Kombs*
6. *Doctor Jekyl and Mr. Holmes*
7. *The Adventures of Picklock Holes*
8. *The Exploits of Sherlock Holmes*
9. *The Return of Herlock Sholmes*
10. *Ten Years Beyond Baker Street*

MAKING THE GRADE

Level	Total Correct Answers
Deductive Genius	41–50
Holmes' Apprentice	27–40
Watson's Apprentice	14–26
Moriarty's Victim	0–13

QUIZ 78

1. He is testing a way to silence gunfire.
2. He plans every detail in his mind before executing it.
3. Administered an anesthetic he was testing
4. She throws a glass of wine in his face and leaves.
5. Watson has developed a gambling problem.
6. He supposedly rises from the dead.
7. She wants Holmes to find a missing dwarf named Luke Reordan.
8. They are blamed for releasing a half-finished

THE SHERLOCK HOLMES QUIZ BOOK

boat from its mooring,
causing it to sink.

9. She drugs his wine.

10. He was testing his theory on
how Lord Blackwell survived
the hanging.

QUIZ 79

1. "The Man with the Twisted
Lip"

2. "The Adventure of the
Copper Beeches"

3. *The Sign of Four*

4. "The Adventure of the
Copper Beeches"

5. "A Scandal in Bohemia"

6. *The Hound of the Baskervilles*

7. "The Adventure of the Abbey
Grange"

QUIZ 80

1. False—Professor James
Moriarty supposedly poisoned
her for betraying him.

2. True

3. False—Mycroft rescues her.

4. True

5. False—Moriarty's target will
be Dr. Watson.

6. False—She is a gypsy fortune
teller.

7. True

8. False—It is Mary Watson.

9. False—It turns out to be
Colonel Sebastian Moran.

10. False—Holmes delivers an
oxygen breathing apparatus

that he took an interest in
earlier in the case.

QUIZ 81

1. "The Adventure of the
Creeping Man"

2. "The Final Problem," and
"The Adventure of the Empty
House"

3. *The Sign of Four*

4. "The Adventure of the
Mazarin Stone"

5. "The Greek Interpreter"

QUIZ 82

1. "Nothing happens to me."

2. The Science of Deduction

3. It's the kindest word for
stupidity.

4. Mrs. Hudson's husband
operated a drug cartel in
Florida.

5. How do you feel about
violins?

6. "You're not haunted by war,
you miss it."

7. A string of murders made to
look like suicides.

8. Moriarty

9. A poison pill

10. He traces the GPS signal
from the victim's phone and
follows Sherlock.

QUIZ 83

1. False—He works at a local
surgery seeing patients.

2. False—It is the Black Lotus.

3. True

4. True

5. True

6. True

7. False—It is a jade hairpin that Sherlock finds in the banker's secretary's hair.

QUIZ 84

1. Firing holes into the wall with his pistol

2. Five orange pips, one representing each puzzle

3. "The Adventure of the Bruce-Partington Plans"

4. His homeless network

5. "Staying Alive"

QUIZ 85

1. Mycroft summons Sherlock to Buckingham Palace to thwart a possible scandal involving intimate photos taken of a royal princess and Adler.

2. He is wrapped only in a sheet because he refuses to get dressed.

3. "How would you know?"

4. As a dominatrix.

5. She is wearing her battle dress, a pair of Christian Louboutin heels, and nothing else.

6. She seduces him, then changes his ringtone to a recording of her suggestive sigh.

7. She sends the information to Moriarty.

QUIZ 86

1. Knight believes the nearby Baskerville military research station is breeding gigantic mutant hounds.

2. He mentions the word "hound" instead of dog, and pleads for Sherlock to investigate the creature with red eyes and black fur.

3. Sherlock claims to be Mycroft Holmes and uses his security pass.

4. Mycroft sent him to keep an eye on Sherlock.

5. It was a chemical-weapon CIA experiment that was conducted in Liberty, Indiana, and later canceled.

6. A dense fog that causes hallucinations

7. Sherlock admits to using John as a guinea pig to test the chemical-weapon theory.

QUIZ 87

1. "The press will turn, and they will turn on you."

2. "Get Sherlock."

3. Moriarty threatened the jury.

4. He arranges a kidnapping, making it appear as if Sherlock committed the

crime, then solves it to make himself look a hero.

5. Journalist Kitty Reiley whom Sherlock insulted at the beginning of the episode

6. Molly Hooper

7. The roof of St. Bartholomew's Hospital

QUIZ 88

1. Syria

2. Waiter

3. Operation

4. Thirteen

5. Lazarus

6. Cyclist

7. Guy Fawkes Day (Bonfire Night)

QUIZ 89

1. She believes she's dating a dead man.

2. They are trying to guess the name of the person written on a note stuck to their foreheads.

3. Sherlock needs help writing his best-man speech for John and Mary's wedding.

4. John's former commander is about to be murdered.

5. He notices the military uniform worn by Major Sholto is similar to one worn by another victim.

6. A razor-thin stiletto knife

7. Mary is pregnant.

QUIZ 90

1. False—It was "The Man with the Twisted Lip."

2. True

3. True

4. False—He's a media tycoon.

5. False—He's threatening to make public the love letters her husband wrote to a fifteen-year-old girl more than thirty years ago.

6. False—He's blackmailing Mary Morstan.

7. False—It was Mary Morstan.

QUIZ 91

1. Moriarty appears to have come back.

2. Mycroft doctors video footage, making it appear as if Magnussen killed himself.

3. Rosamund Mary is her formal name. Rosie is her nickname.

4. A missing item on a table, which he learns is the bust of Margaret Thatcher

5. Mary Watson

6. Morocco

7. Norbury attempts to shoot Sherlock, but Mary jumps in front of him and is shot instead. She dies in John's arms.

QUIZ 92

1. False—She recorded a video for Sherlock, laying out her plan.

2. False—Molly Hooper is taking care of Rosie.

3. True

4. True

5. False—He takes them to his favorite room, the mortuary.

6. False—He views the video Mary sent Sherlock.

7. True

QUIZ 93

1. They disable Mycroft's home security system and frighten him into telling them the truth.

2. In Sherrinford, a maximum-security facility on an island in the North Sea

3. Eurus was a violent child, having supposedly thrown Sherlock's dog, Redbeard, into a well where he drowned. Mycroft was afraid she eventually would harm Holmes.

4. Eurus can reprogram people's minds in order to do her bidding.

5. Mycroft grants Eurus five unsupervised minutes with Moriarty in exchange for her assisting in stopping a national security threat to the British government.

6. Sherlock's childhood friend, Victor Trevor

7. Sherlock visits her often. They play the violin together.

QUIZ 94

1. Holmes is beating a corpse to find out how long after death bruising is still possible.

2. Emelia Ricoletti is reported to have returned to the scene, killing other men. Holmes deduces the murders are committed by a copycat killer and decides to continue the investigation.

3. "Miss me?"

4. By tossing him a cane

5. "No." She doesn't like them because she never says anything, and, according to Dr. Watson, all she does is show people up the stairs and serve breakfasts.

6. It's Mary, John's wife. The reason for her theatrics is that it's the only way she can see her busy husband.

7. "Thank you. I'm glad you liked it. You are very ugly."

8. That Hooper is a woman masquerading as a man

9. Female empowerment; women seeking the vote and more control over their lives

10. He tells Holmes that the country must lose the war because the enemy is right and England is wrong.

11. Mary Morstan

12. Lady Carmichael has "admirably high arches."

13. The Mind Palace, known as an imaginary location in the mind where data, usually in the form of images, is stored

14. A secret organization of militant women in a suffragette movement ceremony

15. Modern-day London

QUIZ 95

1. Sherlock's father hired Joan to be his sobriety companion for six weeks to prevent Holmes from having a relapse.

2. He tells them she is his valet.

3. He burns it.

4. Irene Adler, his former lover, reappears.

5. Clyde

6. The New York Mets

7. Elvis Costello's "Watching the Detectives"

8. Captain Gregson meets Sherlock at Scotland Yard after 9/11 when the Captain is sent to the Yard to study their counter-terrorism strategies.

9. She is a transgender woman.

10. While working for Scotland Yard, Sherlock stopped several of her notorious plans, and she wants to study his methods.

QUIZ 96

1. A. Everyone

2. C. Joan joins an online dating site.

3. C. Detective Bell is shot protecting Holmes for an incident that should not have occurred.

4. A. "The Adventure of the Cardboard Box"

5. D. Bite marks from the same set of teeth

6. C. "The Man with the Twisted Lip"

7. B. Joan decides to leave Baker Street and find her own apartment.

QUIZ 97

1. Singlesticks

2. "The Adventure of the Five Orange Pips"

3. Viewers are warned against flashing bright images that mimic an epilepsy trigger.

4. Joan is in Denmark.

5. Violet DeMervill

6. Joan's boyfriend, Andrew Paek, dies after accidentally drinking a poisoned coffee meant for Joan.

7. Sherlock has had a relapse in his recovery.

QUIZ 98

1. False—Sherlock's father, Morland Holmes, is responsible.

2. True

3. True

4. False—Sherlock becomes involved in a romantic relationship with a computer coder named Fiona Helbron.

5. True

6. False—Paige has MS.

7. False—He announces that he is taking over Moriarty's organization to dismantle it.

QUIZ 99

1. Sherlock suggests that Joan assist Shinwell Johnson, her last patient as a surgeon, in getting back on his feet after being in prison.

2. "The Adventure of the Illustrious Client"

3. Sherlock offers to train Shinwell on how to be an informant and survive.

4. She reappears to warn Sherlock that he is the target of a killer from a case they worked on while in London.

5. Kitty has a child.

6. He gives her a written confession of his past crimes.

7. He directed the episode.

QUIZ 100

1. Post Conclusion Syndrome

2. To save Joan from being arrested for a murder she did not commit, Sherlock confesses and flees to London, where the British government refused to extradite him, claiming he acted in the service of the Queen.

3. He's asked to consider applying for a position with the United States Marshalls Service.

4. She moves to a flat next to Sherlock.

5. In response to a comment Sherlock made earlier, Joan says, "We're not partners. We're two people who love each other."

6. Hill directed episode seventeen, "The Worms Crawl in, The Worms Crawl Out."

7. "The Adventure of the Greek Interpreter"

QUIZ 101

1. D. Sherlock and Joan learn Captain Gregson has been shot and is in critical condition.

2. A. He posed as a researcher for coal tar derivatives.

3. B. She is to destroy his gravestone.

4. C. She receives a message that Moriarty is still alive.

5. C. She fell in love and got married.

6. A. He has been promoted to Captain taking over for Captain Gregson.

7. D. Captain Gregson

8. B. She wrote a book about Sherlock.

9. B. Paige, Captain Gregson's wife

10. A. A report from Joan's doctor

QUIZ 102

1. Sherlock and Wato meet when Wato's colleague, Dr. Mizuno, is murdered, and Sherlock is called to investigate.

2. Performing an unauthorized autopsy on the victim's body

3. The episode loosely follows the storyline of "The Adventure of the Devil's Foot."

4. Syria

5. She is too traumatized by her war experience.

6. Cello

7. Eat, especially chocolate

8. Stella Maris (Star of the Sea)

9. Sherlock, being a stylish dresser, complains that Dr. Wato's clothes are unappealing.

10. He is the Prime Minister's Secretary.

MAKING THE GRADE

Level	Total Correct Answers
Deductive Genius	137–172
Holmes' Apprentice	91–136
Watson's Apprentice	46–90
Moriarty's Victim	0–45

QUIZ 103

1. May 22, 1859

2. Ten

3. Edinburgh University

4. Conan Doyle and Louise "Touie" Hawkins were married in August 1855. Touie died on July 4, 1906.

5. Plymouth

6. His mother

7. Jean Leckie

8. Conan Doyle had two children by his first wife— Mary Louise and Alleyne Kingsley ("Kingsley"), and three children with Jean Leckie—Denis, Adrian, and Lena Jean.

9. 1902

10. Edgar Allen Poe

QUIZ 104

1. *The Stark Munro Letters*

2. *The Coming of the Fairies*

3. *Micah Clarke*

4. *The Exploits and Adventures of Brigadier Gerard*

5. A play about alchemy entitled *The Doings of Raffles Haw*

6. *The White Company*

7. *The Lost World*

8. *Rodney Stone*

9. *The Crime of the Congo*

10. *The Maracot Deep and Other Stories*

QUIZ 105

1. *The New Revelation*
2. Harry Houdini
3. *Light*
4. *The Edge of the Unknown*
5. He operated a psychic book store and museum.
6. *The Vital Message*
7. The medium claimed to be in contact with Conan Doyle's son, Kingsley, and the author's brother, Innes.
8. H. G. Wells
9. *The Wanderings of a Spiritualist*
10. Scientific American

MAKING THE GRADE

Level	Total Correct Answers
Deductive Genius	24–30
Holmes' Apprentice	16–23
Watson's Apprentice	8–15
Moriarty's Victim	0–7

THE SHERLOCK HOLMES QUIZ BOOK

ANSWERS TO CROSSWORD PUZZLES

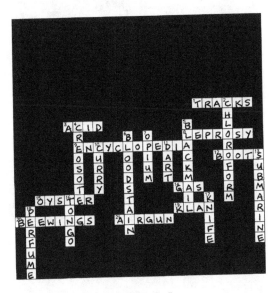

PUZZLE 1

Chemicals, Clues, and Deadly Things

PUZZLE 2

A.K.A.

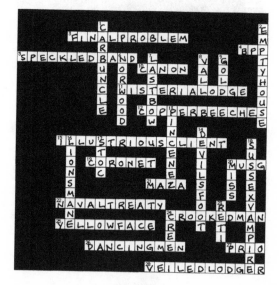

PUZZLE 3

In Other Words

PUZZLE 4

Butlers, Maids, Valets, etc.

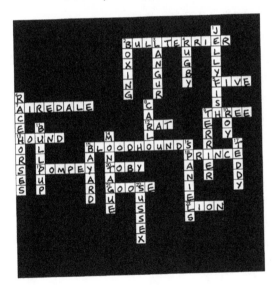

PUZZLE 5

Canines and Other Creatures

APPENDIX I: THE CANON

TITLES ABBREVIATIONS
designed by Sherlockian Scholar Jay Finely Christ

Novels
A Study in Scarlet (STUD)
The Sign of Four (SIGN)
The Hound of the Baskervilles (HOUN)
The Valley of Fear (VALL)

Collections of Short Stories
The Adventures of Sherlock Holmes
"A Scandal in Bohemia" (SCAN)
"The Red-Headed League" (REDH)
"A Case of Identity" (IDEN)
"The Boscombe Valley Mystery" (BOSC)
"The Five Orange Pips" (FIVE)
"The Man with the Twisted Lip" (TWIS)
"The Adventure of the Blue Carbuncle" (BLUE)
"The Adventure of the Speckled Band" (SPEC)
"The Adventure of the Engineer's Thumb" (ENGR)
"The Adventure of the Noble Bachelor" (NOBL)
"The Adventure of the Beryl Coronet" (BERY)
"The Adventure of the Copper Beeches" (COPP)
Memoirs of Sherlock Holmes
"Silver Blaze" (SILV)
"The Yellow Face" (YELL)
"The Stock-broker's Clerk" (STOC)
"The *Gloria Scott*" (GLOR)
"The Musgrave Ritual" (MUSG)
"The Reigate Squires" (REIG)

"The Crooked Man" (CROO)

"The Resident Patient" (RESI)

"The Greek Interpreter" (GREE)

"The Naval Treaty" (NAVA)

"The Final Problem" (FINA)

The Return of Sherlock Holmes

"The Adventure of the Empty House" (EMPT)

"The Adventure of the Norwood Builder" (NORW)

"The Adventure of the Dancing Men" (DANC)

"The Adventure of the Solitary Cyclist" (SOLI)

"The Adventure of the Priory School" (PRIO)

"The Adventure of Black Peter" (BLAC)

"The Adventure of Charles Augustus Milverton" (CHAS)

"The Adventure of the Six Napoleons" (SIXN)

"The Adventure of the Three Students" (3STU)

"The Adventure of the Golden Pince-Nez" (GOLD)

"The Adventure of the Missing Three-Quarter" (MISS)

"The Adventure of the Abbey Grange" (ABBE)

"The Adventure of the Second Stain" (SECO)

His Last Bow

"The Adventure of Wisteria Lodge" (WIST)

"The Adventure of the Cardboard Box" (CARD)

"The Adventure of the Red Circle" (REDC)

"The Adventure of the Bruce-Partington Plans" (BRUC)

"The Adventure of the Dying Detective" (DYIN)

"The Disappearance of Lady Frances Carfax" (LADY)

"The Adventure of the Devil's Foot" (DEVI)

"His Last Bow" (LAST)

The Case Book of Sherlock Holmes

"The Adventure of the Illustrious Client" (ILLU)

"The Adventure of the Blanched Soldier" (BLAN)

"The Adventure of the Mazarin Stone" (MAZA)

"The Adventure of the Three Gables" (3GAB)

"The Adventure of the Sussex Vampire" (SUSS)

"The Adventure of the Three Garridebs" (3GAR)

"The Problem of Thor Bridge" (THOR)

"The Adventure of the Creeping Man" (CREE)

"The Adventure of the Lion's Mane" (LION)

"The Adventure of the Veiled Lodger" (VEIL)

"The Adventure of Shoscombe Old Place" (SHOS)

"The Adventure of the Retired Colourman" (RETT)

APPENDIX II: THE CHRONOLOGY OF SHERLOCK HOLMES

1852	*August 7*	Estimated birth of John Watson
1854	*January 6*	Estimated birth of Sherlock Holmes
1872	*September*	John Watson enters medical school at the University of London and is trained as an army doctor.
	Fall	Holmes enrolls in college.
1874	*Summer*	While attending the university, Holmes solves his first case "The *Gloria Scott*."
1877–1878		Holmes moves to Montague Street in London and sets up practice as a consulting detective.
1878		Watson is dispatched to serve in the Afghan War.
1880	*July 27*	Watson is wounded in the Battle of Maiwand.
	August	Holmes visits America.
	Fall	Watson returns home from the service.*
1881	*January*	Sherlock Holmes and John Watson meet.
	March	Holmes and Watson investigate their first case together, *A Study in Scarlet*.
1886	*November*	Watson marries and starts a medical practice in Kensington.*
1887	*December*	Apparent death of Watson's first wife*
1888	*January*	Holmes and Watson investigate the case known as *The Valley of Fear*.
	September	Holmes and Watson investigate the cases of *The Sign of Four* and *The Hound of the Baskervilles*.
1889	*May*	Watson marries a second time (Mary Morstan). He sets up a second medical practice in Paddington.
1891	*January*	Estimated meeting date of Holmes and Professor Moriarty*
	Spring	Holmes is apparently killed at Reichenbach Falls.
1891–1894		Holmes is presumed dead, the Great Hiatus.
1891–1892		Watson is widowed, once again.
1894	*April 5*	Holmes returns to London.*

	May	Watson moves back to the Baker Street lodging.
1901	*October*	Watson marries again.
1903	*October*	Holmes retires to Sussex Downs on the coast at Fulworth.*
1912		Holmes spies for the government.
1929		Estimated year of Watson's death*
1957		Estimated year of Holmes's death*

*Indicates speculative dates

APPENDIX III: THE CHRONOLOGY OF SIR ARTHUR CONAN DOYLE

1859	*May 22*	Arthur Conan Doyle is born in Picardy Place, Edinburgh, Scotland.
1868		Entered Hodder, Stonyhurst's preparatory Jesuit school in Lancashire
1870–1875		Attended Stonyhurst's secondary school
1876–1881		Studied medicine at the Edinburgh University
1879	*October*	Wrote his first story, "The Mystery of Sarassa Valley," which appeared in *Chamber's Journal*
1880		Spent seven months aboard the *Hope* as the whaling ship's surgeon before he finished his studies at the university
1881	*October 22*	Signed up as a surgeon aboard the SS *Mayumba* bound for Africa
1882–1823		Joined Dr. George Turnavine Budd's medical practice in Edinburgh
1885	*August 6*	Married Louise Hawkins.
1887	*November*	Published the first Sherlock Holmes story, "A Study in Scarlet," which appeared in *Beeton's Christmas Annual*
1890		Published the second Holmes novel, *The Sign of Four*
		Birth of first child, Mary Louise Doyle
		Published his first historical novel, *The White Company*
1891	*Spring*	Retired from medical practice to write full time
1892		Published his first collection of Sherlock Holmes stories, *The Adventures of Sherlock Holmes*
1892		Birth of first son, Alleyne Kingsley
1894		Published his second collection of Sherlock Holmes stories, *Memoirs of Sherlock Holmes*
1894		Visited the United States with his brother, Innes
1896		Published the novel, *The Exploits of Brigadier Gerard*

1900–1903		Volunteered his medical services in the Boer War between Britain and South Africa
1901	*August 9*	Knighted by King Edward VII at Buckingham Palace
1902		Published his third Sherlock Holmes novel, *The Hound of the Baskervilles*
1903		Published the second Brigadier Gerard book, *The Adventures of Brigadier Gerard*
1906	*July 4*	Death of first wife, Louise Hawkins Doyle
1907	*Sept. 18*	Married Jean Leckie
1908		Published the third collection of Holmes stories, *The Return of Sherlock Holmes*
1909		Birth of Denis, first child by Jean Leckie
1910		Birth of third son, Adrian
1912		Birth of fifth child, Lena Jean
		Published the *The Lost World*
1914		Published the last Sherlock Holmes novel, *The Valley of Fear*
1917		Published the fourth collection of Holmes stories, *His Last Bow*
1917	*October*	Death of eldest son, Alleyne Kingsley Conan Doyle
1918		Published his first book on spiritualism, *The New Revelation*
1920	*August*	Began a lecture tour in Australia
1924	*March*	Publication of autobiography, *Memories and Adventures*
1927		Publication of fifth and final collection of Holmes stories, *The Case Book of Sherlock Holmes*
1930	*July 7*	Died at his home in Crowborough

THE SHERLOCK HOLMES QUIZ BOOK

APPENDIX IV: SHERLOCK HOLMES AT HIS BEST

CONAN DOYLE'S FAVORITE SHERLOCK HOLMES STORIES, PUBLISHED IN THE *STRAND MAGAZINE*

1. "The Adventure of the Speckled Band"
2. "The Red-Headed League"
3. "The Adventure of the Dancing Men"
4. "The Final Problem"
5. "A Scandal in Bohemia"
6. "The Adventure of the Empty House"
7. "The Five Orange Pips"
8. "The Adventure of the Priory School"
9. "The Musgrave Ritual"
10. "The Reigate Squires"
11. "Silver Blaze"
12. "The Adventure of the Bruce-Partington Plans"
13. "The Crooked Man"
14. "The Man with the Twisted Lip"
15. "The Greek Interpreter"
16. "The Resident Patient"
17. "The Naval Treaty"

BAKER STREET IRREGULARS' FAVORITE SHERLOCK HOLMES STORIES, TAKEN FROM A 1944 MEMBERSHIP POLL

1. "The Adventure of the Speckled Band"
2. "A Scandal in Bohemia"
3. "The Red-Headed League"
4. "Silver Blaze"
5. "The Adventure of the Dancing Men"
6. "The Musgrave Ritual"

7. "The Five Orange Pips"

8. "The Final Problem"

9. "The Adventure of the Empty House"

10. "The Adventure of the Bruce-Partington Plans"

11. "The Adventure of the Second Stain"

12. "The Adventure of the Devil's Foot"

BAKER STREET JOURNAL READERS' FAVORITE SHERLOCK HOLMES STORIES, PUBLISHED IN THE JOURNAL IN 1959

1. "The Adventure of the Speckled Band"

2. "The Red-Headed League"

3. "The Adventure of the Blue Carbuncle"

4. "Silver Blaze"

5. "A Scandal in Bohemia"

6. "The Musgrave Ritual"

7. "The Adventure of the Bruce-Partington Plans"

8. "The Adventure of the Six Napoleons"

9. "The Adventure of the Dancing Men"

10. "The Adventure of the Empty House"

APPENDIX V: SHERLOCK HOLMES'S LETTER TO WATSON IN "THE FINAL PROBLEM"

MY DEAR WATSON:

I write these few lines through the courtesy of Mr. Moriarty, who awaits my convenience for the final discussion of those questions which lie between us. He has been giving me a sketch of the methods by which he avoided the English police and kept himself informed of our movements. They certainly confirm my very high opinion which I had formed of his abilities. I am pleased to think that I shall be able to free society from any further effects of his presence, though I fear that it is at a cost which will give pain to my friends, especially, my dear Watson, to you. I have already explained to you, however, that my career had in any case reached its crisis, and that no possible conclusion to it could be more congenial to me than this. Indeed, if I may make a full confession to you, I was quite convinced that the letter from Meiringen was a hoax, and I allowed you to depart on that errand under the persuasion that some development of this sort would follow. Tell Inspector Patterson that the papers which he needs to convict the gang are in pigeonhole M., done up in a blue envelope and inscribed "Moriarty." I made every disposition of my property before leaving England and handed it to my brother Mycroft. Pray give greetings to Mrs. Watson, and believe me to be, my dear fellow,

Very sincerely yours,
SHERLOCK HOLMES

APPENDIX VI:
SHERLOCK HOLMES SOCIETIES

There are over 500 active Sherlock Holmes societies worldwide. Members are devoted to reading, studying, and analyzing the Great Detective's every move, speculating on events that might have occurred, and discussing the nuances of Conan Doyle's literary creations. Below is a list of several Sherlock Holmes societies.

United States

The Agra Treasures (Dayton, Ohio): http://www.agratreasurers.net/

The Baker Street Irregulars (New York, New York): https://bakerstreet irregulars.com/

The Crew of the Barque Lone Star (Dallas/Fort Worth, Texas): https://www.dfw-sherlock.org/

The Dogs in the Nighttime (Anacortes, Washington): https://dogsin thenighttime.weebly.com/

The Giant Rats of Sumatra (Memphis, Tennessee): http://www.sherlock-holmes.com/giantrat.htm

The Greek Interpreters (East Lansing, Michigan) http://thegreek interpreters.org/

The Hounds of the Baskerville (Chicago, Illinois) http://www.hounds ofthebaskerville.org/

The John Openshaw (Houston, Texas) https://johnopenshaw.org/

The Noble and Most Singular Order of the Blue Carbuncle (Portland, Oregon): https://sites.google.com/site/bluecarbunclesociety/

The Norwegian Explorers of Minnesota: http://www.norwegian explorers.org/

The Pleasant Places of Florida: http://ppofl.net/

The Red Circle (Washington, DC): http://www.redcircledc.org/

The Sherlock Holmes Society of Cape Fear (North Carolina): http://www.sherlockholmessociety.com/

The Sound of the Baskervilles (Seattle, Washington): http://soundof thebaskervilles.com/

United Kingdom

The Retired Beekeepers of Sussex: https://retiredbeekeepers.tumblr.com/

The Sherlock Holmes Society of London: http://www.sherlock-holmes.org.uk/

The Sherlock Holmes Society of Scotland: http://sherlockscotland.blogspot.com/

Asia

Japan Sherlock Holmes Club: http://www.holmesjapan.jp/

Sherlock Holmes Club in Japan: http://www.nextchurch.org/resources/shj/shjindex.html

Australia

The Sherlock Holmes Society of South Australia: https://sites.google.com/site/sherlocksa/

The Sydney Passengers: http://www.sherlock.on.net/

Canada

The Singular Society of the Baker Street Dozen (Calgary, Alberta): http://www.bakerstreetdozen.com/

The Stormy Petrels of British Columbia: (https://thestormypetrels.com/

Switzerland

The Bootmakers of Toronto https://www.torontobootmakers.com/

The Reichenbach Irregulars: http://www.221b.ch/index_e.html

Online

The Hounds of the Internet: http://www.sherlockian.net/sharing/hounds/

The John H. Watson Society (Seattle, Washington): https://www.johnhwatsonsociety.com/

APPENDIX VII: SHERLOCK HOLMES WEBSITES, BLOGS, AND PODCASTS

The following is a select list from the dozens of Sherlock Holmes websites devoted to the study of the Great Detective and to the discovery of Holmes collectables and memorabilia.

1. Sherlock Holmes Shoppe: Home Page
   http://www.sherlock@sherlock-holmes.com/

2. Sherlock Holmes Museum
   http://www.sherlock-holmes.co.uk/

3. Sherlock Holmes Mystery Books
   http://members.tripod.com/~Sherlock_Tomes/index.html

4. The Arthur Conan Doyle Encylopedia
   https://www.arthur-conan-doyle.com

5. The Baker Street Journal:
   http://www.bakerstreetjournal.com/

6. Dan Andriacco's The Baker Street Beat:
   http://bakerstreetbeat.blogspot.com/

7. Sherlock Peoria
   http://sherlockpeoria.blogspot.com/

8. The Shigle of Southsea
   http://shingleofsouthsea.blogspot.com/

9. The Sherlockian
   https://www.sherlockian.net/

10. The Well Read Sherlock Holmes:
    https://wellreadsherlockian.com/

11. I Hear of Holmes Everywhere Podcast:
    https://www.ihearofsherlock.com/

12. Sherlock Holmes Adventures Podcast:
    https://www.stitcher.com/podcast/sherlock-holmes-adventures-podcast

13. Sherlock Holmes Podcast:
    https://www.sherlockholmespodcast.com/

14. The Jeremy Brett Sherlock Holmes Podcast:
    http://sherlockpodcast.com/

15. The Baker Street Babes Podcast:
    https://bakerstreetbabes.com/podcast/

16. Talk About Sherlock: Mattias Boström Podcast:
    https://podcasts.apple.com/us/podcast/talk-about-sherlock/
    id1450398363

APPENDIX VIII:
RECOMMENDED READING

Arthur and Sherlock: Conan Doyle and the Creation of Holmes, by Michael Sims

Encyclopedia Sherlockiana: An A–Z Guide to the World of the Great Detective, by Matthew E. Bunson

From Holmes to Sherlock: The Story of the Men and Women Who Created an Icon, by Mattias Boström

The Ultimate Sherlock Holmes Encyclopedia: A Universal Dictionary of Sherlock Holmes and His Biographer, Dr. Watson, by Jack Tracy

The Adventures of Conan Doyle: The Life of the Creator of Sherlock Holmes, by Charles Higham Conan Doyle, by Michael Coren

BIBLIOGRAPHY

Arnold, Martin. "Making Books—Serial Sleuth, Spreading Glee." *New York Times*, October 8, 1998, p. B3.

Baring-Gould, William S. *Sherlock Holmes of Baker Street*. New York: Clarkson N. Potter, 1962.

Blackbeard, Bill. *Sherlock Holmes in America*. New York: Harry N. Abrams, Inc., 1981.

Brennan, Steve. "Ani 'Sherlock,' 'Sonic' are on MIPCOM case." *Hollywood Reporter*, September 10, 1998.

Bostrom, Mattias. *From Holmes to Sherlock*. New York: Mysterious Press, 2013.

Bunson, Matthew E. *Encyclopedia Sherlockiana*. New York: Macmillan, 1994.

Carr, John Dickson. *The Life of Sir Arthur Conan Doyle*. New York: Carroll & Graf, 1987.

Coren, Michael. *Conan Doyle*. London: Bloomsbury, 1995.

Costello, Peter. *The Real World of Sherlock Holmes*. New York: Carroll & Graf, 1991.

Gennusa, Chris. "Col aboard Holmes–Dracula tale." *Hollywood Reporter*, November 5, 1999.

Haining, Peter, ed. *The Sherlock Holmes Scrapbook*. New York: New English Library, 1973.

Hall, Trevor. *Sherlock Holmes and His Creator*. New York: St. Martin's Press, 1977.

Hammer, David. *The Game Is Afoot*. Bloomington, Indiana: Gaslight Publications, 1983.

Hardwick, Michael. *The Complete Guide to Sherlock Holmes*. London: Weidenfeld & Nicholson, 1986.

————. *The Private Life of Dr. Watson—Being the Personal Reminiscences of John H. Watson, M.D.* New York: E. P. Dutton, 1983.

Harrison, Michael, ed. *Beyond Baker Street: A Sherlockian Anthology*. Indianapolis and New York: Bobbs–Merrill, 1976.

————. *I, Sherlock Holmes*. New York: E. P. Dutton, 1977.

Haydock, Ron. *Deerstalker! Holmes and Watson on Screen*. Metuchen, New Jersey: Scarecrow Press, 1978.

Higham, Charles. *The Adventures of Conan Doyle: The Life of the Creator of Sherlock Holmes.* New York: W. W. Norton, 1976.

Keating, H. R. F. *Sherlock Holmes: The Man and His World.* New York: Charles Scribner's Sons, 1979.

King, Susan. "The Two Faces of Sherlock." *Los Angeles Times*, November 3–9, 1991, p. 82.

Lellenberg, Jon Daniel Stashower, and Charles Foley. *Arthur Conan Doyle: A Life in Letters.* New York: Penguin Books, 2007.

Liebman, Arthur. *The Biographical Sherlock Holmes: An Anthology/Handbook.* New York: The Rosen Publishing Group, 1984.

McKenna, Kristine. "Sherlock Holmes' Greatest Interpreter." *Los Angeles Times*, June 9, 1998.

Moss, Marilyn. "TV Reviews—Sherlock Holmes in the 22nd Century." *Hollywood Reporter*, September 17–19, 1999, p. 18.

Nepodahl, Lawrence. "Sherlock Holmes on American Radio, Part 2." *Past Times*, 1998, p. 22.

Nordon, Pierre. *Conan Doyle: A Biography.* New York: Holt, Rinehart, and Winston, 1967.

Oliver, Myrna. "Jeremy Brett: TV Series' Sherlock Holmes." *Los Angeles Times*, September 19, 1995.

Pohle, Robert W. and Douglas C. Hart. *Sherlock Holmes on the Screen: The Motion Picture Adventures of the World's Most Popular Detective.* South Brunswick, New Jersey and New York: A. S. Barnes, 1977.

Pointer, Michael. *The Public Life of Sherlock Holmes.* Newton Abbot, U.K.: David & Charles, 1975.

Shreffler, Philip A., ed. *Baker Street Studies: Cornerstone Writings About Sherlock Holmes.* Westport, Connecticut and London: Greenwood Press, 1984.

Sims, Michael. *Arthur and Sherlock: Conan Doyle and the Creation of Holmes.* New York: Bloomsbury, 2017.

Symons, Julian. *Conan Doyle: Portrait of an Artist.* New York: The Mysterious Press, 1979.

Tracy, Jack. *The Ultimate Sherlock Holmes Encyclopedia.* New York: Gramercy Books, 1977.

Viney, Charles. *Sherlock Holmes in London.* Boston: Houghton Mifflin, 1989.

Weller, Philip. *The Life and Times of Sherlock Holmes.* London: Crescent, 1993.

CPSIA information can be obtained
at www.ICGtesting.com
Printed in the USA
FSHW011253221020
75125FS